From popular enlightenment
to lifelong learning

with Best wisler

Clay Cooks

To the members of the New Opportunities classes,
Dundee University, 1980-2000

From popular enlightenment to lifelong learning

A history of adult education in Scotland 1707-2005

Anthony Cooke
**Formerly Senior Lecturer in Continuing Education,
University of Dundee**

promoting adult learning

© 2006 National Institute of Adult Continuing Education
(England and Wales)

21 De Montfort Street
Leicester
LE1 7GE

Company registration no. 2603322
Charity registration no. 1002775

NIACE has a broad remit to promote lifelong learning opportunities for adults. NIACE
works to develop increased participation in education and training, particularly for those who
do not have easy access because of class, gender, age, race, language and culture, learning difficulties or disabilities, or insufficient financial resources.

You can find NIACE online at **www.niace.org.uk**

Cataloguing in Publication Data
A CIP record of this title is available from the British Library

Designed and typeset by Book Production Services, London
Printed and bound in the UK by Cromwell Press Ltd, Trowbridge
ISBN: 1 86201 267 9

Contents

List of illustrations

Acknowledgements

This book has been a long time in the making. It combines two of my main interests – a career in adult and continuing education in Scotland and a professional interest in Scottish social and economic history. I taught my first adult class at the tender age of 23, for the University of the West Indies, on the island of Carriacou, where I was working as a volunteer for VSO. The following year, I enrolled for a diploma in Adult Education at Manchester University and was taught the history of British adult education by the estimable Derek Legge. I came to Dundee in 1968 and taught adults in further education before moving into the Department of Extra-Mural Education at Dundee University. In 1980, I started a 'New Opportunities' (adult access) course in Dundee, the second to be established in Scotland, and taught history on it for the next 20 years. Some remarkable people came through the course, many of whom triumphed over considerable odds to go on to university or further education, or to change jobs. They were carrying on a long Scottish tradition of self-improvement, which this book attempts to document and explain.

I had a long and rewarding connection with the Scottish Institute of Adult Education and was Editor of the *Scottish Journal of Adult Education* for ten years. Elisabeth Gerver, who was Director of the Institute and then Professor of Continuing Education at Dundee University, was a supportive colleague who encouraged me to take two much needed sabbatical terms for research. I met some congenial and like-minded people through a series of international conferences on the history of adult education held in Jena, Dundee, Pecs and Leiden, particularly Franz Poggeler of Aachen University of Technology.

I have made heavy use of the University Library, Dundee, particularly the Kinnear and the Joan Auld Memorial Collections. I have made extensive use of the Mitchell Library, Glasgow and the National Library of Scotland, Edinburgh, which both have outstanding collections in this field. I have also used Cambridge University Archives, Dundee City Archives, the excellent University Library at St Andrews and the Local History Libraries in Dundee and Perth. I would like to thank librarians and archivists in these collections for all their help and support. Anna Grant, of the Centre for Learning and Teaching, University of Dundee, has answered my IT queries with patience and forbearance. A number of colleagues and friends have read chapters in draft and made many helpful comments and suggestions. I would like thank Ian Donnachie of the Open University in Scotland, John Stocks, formerly of Dundee University, Rob Duncan of the Workers' Educational Association and Ian Martin of Edinburgh University for their help in these matters. Jim Gallacher of Glasgow Caledonian University recommended approaching NIACE to publish the book and Virman

Man of NIACE showed enthusiasm for the project from the start. I would like to thank Tom Steele, formerly of Glasgow University, for recommending Jonathan Rose's book *The Intellectual Life of the British Working Classes* to me, and Murdo Macdonald, of Dundee University, for drawing my attention to Kemp Smith and the Edinburgh WEA.

I would like to thank my wife Judith for her support over the years. She has read every word of this book with an eye for the sweeping generalisation. I owe her a special debt of gratitude here, as her grandfather and great grandfather were both editors of the *People's Friend*, a highly successful example of popular journalism, published by the remarkable firm of John Leng in Dundee. David Pae Senior began life in a meal mill at Buchanty, Perthshire, moved to a farm in Berwickshire on his father's death, became an apprentice printer in Edinburgh and a member of the Bristo Young Men's Mutual Improvement Society. Eventually, he established himself as a prolific writer of popular novels and founding editor of the *People's Friend*. His son, also David Pae, was editor of the same publication for over fifty years. David Pae Sr was the subject of detailed discussion in William Donaldson's *Popular Literature in Victorian Scotland* and I have used the Pae family papers in this book.

I would like to thank my sons, Alistair and Michael, and my daughters-in-law, Louise and Gill, for their warm hospitality during my research trips to Glasgow. My friend and colleague, Antony Black, has been helpful and supportive as always, as have other friends such as Roy Partington, John Cheyne and Russell Meek.

Introduction

Approaches and definitions

Historically, most types of adult education in Scotland have taken the form of part-time education fitted in on top of a working life. The 'classic' form of adult education provision was evening classes, but there were many others, including day schools, summer schools, mutual improvement societies, and self-education, often linked to library provision. In this book, I have tried to write more than simply a history of adult education institutions or a hagiography of 'great men' in adult education. I have been concerned to give a flavour of the learners' experience over the years and to cast light on the largely unsung army of part-time teachers who taught them. Here, Jonathan Rose's *The Intellectual Life of the British Working Classes* has been of great help in suggesting an approach to the subject through working-class autobiographies, diaries, and memoirs (Rose, 2002). Scotland is particularly rich in such literature and I have been able to add considerably to Rose's original list. By using this method, one can begin to see that adult learners used a great variety of methods to further their education, from self-education based on home learning and the use of libraries, through mutual instruction to the more formal class teaching. This approach also highlights the strongly utilitarian nature of much adult education in Scotland, at least from the learners' point of view.

A powerful motivation behind many of the learners, at least the ones who have left accounts behind, was the desire to 'get on' in life. This motivation can crop up in some unexpected quarters. There is little surprise in finding Samuel Smiles (the author of *Self Help*) describing how the Haddington School of Arts, where Smiles lectured on chemistry, helped men from his native town to 'get on' in life (Smiles, 1905, p.31). More surprising, perhaps, is the way in which the many forms of radical/socialist education on offer in late nineteenth and early twentieth-century Scotland, combined with the Labour Movement itself, acted as a ladder of social mobility for a significant number of Scots (Knox, 1984, p.19). Here, the role of Calvinism, which believed that 'getting on' in life was a sign of spiritual as well as material advancement, is important. The tradition of the 'lad o' pairts' is well rooted in Scottish mythology, and has considerable basis in fact. Less obvious in this discourse is the role of women, who play a largely hidden role for much of the period. There are very few autobiographies, diaries or memoirs by working-class women, although there are hints at their roles in male-generated sources.

Changing notions of childhood and adulthood also come into the equation. In the late eighteenth and early nineteenth centuries, when working-class children might start full-time work as early as seven or eight, evening classes were often provided for older children who were employed during the daytime, particularly factory workers in cities like Aberdeen, Dundee, Paisley, and Glasgow or villages such as Blantyre, Catrine, New Lanark, and Stanley. The Sunday School Movement, which began in Scotland in the 1760s, started out targeting similar groups of working-class children or young adults, although later their audience became more middle class. (Sinclair, 1826, p.96; Brown, 1981, p.19)

Surprisingly, there is no detailed history of adult education in Scotland. Bryant produced a pamphlet-sized guide and there are detailed references to Scotland in Kelly's large-scale history of British adult education (Bryant, 1984; Kelly, 1992). The history of modern British adult education by Fieldhouse and others is largely English-orientated although it does have a short section on the Scottish community education service (Fieldhouse, 1996). Too many historians of Scottish education have written as though the words 'education' and 'schooling and universities' were synonymous. Recently, writers such as Anderson and Paterson have begun to redress the balance by giving more attention to adult and technical education (Anderson, 1995; Paterson, 2003). Prior to this, the outstanding exception was Saunders in his *Scottish Democracy 1815–1840*, published as long ago as 1950. Saunders used the term 'popular enlightenment' to define characteristically Scottish forms of self-improvement such as the itinerating library scheme of Samuel Brown of Haddington, Thomas Dick's early proposals for adult education institutes, and the activities of George Miller, the Dunbar bookseller, who published improving tracts and the *Cheap Magazine* (Saunders, 1950). In the 1930s, Marwick published a string of articles on adult education in nineteenth-century Scotland, and Smith, in the early 1980s, carried out a critique of Saunders' views, by discussing the ways in which popular enlightenment could act as a form of social control (Marwick, 1930, 1931, 1932, 1933a, 1933b; Smith, 1983a, 1983b).

One reason why the history of adult education in Scotland is under-researched is that many educational historians have believed that there is little history to write about. A recent book on Scottish education, for example, sums up the general consensus by puzzling over, 'the relative failure of adult education' in Scotland (Paterson, 2003, p.89). This belief goes back a long way. The Report of the Ministry of Reconstruction on Adult Education in 1919 contained a confident assertion by a Scottish educationalist that, 'it would be wise to assume therefore that non-vocational adult education of an organised nature is at present non-existent in Scotland' (Ministry of Reconstruction, 1980 edition, pp.294-5). This in spite of the fact that in 1919 Scotland was the stronghold of independent (Marxist) working-class adult education in Britain, with some 2,500 people enrolled in such classes in the West of Scotland, and the Fife coalfields (McIlroy, 1996, p.226). Similarly, the Committee of Inquiry on Adult Education, which reported in 1975, concluded, 'the inescapable fact is that Scotland was very much slower than England to develop adult education in an organised way' (SED, 1975, p.3).

In fact, adult education in Scotland took different forms to that in England and Wales. The concept of 'popular enlightenment,' for example, had resonance in Scotland in a way that it did in the Scandinavian countries or Germany, but not in England and Wales (Jacobsen, 1992, p.278). An American historian has recently pointed out that, 'in the eighteenth century, autodidact culture flourished especially in Scotland, particularly among weavers,' and that 'unsurprisingly, mutual improvement was Scottish in origin' (Rose, 2002, pp.16, 59). Similarly, one of the main reasons that the Workers' Educational Association initially failed to take root in Scotland was the strength of independent working-class education in the West of Scotland and the Fife coalfields, with its more radical vision of society and consequent distrust of collaboration between working-class organisations and the educational establishment (Cooke, 2000, pp.267-277). Scots-born or Scots-educated people also played a prominent role in many English adult education ventures, from George Birkbeck and the Mechanics' Institutes, Henry Brougham and the Society for the Diffusion of Useful Knowledge, to writers like Samuel Smiles, and the academic/politician/industrialist James Stuart and the Cambridge University Extension movement. Similarly, Robert Owen's ideas on education, developed and articulated whilst he was managing partner at New Lanark cotton mills, owe a good deal to the ideas of the Scottish Enlightenment.

Adult education has fulfilled a variety of functions including remedial education, improving the skills of the workforce, and education for citizenship. In all three areas there has been ongoing debate over who controlled the finances, management, and organisation of adult education institutions and, by implication, the curriculum. At different times adult education has been seen as a means of maintaining the existing social and economic system or as a way of challenging or modifying it. There have always been difficulties in defining the concept of 'adult education'. In the UK, it has often been defined narrowly as 'non-vocational'. In Scotland, for example, the Committee of Inquiry into Adult Education, otherwise known as the Alexander Report, which reported in 1975, was given a remit to examine, 'voluntary leisure time courses for adults which are educational but not specifically vocational' (SED, 1975, p.vi). However, many adults have studied for qualifications in technical and vocational education and in Scotland the universities were traditionally more accessible to adult students than many elsewhere in Europe.

In his history of the adult education movement in Yorkshire, Harrison identified four broad themes:

First, adult learning has been the outcome of a movement, largely volun-tary and not just a series of organisations. Second, it has been in the main regarded as a movement for freedom and liberation, both personal (in the sense of widening horizons) and social. Third it has been an ernest, seri-ous affair, there has been comparatively little of the 'learning for leisure' approach and a great deal of emphasis on striving and struggle by people who had very little leisure. Lastly, adult education has reached out to a minority of the people only; it has been, in several senses, an elite move-ment. (Harrison, 1961, xiv)

To these four major strands, I would add the provision of adult education by individual teachers at commercial rates to largely middle-class audiences, which is under-recorded by historians but whose importance is obvious to anyone who looks through the advertisements in Scottish newspapers from the 1750s onwards. In the middle of the eighteenth century, those included academic (but 'useful') subjects, such as writing and arithmetic, vocational subjects, such as bookkeeping, surveying or navigation, and academic/cultural subjects, such as French, Latin and other languages, often aimed at women. By the early nine-teenth century, more exotic subjects begin to appear, such as spiritualism, mesmerism or phrenology.

By the late twentieth century, a report on *The Education of Adults in Scotland* took as its focus, 'adults over 20 who wish to re-engage in learning on a part-time basis' (SOED, 1992, p.1). The Scottish Office defined a 'mature student' in higher education as over 21 whereas the same organisation defined the same group in full-time vocational further education as those over 20 (Munn, Tett and Arney, 1993, p.8). The Scottish Council for Research in Education defined adult learners as those over 20 who had taken a break of over two years from initial full-time education (Gerver, 1992, p.390). This concept of a break after full-time education is a useful one and was used by the Open University's *Venables Report* in 1976, when it defined continuing education as, 'learning opportunities which are taken up after full time compulsory schooling has ceased' (Open University, 1976, p.6). It has recently been claimed that, with the growing influence of post-modernist ideas and of concepts of lifelong learning, the landscape of adult and continuing education has shifted from an emphasis on structured 'adult educa-tion' to 'adult learning', from 'the "field" of adult education to a "moorland" of adult learning' (Usher, Bryant and Johnston, 1997, p.1; Edwards, 1997, p.67). However, this emphasis on adult learning rather than the more narrowly defined institutions of adult education pre-dates postmodernist thinking and indeed, was a staple of Diploma in Adult Education courses in British universities in the 1960s. This has influenced my approach in this book, where I have used a broad definition of adult education to include learning activities by adults, mainly on a part-time basis, taken up after a break from full-time schooling.

This lack of clarity and uncertain status extends to concepts used in the field of adult and continuing education. 'Lifelong learning' is an over-arching concept that has been adopted by New Labour. Strictly speaking, it is a holistic concept embracing learning from the cradle to the grave but tends to have been used as a form of shorthand by governments throughout Europe to signify vocational updating for adult employees. 'Continuing education' encompasses education and training for adults for personal, vocational, and professional purposes, both credit and non-credit bearing, although it tends to be particularly associated with higher education. 'Access' can refer to a more open system of higher education or to specially designed courses for entry to higher education, usually for adults or disadvantaged school leavers. 'Community education' refers to more informal education, particularly community rather than institutionally based, often carried out by local authorities or voluntary organisations. 'Open learning' can straddle both these fields, being concerned with flexible methods of study using print or electronic media with the emphasis on the learner setting his or her own pace of study.

'The Godly Commonwealth' – the legacy of the Scottish Reformation

Religion played a major role in eighteenth-century Scotland, as in most other European countries. The Revolution Settlement of 1690 established Presbyterianism as the state church, with a degree of tolerance for Episcopalianism in the early part of the eighteenth century. Presbyterianism was founded on a literal interpretation of the Bible as the word of God and the belief that the head of the church was Christ, not the monarch. It was governed by a 'democratic' hierarchy of courts, stretching from the kirk session, through the local presbytery, to the synod and finally to the General Assembly at national level. At local level the kirk session was responsible for education (parish schools) and poor relief. Although the minister and elders were initially selected by the congregation, the local landowner in the countryside and the provost and the town council in the burghs increasingly expected to control patronage, particularly the appointment of the minister and the schoolmaster, leading to numerous disputes and breakaway movements as the century progressed (Brown, 1997, 1998a). The Act for Settling of Schools (1696) gave the right of appointing the schoolmaster to the heritors and minister of the parish (Withrington, 1998, p.276).

From the beginnings of the Reformation, John Knox and his fellow reformers had seen an important role for schools and universities in the fight to establish and defend the reformed faith in Scotland. In the *Book of Discipline*, dated 1561, and addressed to the Great Council of Scotland, a convention of nobility and lairds, Knox and a group of fellow reformers drafted a national programme for spiritual reform. They wanted a strict system of religious discipline, backed up by a national system of education, based on a school in each parish. Whilst this was an ideal, rather than a proven achievement, it may suggest a continuing influence on the idea of a national curriculum based on a centralist view of education. A section of the *Book of Discipline* entitled 'The Necessity of Schools' argued:

> Seeing that God hath determined that his Church here in earth shall be taught not by angels but by men; and seeing that men are born ignorant of all Godliness…of necessity is it that your Honours be most careful for the virtuous education and godly upbringing of the youth of this Realm. (Dickinson, 1949, II, p.295)

Every church should have a schoolmaster who should be able to teach at least grammar and Latin, as well as instruct young people in the catechism. In every notable town a college should be established to teach the arts and at least logic and rhetoric, 'together with the tongues'. Detailed regulations were also laid down for the conduct of the universities – the subjects to be taught, how long they were to be taught for, even salary levels for members of staff from principals (£200 a year), to gardeners, cooks and porters (10 marks) (Dickinson, 1949, II, pp.296-302).

Weber argued that Protestantism was peculiarly suited to the development of capitalism, through, 'the idea of proving one's faith in worldly activity' (Weber, 1992 edition, p.121). Calvinism seems to have had a particularly strong attachment to ideas of thrift, self-denial, and 'getting on' in life or self-improvement. There was a darker side to this, of course. The consciousness of divine grace of the elect and holy was accompanied by a lack of sympathy for the failings of others. The Scottish Poor Laws were noticeably harsher than those in England and English radicals such as William Cobbett railed against the 'Scotch feelosofers' whom they suspected of wishing to reduce England to a similar state (Cobbett, 1833, pp.48, 140). As the example of Ulster suggests, sectarianism and anti-Catholic feelings could reach particular intensity amongst a Presbyterian population, and this situation was replicated on a smaller scale in the west of Scotland.

Calvinist ideas were also influential in seventeenth-century England, both in breakaway sects and in the Church of England. The English puritan thinker, Baxter, believed that:

> labour came to be considered in itself the end of life, ordained as such by God. St. Paul's 'He who will not work shall not eat' holds unconditionally for everyone, Unwillingness to work is symptomatic of the lack of grace. (Weber, 1992 edition, p.159)

These Calvinistic attitudes come through strongly in the writings of some early Scottish adult educators. George Miller, the Dunbar bookseller who produced *The Cheap Magazine* and other improving tracts aimed at the working classes, quoted this saying of St Paul approvingly in his autobiography and added a passage from Timothy, 'if any provide not for his own, and especially for those of his own house, he hath denied the faith, and is worse than an infidel' (Miller, 1833, pp.56-7).

However, Calvinism had a more positive side in its encouragement of study, debate, and controversy. The Rev. James Lapslie, minister of Campsie parish in Stirlingshire, wrote in the 1790s:

> Upon the whole, I would style the common education of Scotland, partly religious and partly philosophical; it would not be in our interest to see it violently broken in upon; it is this mode of education which gives the Scotch nation such an attachment to speculation in religion. (*Old Statistical Account, (OSA)*, 1978 edition, IX, p.261)

Hugh Miller (1802-56), the Cromarty stonemason who became a self-taught geologist and journalist, would have agreed with this analysis. Miller was born into a Secession Church family and after the Disruption in 1843 he became an activist in the Free Church and edited the Free Church publication, *The Witness*. In his *First Impressions of England*, Miller defended the prevalence of religious controversy in Scotland against English criticism. In response to an English questioner who had asked, 'What good does all your theology do you?' Miller replied, 'Independently altogether of religious considerations, it has done for our people what all your Societies for the Diffusion of Useful Knowledge, and all your Penny and Saturday Magazines, will never do for yours: it has awakened their intellects, and taught them how to think' (Miller, 1847, pp.10-11).

David Kirkwood was born in 1872 in Parkhead, in the east end of Glasgow, into a family of labourers. The area had been a handloom weaving centre and Kirkwood described how:

> These old weavers were Radicals, and like all Radicals, they dearly loved an argument. Unlike their English cousins, they could all read and write. The Old Church Parish Schools taught their pupils how to learn and long before education was made compulsory by law, it had become a necessity by tradition. To be illiterate was to lack dignity and dignity was and is, to the Scot as essential a feature as it was to the Roman. (Kirkwood, 1935, pp.3-4)

Born in 1885, Patrick Dollan grew up in Baillieston, Lanarkshire, a mining village on the southern edge of Glasgow. He recalled:

> The elderly colliers knew more about theology and the Catechism in those days than football coupons and I have heard them competing as to who could recite most of the Catechism without a memory fault. They had all attended schools in the village or in Shettleston and had received some kind of tuition for which they paid fourpence a week. They were known as the fourpenny professors. (Mitchell Library, Dollan Ms., 1952, p.13)

A similar claim about the impact of the Presbyterian tradition was made by an outside observer, the London-born printer and socialist T.A. (Tommy) Jackson, writing about the teaching of Marxian economics to working-class adults in Scotland in the period before, during, and after the First World War:

> I have often noticed a difference between Scottish and English practice in the matter of economics classes. This difference turned upon a fact of which I have plenty of evidence – a fact that the 'traditional distrust of theory' which Engels noted and deplored as a peculiarity of the move-ment in England, was nothing like so evident in Scotland. In my day, the level of education in the public elementary schools was definitely higher in Scotland than in England; and in addition, for historical reasons, there was in Scotland a popular respect for learning that had no counterpart in England. I fancy – though this is only my guess – that an early drilling in the Shorter Catechism had something to do with giving our Scottish com-rades their taste for, and respect of logic. And while this can at times, develop into pedantry and a metaphysical bias favourable to doctrinaire dogmatism, it was a quality that helped the Scottish comrades to play the notable part they have played in the development of the Socialist move-ment in Britain. (Jackson, 1953, p.64)

Many Scottish Radicals and early socialists were heavily influenced by the Presbyterian tradition, particularly the Covenanter version of it, which dated back to the religious struggles of the seventeenth century between Presbyterianism and Episcopalianism. Sometimes the connection was quite explicit. For example, when Sir John Dunlop, a Tory, but from a family with a famous Covenanter tradition, was elected the first MP for Kilmarnock after the 1832 Reform Act, he was driven in the family coach, 'and beside the coachman waved an old, worn flag, that had been with the Laird of Dunlop at the battles of Drumclog and Bothwell Brig. The effect produced on the people of Kilmarnock - who still remembered the covenanting times of their ancestors – as the procession passed along the main streets, was exciting in the extreme' (Paterson, 1871, p.111). Similarly, the main intellectual influences on Keir Hardie were said to be, 'the Covenanters, Burns and Carlyle'. In his obituary of Hardie, Ramsay MacDonald claimed:

If Hardie had ever written a historical introduction to the history of the Labour Movement, he would not have begun with the Reform Bill or such insignificant superficiality, but with Aird's Moss, the Declaration of Sanquhar and that time and such happenings. (Maclean, 1975, p.162)

With this tradition, it is small wonder that early advocates for Owenism were described as 'Socialist missionaries', or that the Eclectic Society, a Glasgow secularist organisation, held annual meetings 'to commemorate the birth of the two prophets, Owen and Payne, who had inspired their movement' (*Forward,* 11 June 1910). Even self-proclaimed atheists and historical materialists could pepper their correspondence with Biblical allusions. Amongst the Scottish Labour College correspondence in the National Library of Scotland is a letter, dated 20 January 1925, from Archibald Bain of Helensburgh, congratulating a fellow activist on getting the better of an argument with a local Labour Party worthy:

It is generally admitted that you justified the materialistic conception on Tuesday in your passage with Bryan. He is the Caiaphas of the Local Labour Party so you ought to feel thankful you escaped the punishment that was meted out to the Nazarenes. (NLS, Acc. 5120, Box 6, No 4)

The role of the churches – the Church of Scotland, the Secession Churches, the Free Churches, the Roman Catholic Church

The patronage issue divided Presbyterianism in Scotland throughout most of the eighteenth century and into the nineteenth. The right to select a minister in the parish church had passed to elders and heritors at the settlement of 1690 but was reinstated by the Patronage Act of 1714 to pacify Scottish landowners during the Jacobite crisis. Landowners increasingly selected ministers who were sympathetic to their political and social views, usually those belonging to what became known as the Moderate faction of the Church of Scotland, and came into conflict with their parishioners, who disliked losing control of appointments and often favoured Evangelical candidates. In 1733, four Church of Scotland ministers denounced patronage and began to form a breakaway church. After expulsion from the Church of Scotland in 1756, the Secession Church was formed, with a reputation for strict Calvinism. This began a long process of internal division and a proliferation of breakaway denominations and sects (Brown, 1998a).

The Secession Churches recruited heavily in certain areas of Scotland and amongst certain social groups. Up to the 1780s their strength lay in rural areas, particularly amongst agricultural labourers, weavers and others who were feeling the upheavals of agricultural change and increasing social divisions. After the 1790s, their strongholds were increasingly in the growing industrial centres

Table 1: Religious backgrounds of parents of autobiographers born between 1741 (John Macdonald) and 1891 (Harry McShane)

Religious background of parents	Numbers
Church of Scotland	9
Dissenting Protestant/Free Church	19
Episcopalian	1
Roman Catholic	1
Mixed RC/Protestant	3
Jewish	1
Non-Religious	2
Not Given/Unknown	26
Total	**62**

such as Dundee, Edinburgh, Glasgow, Paisley and their surrounding villages (Brown, 1998a). In some areas, they were building on a tradition of religious dissent and strict Presbyterianism that went back to the Covenanters, who had signed a National Covenant in 1638 to defend the church against 'popery' and any changes in worship not approved by free assemblies and parliaments.

It is striking how many of the autobiographies, usually describing a self-education or adult education experience, that were written by Scots-born men and women, come from this background of Dissent. My own sample (Table 1) of 62 such autobiographies, diaries and memoirs reveals that no less than 19 (31 per cent) of the writers came from a religious background of Dissenting Protestant/Free Church, with only nine coming from family backgrounds that were Church of Scotland. A further 26 came from backgrounds where the religious affiliation was not given or not known. This means that of those whose parents' religious background is known, a majority (53 per cent) came from a Dissenting/Free Church background.

David Livingstone, for example, born in a 'single end' in Shuttle Row, Blantyre, a cotton manufacturing village in Lanarkshire, described how his father walked out of the Church of Scotland, after being repelled by a sermon on infant damnation, and joined an independent church, which rejected strict Calvinistic notions of election and limited atonement (Ross, 2002, p.5). Livingstone's sister recalled that her grandfather was the manager of the building of the first Secession Church at Airdrie and the arguments in his house about New Light and Old Light, Burgher and Anti-Burgher and the Solemn League and Covenant were so heated that her mother 'could never bear religious controversy' (NLS, Ms 10767, Janet Livingstone's Notes for Dr Blaikie). Similarly, Andrew Carnegie, born into a family of radical weavers in

Dunfermline, Fife, boasted 'we had not one orthodox Presbyterian in our family circle,' which included Swedenborgian uncles and aunts (Carnegie, 1920, p.22).

Religious radicalism had other spin-offs too, one of them being a decline in social deference. In Galt's *Annals of the Parish* (1821), the Rev. Micah Balwidder, in his fictional Ayrshire parish of Dalmailing, described the resistance to his installation as minister in 1760, 'for I was put in by the patron and the people knew nothing whatsoever of me, and their hearts were stirred into strife on the occasion and they did all that lay within their power to keep me out, insomuch that there was obliged to be a guard of soldiers to protect the presbytery'. When a cotton mill was built in the parish in 1788, a new spirit of enterprise entered the area, accompanied by, 'unsettled notions of religion' amongst the textile workers, who disliked Balwidder's sermons and challenged his attempts to 'convince them of their error with regard to the truth of divers points of doctrine' (Galt, 1919 edition, pp.7, 179).

John Ramsay, a Perthshire landowner, made similar comments about the Anti-Burghers, the largest Seceder group:

> Not many years ago, in walking upon the highroad, every bonnet and hat was lifted to the gentry whom the people met. It was an unmeaning expression of respect. The first who would not bow the knee to Baal were the Antiburghers when going to church on Sunday. No such thing now takes place, Sunday or Saturday, among our rustics, even when they are acquainted with gentlemen. It is connected with the spirit of the times. (Ramsay, 1888, p.557)

In the early 1840s, the long-running disputes between the Moderates and the Evangelicals in the Church of Scotland came to a head. The Evangelicals won control of the General Assembly in 1834 and sought to get Parliament to abolish patronage. When, in 1842, the government refused to abolish patronage, church schism seemed inevitable. On 18 May 1843, the Evangelicals, led by the Rev. Thomas Chalmers, staged a walkout from the General Assembly and inaugurated the Free Church of Scotland. After the Disruption, the state church lost 37 per cent of its clergy and between 40-50 per cent of its church membership. In 1847, the majority of 'old' Presbyterian dissenters – those in the Secession and Relief churches, came together in the United Presbyterian Church (Brown, 1998a, pp.75-6, 1998b, p.142). The result of all these changes meant that the Church of Scotland was no longer the dominant national voice in religion that it had been in the eighteenth century, particularly in the growing towns and cities.

Throughout the eighteenth century, Catholicism was confined to the remoter corners of Scotland, particularly the western Highlands and the rural North-East. In the Barony parish of Glasgow, for example, out of a population of 18,451 in 1794, there were only 20 Roman Catholics, compared to 12,369 members of the Church of Scotland and 5,631 belonging to secession churches (*OSA*, 1973 edition, VII, p.350). This began to change with Irish immigration into the west of Scotland, starting often on a seasonal basis as harvesters, then coming as more permanent migrants, aided by cheap steamboat travel. In Glasgow, the Catholic population rose from a reputed 30 in 1778, to 2,300 in 1808, to 27,000 in 1831, to be followed by an even larger wave after the Irish Famine (Brown, 1998a, p.80).

These poor Irish migrants met racist and sectarian responses from the host population. They occupied the lowest paid and least skilled jobs and their low level of initial education was contrasted unfavourably with that of the native Scots. Thomas Malthus, in *An Essay on the Principle of Population* (1798), praised the generally high level of education in Scotland and its effectiveness as a method of social control compared with the situation in Ireland. He argued:

> The quiet and peaceable habits of the instructed Scotch peasant, compared with the turbulent disposition of the ignorant Irishman, ought not to be without effect on every impartial reasoner. (Malthus, 1986 edition, p.527)

Not all the hostility towards Irish immigrants was based on anti-Catholicism. For example, William Hutton's family were Presbyterians from Dumfries but he was born and grew up in County Tyrone in Ulster. As a young man, he moved to Glasgow in the 1840s, travelling first by paddle steamer from Belfast to Ardrossan, then in an open cattle truck from Ardrossan to Glasgow 'completely filled with Irish immigrants like myself'. He was taken on as a weaver in Glasgow and found that, 'Some lads, weavers like myself, helped me to better my skill at the craft, so did the old men with whom I worked, but some of the baser sort made me understand that it was not an advantage to have been born in Ireland' (Hutton, 1904, p.20).

However, the greatest hostility was directed towards the Roman Catholic Irish, reflecting the prejudices of the Presbyterian Scot towards the living standards, behaviour and perceived lack of education of the incomers, as well as their religion. Thomas Carlyle, for example, from a Burgher Seceder background in the Scottish Borders, used his 1839 essay on Chartism and the condition of the English working class to fulminate against 'the uncivilised Irishman, (who) not by his strength but by the opposite of strength, drives out the Saxon native, takes possession in his room. There abides he, in his squalor and unreason, in his falsity and drunken violence, as the ready made nucleus of degradation and disorder' (Carlyle, 1894 edition, Vol. VI, p.127). Similarly, James Myles, a radical Dundee bookseller, (Whatley, 2000b, p.73) writing in 1850, displayed many of the prejudices of the Presbyterian Scot towards the Irish incomers:

> It is deeply to be lamented that the vast hordes who have migrated to the Scouringburn are composed of the most debased and ignorant of their countrymen. Their vile slang and immoral habits have seriously injured the general character of the poor population of Dundee, and I believe throughout Scotland. The low Irish are not a very improvable race. They cling to their rags, their faith and their filth with all the besottedness of perfect ignorance and stupidity. (Myles, 1850, p.25)

In the west of Scotland, the Rev. Patrick Macfarlan, writing about the Clyde port and sugar-refining centre of Greenock, gave vent to similar feelings, but in more euphemistic language:

> it is no more than justice to the inhabitants of Greenock to remark, that where the population is dense, intemperance and licentiousness are too frequently the vices of persons of all ranks; and seaport towns are more than others exposed to that moral contagion. To this we may add that association for other purposes, by bringing together men of very different and opposite principles, have exerted a most injurious influence on the working classes; and the immigration from other quarters, of families unaccustomed in their infancy to the habits of a well-educated Scottish population, has tended not a bit to lower the standard by which they are wont to regulate their conduct. (*New Statistical Account*, 1845, p.429)

The Irish were seen as threatening not only the jobs and living standards but also the cultural identity of the native Scots. In 1838, the Commission on Handloom Weaving, reporting on the long decline of the industry, commented, 'Those of the Scotch weavers who come much in contact with the Irish, are almost invariably worsened by fellowship with them. The Irish weavers are a little in advance in the career down hill, for they are the main cause of pulling the Scotch down after them' (*Parliamentary Papers*, (1970 edition), Industrial Revolution, Textiles, Vol. 9, p.31).

In 1846, it was claimed that out of 600 railway workers lodged at Lockerbie, Dumfrieshire, the evening school was attended almost exclusively by Irish workers, as almost all the native Scots could read and write (Webb, 1954, p.101). Similarly, the Commissioners on Education reported in 1867 that in the south of Scotland, particularly Dumfriesshire, Peebles, Roxburgh, Edinburgh, Ayr and Kirkcudbright, 'nearly all the native population can read with ease, and the majority can write, but the Irish settlers are in great ignorance, and as a result can neither read nor write' (*Parliamentary Papers*, 1867, XXV, p.xxii).

Patrick Dollan, born into a Roman Catholic family in the coal-mining village of Baillieston in Lanarkshire, remembered his grandmother, an Irish peasant who had been evicted during the Famine, as being the only woman of her generation who could read and write. As a result she 'acted as political tutor and adviser to all the emigrants who came seeking for aid and advice' (Mitchell Library, Dollan Ms., 1952, p.23). As late as 1910, Harry McShane recalled that most of the Catholics in the tenement close in Tradeston, Glasgow, where he grew up, were unable to read, and he 'had to read the papers out every night' during a particularly lurid murder trial in Glasgow (McShane, 1978, p.7).

Chapter 1
'An instructed and intelligent people'
– Scotland from the Union of 1707 to 1790

An instructed and intelligent people besides, are always more decent and orderly than an ignorant and stupid one.

(Adam Smith, *The Wealth of Nations,* 1776)

The Union of 1707

Social and intellectual history does not divide easily into periods but the Act of Union of 1707 can be viewed as a crossroads for Scotland in many ways. The Act, which abolished the Scottish Parliament, forged an economic union with Scotland's larger and richer southern neighbour, England, whilst largely preserving Scotland's distinctive systems of law, religion and education. The economic benefits of Union were slow to appear at first but the available evidence suggests that Scotland's population grew from just over one million in the late 1690s to 1.6 million in 1801 (Tranter, 1998, p.112). The same period saw agricultural change, population movement to the central belt of Scotland, particularly west central Scotland, growing urbanisation and industrialisation. Eighteenth-century Scotland was a nation divided linguistically between the English (or Scots) speaking Lowlands and the Gaelic speaking Highlands and Western Isles. One result of the Union was a growing tension between the use of the Scots tongue and more 'polite' English. Indeed, an early form of adult education provision in Edinburgh was a series of lectures on 'Elocution and the English Tongue' by Thomas Sheridan, the father of the playwright, held in 1761 under the auspices of the Select Society. The lectures were aimed at upwardly mobile Scots, in the belief that: 'gentlemen educated in Scotland have long been sensible of the disadvantages under which they labour, from their imperfect knowledge of the ENGLISH tongue, and the impropriety with which they speak it' (Simpson, 1988, pp.77–9). Ironically, Sheridan was Irish.

The Society in Scotland for Propagating Christian Knowledge

As one might expect from the ideas discussed in the introduction, the earliest organised adult education movement in Scotland had a religious impulse. In

1704, the General Assembly of the Church of Scotland sponsored a library scheme for the Highlands, thanks to the initiative of James Kirkwood, an ejected Episcopalian minister, who had become Scottish correspondent for the Society for Promoting Christian Knowledge (SPCK) in 1702. Kirkwood had come up with an ambitious scheme in 1699 to set up a free public lending library in every parish, containing at least one copy of every valuable book extant. The scheme would be funded by a levy on church income and would rely on the parish schoolmaster to act as librarian. This scheme was too ambitious for the General Assembly but, nothing daunted, Kirkwood collected £650 and the scheme went ahead with small libraries of less than a hundred volumes in some 77 centres in the Highlands and Islands. The library collections included theology, history, medicine, astronomy and agriculture. Books could be borrowed by any Protestant, with a deposit of a quarter of the value of the book borrowed. By 1826, most of these libraries had disappeared (Kelly, 1992, p.69).

The SSPCK, founded in 1709, was modelled on the SPCK in England, which had been founded ten years earlier. The Scottish Society worked closely with the Church of Scotland and by the end of the eighteenth century, had established over 300 'ambulatory schools', mainly in the Highlands. These schools were not only aimed at children but also provided 'night schools for servants and adults who could not leave their work in the daytime'. In the Gaelic-speaking areas, they also had to grapple with the problems of teaching English as a second language. Until 1766, the Society insisted that children were taught in English but Gaelic books were provided for older people. In 1767, the Society printed 10,000 copies of a Gaelic version of the New Testament by James Stuart of Killin. It seems that it was from the SSPCK that Griffith Jones copied the idea of circulating schools for his Circulating Welsh Charity Schools, built up in the 1730s, to teach children and adults to read the Bible in Welsh (Kelly, 1992, p.68; Withers, 2000, pp.397–403).

The SSPCK made a considerable impact on the education of the Highland population, particularly on the eastern fringes of the Highlands. For example, in 1792, in Glengairn parish in Highland Aberdeenshire, part of the combined parish of Glenmuick, Tulloch and Glengairn, the two Society schools were said to be 'an unspeakable advantage to the people. I am told that 60 or 70 years ago, it was rare to find one in all these three parishes who could read. But now all the young people read distinctly and understand the principles of religion; and many of the young men leave school and immediately enter as clerks to commercial companies in different corners of the world' (OSA, 1982, XIV, p.513). Further north, in Urquhart parish in Ross and Cromarty, on the north-eastern shores of Loch Ness, the Rev. Charles Calder reported in the same year, 'The early establishment of a school in it, by the Society for the Propagation of Christian Knowledge, at which, for a long tract of years, about 100 children, (besides those enjoying similar advantages at the parochial school), have annually received instruction in the great duties of religion and morality, as well as the first principles of literature, could hardly fail, in such a course of time, to have a happy influence on the character and manners of the people' (*OSA*, 1981, XVII, pp.666–7).

Official attitudes towards the Gaelic language varied from ambivalent or indifferent to downright hostile. In the seventeenth century, the Gaelic speaking Highlands and Western Isles were often seen as strongholds of irreligion and violence, or bastions of Episcopalianism or Catholicism and a threat to the Presbyterian faith. An Act of the Privy Council of 10 December 1616 stated in its preamble that:

> Forsameikle as the Kingis Majestie having a speciall care and regaird that the trew religioun be advanceit and establisheit in all pairtis of this king-dome and that all his Majesties subjectis, especiallie the youth, be exercised and trayned up in civilitie, godlines, knowledge and learning, that the vulgar Inglishe toung be universalie plantit, and the Irische lan-guage, whilk is one of the cheif and principall causis of the continewance of barbaritie and incivilitie amongis the inhabitantis of the Ilis and Heylandis, may be abolisheit and removit; and quhair as thair is no meas-ure more powerful to further his further his Majesties princelie regaird and purpois that the establiseing of Schooles in the particular parroches of this Kingdom whair the youth may be taught at least to write and reid, and be catechised and instructed in the groundis of religioun. (Burton, (ed.), X, 1616, pp.671–2)

A similar assault on minority languages was taking place in many other parts of Europe at this time. In France, for example, the centralisation of the French state was being carried through at the expense of the 'fringe' languages such as Basque, Breton, Catalan, and Provencal. The Academie Francaise was founded in 1635 to act as the official guardian of the purity of the French language (Davies, 1997, p.623).

Literacy rates – the historical debate

Historians have been engaged in an ongoing debate about the extent and limi-tations of literacy in Scotland in the eighteenth and nineteenth centuries. Houston sampled those able to sign their names in court depositions in England and Scotland for the period 1640–1770 and found that signing ability was closely associated with occupation and with socio-economic status. There were significant differences between Scotland and the north of England only in the seventeenth century, when Scotland enjoyed a superior signing rate, but the gap narrowed in the eighteenth century. Mirroring the English experience, there were higher signing levels in Scottish towns than in the countryside. The Highlands of Scotland presented particular problems of low levels of signing ability, probably due to the prevalence of Gaelic. In England between 1640 and 1760, 42 per cent of all male assize deponents were unable to sign their names, whilst in Scotland, between 1650 and 1770, the comparable figure was 32 per cent. The level for women in both countries was identical, with 81 per cent unable to sign their names (Houston, 1985, pp.34–57).

Houston believed that Scotland's achievements in literacy were comparable to those of Northern England and that, internationally, Scotland's literacy rates were not dramatically different from those of a number of other European countries and were probably outstripped by Sweden and New England (Houston, 1985, pp.21–2). An American historian, by contrast, has argued that Scotland, New England and Sweden, 'stood out among the western states of the early modern era for the rapidity, breadth and pace of their rise in literacy' (Lockridge, 1981, p.188).

Houston's stress on the significance of the ability to sign one's name has been challenged by historians such as Smout and Withrington, who believed that the ability to read and understand was much more important. The ability to read the Bible was considered particularly important in a Calvinist country. Smout used evidence from a 'born-again' Christian group in Cambuslang, in 1742, where out of 109 cases all the women (74) and all the men had been taught to read but only 11 per cent of women and 60 per cent of men could write. This is in line with evidence from Sweden, where by 1750, 80 per cent of the population could read but only from 5 to 20 per cent could write. The 'born-again' Christians at Cambuslang came from fairly humble backgrounds – most of the women were live-in servants, whilst the men were mainly small crafts-men. However, revivalists may not be typical of the general population in educational background. A fascinating insight from the Cambuslang study is the way in which schools tend to be over-rated as a medium of instruction in this period. Many of the Cambuslang witnesses were taught to read the Bible by their parents, many had a broken schooling because of poverty, and one woman was only at school for 20 days. There were nine cases of 'post-school learning' – either learning to read the Bible in church as a young adult or being taught in houses where they worked as servants (Smout, 1982, pp.122–3). This pattern recurs in many of the working-class autobiographies of the eighteenth and nineteenth centuries. It seems likely that in many of these revivalist groups, the Bible may have been the only form of reading available or sanctioned by the group.

One result of the modest amount of schooling received by many Scots was that reading and writing skills could easily lapse. James Hogg, the 'Ettrick Shepherd', who was born in 1770, became a cow herd at the age of seven, then had about six months of schooling and went back to shepherding. From then until the age of 15, Hogg claimed, 'I neither read nor wrote, nor had I any access to any book save the Bible'. At the age of 18, Hogg started to work as a shepherd with a Mr Laidlaw of Elibank on Tweed. Here, he began to read Blind Harry's *Wallace* and Allan Ramsay's *Gentle Shepherd*. Hogg recalled, 'the little reading I had learned I had nearly lost' and that writing was more difficult still. He had 'no method of learning to write, save by following the Italian alphabet' and found he got cramp after writing four or five lines. On trying to write a letter to his elder brother, Hogg found that, 'never having drawn a pen for such a number of years, I had actually forgotten how to make sundry letters of the alphabet'. In 1790, he went to work for another Mr Laidlaw, this time of Black Howes, where he worked as a shepherd for ten years. Laidlaw had a collection of books, which Hogg was allowed to use and he wrote his first poem in 1796. Not until 1797, when Hogg was 27, did he discover the poetry of Robert Burns (Hogg, 1972 edition, pp.vii, 4–10).

Others took even longer to acquire the basics of literacy. John Duncan, for example, a Stonehaven weaver and self-taught botanist, was born in 1794 to an illiterate single mother. At the age of 16, he learned to read his ABC at the home of a female neighbour, Mrs Clark. However, it was not until 1828, at the age of 34, that Duncan began to learn to write and he completed his formal education by attending evening school for five or six weeks 'to improve his scholastic attainments' (Jolly, 1883, pp.39-43).

The evidence of the *Statistical Accounts*, 1790

Certainly, many contemporaries, whether Scots or English, believed that the Scottish educational system was superior to the English and that as a consequence literacy rates were higher, crime lower and even behaviour better. Daniel Defoe, for example, praised the role of the Church of Scotland, which policed behaviour such as, 'swearing, drunkenness, slander, fornication, adultery and the like'. Writing in 1717, he claimed, 'you may pass through twenty towns in Scotland without seeing any broil or hearing an oath sworn in the streets; whereas if a blind man was to come from thence into England, he shall know, the first town he sets his foot in, within the English border, by hearing the name of God blasphemed, and profanely used even by the very little children in the streets' (Defoe, 1844 edition, p.351). Defoe returned to this theme in his *Tour Through the Whole Island of Great Britain*, published in 1724–6. In Kirkcudbright, he observed, 'far from what it is in England, you hear no oaths, or profane words in the streets; and if a mean boy, such as we call shoe-blackers, or black-guard boys, should be heard to swear, the next gentleman in the street.... would cane him and correct him, whereas, in England, nothing is more frequent, or less regarded now, than the most horrid oaths and blasphemies in the open streets, and that by the little children that hardly know what an oath means'

(Defoe, 1971 edition, p.597). This suggests either that the role of the Kirk in policing morality was highly effective, or that, as an English Dissenter, Defoe was making a religious point as much as a social observation.

The *Statistical Accounts of Scotland*, published under the direction of Sir John Sinclair in the 1790s, provide a unique record of many aspects of Scottish life in a period of rapid social and economic change. Compiled on a parish basis mainly by the local minister, but also on occasion by the local schoolteacher or landowner, the *Statistical Accounts* took considerable interest in schooling, teachers' salaries, and general levels of literacy, often contrasted favourably with England. For example, the Rev. James Wilson, minister of Mid Calder parish in Midlothian, boasted in the early 1790s:

> I know nobody in the parish, above eight or ten, who cannot read, and not a few can write and do a little in accounts. These acquirements, which are so common among the people of Scotland, are easily seen to proceed from the important regulation of having a school with a fixed salary annexed to it, in every parish. *(Old Statistical Account,* hereafter *OSA,* 1975 edition, II, p.94)

A similar claim was made by the Rev. John Burns, writing in 1794 about the rapidly industrialising parish of the Barony of Glasgow:

> There are few of the inhabitants who have been bred in this parish, who have not been taught to read; and most of them can write, and understand the common rules of arithmetic. Education is so cheap, as not to be placed beyond the reach of the poorest. And the people are so impressed with a sense of its importance that most parents, if not most profligate themselves, are exceedingly anxious to have their children instructed in reading. They often cheerfully deny themselves many of the comforts of life to give their children education; and many of them have been rewarded, by seeing them rising to affluence and respect in society. (*OSA,* 1975, VII, p.351)

In the Fife parish of Auchterderran, a coal mining area, the Rev. Andrew Murray described the poverty of his parishioners, the inadequacy of their housing and their bad diet. In spite of this:

> The people are not illiterate. In common with the rest of Scotland, the vulgar are for their station, literate, perhaps, beyond all other nations. Puritanic and abstract divinity comes in for a sufficient share in their little stock of books; and it is perhaps peculiar to them as a people that they endeavour to form opinions by reading as well as frequent conversation,

on some very metaphysical points connected with religion and on the deeper doctrines of Christianity. They likewise read, occasionally, a variety of other books unconnected with such subjects. (*OSA*, 1978, X, pp.48-9)

In the south-west of Scotland, in the Dumfriesshire parish of Kirkpatrick-Juxta, the minister, writing in the early 1790s, contrasted the present levels of literacy amongst his parishioners very favourably with the position 50 years earlier:

The common people were certainly more ignorant 50 years ago than at present. Several at that time had not learned either to read or write; now they can all read pretty well, and all the men at least can write. Several of the farmers read history, magazines and newspapers. The vulgar read almost nothing but books on religious subjects. Many of them are too fond of controversial divinity; a taste which the Dissenters are very diligent in promoting, and which the few books they are acquainted with, are rather calculated to confirm. To discourage this unhappy propensity, so common through a great part of Scotland, and to recommend books of a more rational and instructive nature, seems an object worthy of a clergyman. *(OSA*, 1978, IV, p.349)

A similarly optimistic view of the spread of popular enlightenment was given by the Rev. John Bruce, parish minister of Forfar in Angus, where he claimed:

A spirit of enquiry and a taste for reading is springing up and popular superstitions begin to hide their heads. The subscription to the *Encyclopedia Britannica*, the *Bee* and several periodical and other publications, scientific, religious, moral and political, are more numerous of late than could well have been expected; and they already shed an evident lustre on the conversation of many. (*OSA,* 1976, XIII, p.273)

The Gaelic speaking parts of the Highlands and Islands faced particular difficulties in terms of language problems, scattered populations, transport difficulties and poverty. However, even here changes were taking place, particularly on the eastern fringes of the Highlands. For example, in Glenmuick, Tulloch and Glengairn parish in Highland Aberdeenshire, the Rev. William Spence observed, 'The people, in general, have got a taste for education, and as the parishes are extensive, they engage young men in the winter season in those places which are at a distance from the established schools.' (*OSA,* 1982, XIV, p.513)

Further north, in Cromdale, Invernesshire, the Rev. Mr Lewis Grant claimed in 1792, 'In a few years hence, English will be the only language, as the people ardently wish their children to read the scriptures; and for this purpose, often, in the winter, four or five schools are employed at once in the parish at their expense' (OSA, 1981, XVII, p.41). Another minister, writing about the parish of Urray in Ross and Cromarty, took a different view, 'Several of the inhabitants read the English Bible and can transact business in that language; but they, as well as the bulk of the people, prefer religious instruction in Gaelic; and there-fore are at pains to read the Gaelic New Testament and Psalm Book'. In this Highland parish, the parochial school was supplemented by a SSPCK charity school and a spinning mistress (OSA, 1981, XVII, pp.682, 676).

How typical, impartial and accurate were these descriptions by ministers? Some of them were undoubtedly trying to make a point about the desirability of keeping the parochial system of schools going in the face of increasing pres-sures brought about by urbanisation, industrialisation, population increase and shifts of population. Many of them stressed the difficulties of recruiting and retaining schoolmasters when salaries were so low. Others argued that education acted as a check on crime and other social evils and a bulwark against revolu-tion. William Barclay, for example, the schoolmaster of the Lanarkshire parish of Cadder, north-east of Glasgow, contrasted Scotland with England to defend the role of the schoolmaster:

> The good behaviour of the lower orders in Scotland, in general, con-trasted with the immoralities, crimes and annual executions, of many of the same class, in the sister kingdom, can be ascribed to nothing so much as the superior advantages the former enjoy, of early education and proper instruction, in the first principles of moral and religious duty. Deprive them of those and they will soon become as great savages, as the most ignorant rabble of London, Paris or Birmingham. (OSA, 1973, VII, p.77)

However, not all ministers or schoolmasters were quite so optimistic about Scottish education and levels of literacy. The Rev. Alex Carlyle, of Inveresk parish, Midlothian, reported in 1792 that Sunday schools had been established in the last three years in the fishing communities of Musselburgh and Fisherrow:

> which though unnecessary in general in Scotland, where the parish schools are sufficient, yet are of much general utility here, where, on account of the poverty and constant occupations of the parents, the instruction of many children was neglected. (OSA, 1975, II, p.309)

Against this background, when poverty meant there was pressure on parents to send their children out to work early, Sunday schools and evening classes could perform a useful compensatory function, often supplemented by teaching at home by parents and by mutual instruction and local libraries. In Renfrew in 1791, for example, the Rev. Thomas Burn claimed that:

> Not only tradesmen, but even day labourers, give their children a good education. Scarce a boy who is not taught reading, writing, and arithmetic, a little church music &etc. And should any of them be neglected in their youth, when they come to the years of discretion, they go to school at their own expense, in order to acquire these branches. This is an important advantage which the Scots, as a nation, enjoy over the inhabitants of other countries. (*OSA*, 1973, VII, p.864)

Similar claims were made by the minister of Newburgh in Fife, a river port and weaving town, where there were two schools, one parochial, the other run by the secession church. The Rev. Thomas Stuart described how:

> During the winter season, both schools are resorted to, after the ordinary hours of labour, by a considerable number of grown up persons, for the purpose of learning English, writing, arithmetic, book-keeping and navigation. (*OSA*, 1978, X, p.681)

Hugh Miller, in his portrait of an outstanding schoolmaster at Cromarty Grammar School in the early 1800s, had a similar tale to tell:

> There were usually a few grown up lads under his tuition – careful sailors, that had stayed ashore during the winter quarter to study navigation as a science - or tall fellows, happy in the patronage of the great, who in the hope of being made excisemen, had come to school to be initiated in the mysteries of gauging – or grown young men, who on second thoughts and somewhat late in the day, had recognized the Church as their proper vocation. (Miller, 1874, p.45)

It is hard to tell whether evening schools were a long standing part of the Scottish tradition or a response to the changing social and economic circumstances of late eighteenth-century Scotland. They seem to have had a particular resonance in the industrial towns and villages, where there was financial pressure to send children into employment as early as seven or eight. In the early 1790s, Campsie in Stirlingshire was a parish with coal mines and two large print-fields. From there, the Rev. James Lapslie reported the high wages paid to adult textile printers (up to 21 shillings a week) and the demand for evening schools by adults:

There being several public works in the parish, the night school is considerable, being wholly made up of grown up persons, who attend for the purposes of writing and arithmetic. (*OSA*, 1978, IX, p.261)

However, evening schools were also a feature of rural parishes. At Pencaitland in East Lothian the Rev. Henry Sangster, minister of Humbie, claimed that:

It is not remembered that an inhabitant of this parish has been punished by the civil magistrate for any crime. All of them at least can read the Bible; and the greatest part of the young men, whose parents could afford but little for their education, attend the schoolmaster in the winter evenings; who for a small consideration, teaches them writing and the common rules of arithmetic, by which means they acquire good habits, and become useful as farm and family servants. (*OSA*, 1975, II, p.558)

School masters trying to eke out an existence on the small salaries and fees paid by most parish schools found evening classes and Sunday schools a useful source of extra income. The minister of Nielston in Renfrewshire explained:

By keeping evening schools for arithmetic, church music &c every schoolmaster, especially in large landward parishes, may greatly increase his emoluments. (*OSA*, 1973, VII, p.815)

While these examples may not be typical, they do suggest that in the early stages of industrialisation, there was a demand for adult education in a wide range of localities where schooling was neglected or shortened, due to economic pressures and the demand for child labour. Adult education fulfilled a compensatory function for many young adults and also acted as a way of preventing hard won skills in reading and writing from lapsing through disuse.

The supply of reading material – chapbooks, newspapers, pamphlets, books and early libraries

Crucial to most forms of adult learning in this period – self-education, mutual improvement and more formal types of education - was the supply of reading material in the form of chapbooks, newspapers, pamphlets and books. The most basic type of reading material for the masses was the cheaply produced chapbook, a favourite target for early adult educators such as George Miller, the Dunbar bookseller. In his autobiography, Miller recounted how he opened his first circulating library in 1789 and published his first catalogue two years later. He produced up to 100,000 *Cheap Tracts* from the Dunbar Press in 1802 and 1803, 'to counteract the dangerous tendency of that noxious description, which were then so abundantly scattered about the country, through the medium of what has been so emphatically styled, that copious source of mischief, THE HAWKER'S BASKET' (Miller, 1833, p.49; Macgregor, 1883).

Strangely, Violet Croumbie, the mother of another early adult educator, Samuel Brown of Haddington (born 1799), the founder of the East Lothian Itinerating Library Scheme, came from a pedlar family from Stenton, East Lothian, who were members of the Guild of Travelling Packmen and presumably sold chapbooks. Brown's father had been orphaned at ten and earned his living as a herd boy and shepherd, 'followed by a short trial of the pedlar life'. He then became, 'a Student of Divinity, Preacher of the Word, Minister of the Gospel, Professor of Divinity and widely-respected Author'. Brown's mother, Violet, was a voracious reader and when the family moved back to Haddington from Edinburgh, she 'literally read the libraries of the burgh dry after her return from the metropolis this time' (Brown, 1856, pp.3-13).

Newspapers experienced a modest expansion in Scotland up to the 1780s, after which there was a boom in their numbers. By 1785, there were about a dozen newspapers in Scotland, compared to about 50 provincial newspapers in England. The geographical spread included a cluster in Edinburgh, Glasgow (from 1715), Dumfries (1721), Aberdeen (1747) and Kelso (1783) (Kelly, 1992, p.83). Between 1782 and 1790, the number of newspapers in Scotland jumped from eight to 27 and there was a further expansion in the years 1791–2, in response to the ferment of ideas coming from revolutionary France (Lenman, 1981, p.101). Although newspaper sales were modest in this period and their readership largely upper and middle class, there is some indication that readership was widening, through libraries and reading aloud in pubs, coffee shops and workplaces, which will be more fully discussed in the next chapter.

One index of the growing popularity of reading was the spread of the printing, publishing and book trade. In 1688 there were printers, booksellers and binders in only six places in Scotland but by 1775 this had expanded to 75 places. In Edinburgh, the centre of the Scottish publishing trade, the six printing houses in 1763 had increased to 16 by 1790 (OSA, 1975 edition, II, p.35). It seems likely that the bulk of the market for book sales was middle class. Analyses of inventories and wills for Lasswade in Midlothian from 1660 to 1760 and for Orkney, Shetland, Argyll and the Isles up to 1750 suggested that ownership of books was, 'very much a preserve of the upper middle class' (Houston, 1985, p.164, 169). By contrast, the market for religious books may have been different. An analysis of the subscription lists of two religious works reprinted in Glasgow (Isaac Ambrose, *Prima Media* 7th edition, 1757 and Thomas Watson, *A body of Practical Divinity*, 5th edition, 1759) showed that most of the 1004 subscribers were craftsmen and tradesmen, with weavers making up 37 per cent and 45 per cent of subscribers of known occupation on the two dates. The number of female subscribers was tiny. Only 12 women bought the

1757 volume (3 per cent) and 11 the 1759 one (2 per cent) (Laslett, 1969). However, readership, as opposed to ownership, of books was probably much wider than these figures suggest.

The earliest public library in Scotland was Innerpeffray Library, near Crieff in Perthshire, founded in 1680 by David Drummond, 3rd Lord Madertie. Its borrowing record was modest. Between 1747 and 1757 only 241 book loans were made to a mere 130 individuals. Of these, only nine were women. Out of the 121 men, the occupations of 88 were listed. The dominant groups amongst borrowers were professionals – ministers, schoolmasters, students and lairds (41), and craftsmen and tradesmen (40). Other borrowers included servants (6) and only one farmer in a heavily agricultural area. The bulk of the books borrowed were religious and even the historical books had a religious flavour, such as Knox's *History of the Reformation* (Houston, 1985, p.176).

Scotland led the way in the development of commercial circulating libraries. The first of its kind in Britain was established in 1726 by Allan Ramsay, poet, wigmaker and bookseller, in his shop in the High Street in Edinburgh. By the end of the eighteenth century, there were over 1000 circulating libraries in Britain, catering mainly for the middle classes and concentrating on fiction. As such, they were condemned for corrupting morals and it was said that, 'all the villainous, profane and obscene books of plays, as printed in London, are got down by Allan Ramsay and lent out for an easy price, to young boys, servant women of the better sort and gentlemen,' the end result being 'vice and obscenity dreadfully propagated' (Houston, 1994, p.208). Particularly worrying to the moralists was the involvement of women in reading. It was claimed, in 1783, that the daughters of Edinburgh tradesmen no longer cooked or sewed but 'employed those heavy hours when she was disengaged from public or private amusements, in improving her mind from the precious stores of a circulating library; and all, whether they had taste for it or not, were taught music at a great expense' (*OSA*, 1975, II, p.55).

These criticisms were less likely to be levelled against the private subscription libraries, which were thought to be eminently respectable. Again, Scotland led the way, the first example in Britain being a working-class library formed by the lead miners of Leadhills in Lanarkshire 'wholly at their own suggestion' in 1741. This was followed by middle-class subscription libraries in Dumfries in 1745 and in Kelso in 1751. In 1756, another library for lead miners was established at Wanlockhead in Dumfrieshire, just over the county border from Leadhills (Kelly, 1992, p.86).

Lead miners in this period enjoyed high wages, a relatively short working day and a good level of basic schooling (Smout, 1967). At Leadhills, in 1792, the Rev. James Maconochie explained, 'They work in the mines only 6 hours out of 24. Having therefore a great deal of spare time, they employ themselves in reading, and for this purpose have been at the expense of fitting up a library, out of which everyone who contributes to the expense receives books' *(OSA*, 1973, VII, p.210). Another minister, the Rev. William Peterkin, described the miners' library in glowing terms, 'The Leadhills library contains some trash, but as many valuable books as might be expected to be chosen by promiscuous readers. They are the best informed and therefore the most reasonable common people that I know'. He also praised the effects of temperance on the lead miners, 'About thirty years ago, most of the smelters died either madmen or idiots. Now they retain their senses as well as other people. The reason given is: formerly spirits were cheap and the smelters partook them liberally at their work. For many years past they drink nothing at their work, but pure spring water; they now live as long and rationally as others' (*OSA,* 1973, VII, p.216). The books in the Leadhills Library included philosophical but not scientific subjects, and the engineer and inventor William Symington was a library member in 1783 (Harvey and Downs-Rose, 1980, pp.5–6).

Undoubtedly, many private subscription libraries must have functioned as cultural enclaves for the middle classes. For example, the Speculative Society was founded in 1764 by six Edinburgh students to improve their composition and public speaking skills. It built a hall within Edinburgh University and furnished a library. The Society flourished as part of a network of clubs within the intensely clubbable atmosphere of eighteenth-century Edinburgh and, it was claimed, 'can boast of eminent members in the Senate, in the Pulpit, in Professors' chairs in the Universities, at the Bar, in Medicine and in various departments of life' (*OSA,* 1975 edition, II, p.28). Nor were such activities confined to the cities. Ayr had a Library Society as early as 1761, with the town's two ministers as sponsors (Boyd, 1961, p.124). In Montrose, a public library was founded by 'some literary gentlemen' in 1785 (*OSA,* 1976, XIII, p.547).

Reading tastes appear to have differed between middle-class and working-class libraries. Rose carried out an analysis of holdings in eighteenth-century Scottish libraries, based on statistics collected by John Crawford. His sample included James Sibbald's circulating library in Edinburgh's Parliament Square, which served a middle-class clientele, four middle-class libraries in smaller towns (Greenock, Forfar, Hawick and Duns) and two libraries run by and for lead miners in Leadhills and Wanlockhead in 1790 and 1800. They reveal that libraries catering for the middle classes favoured fiction, whilst working-class run libraries were much more likely to stock religious literature (Rose, 2002, p.117).

However, subscription libraries were not confined to lead miners and the urban middle classes. By 1790, Robert Burns (1759-1796) was ordering books for the library of the Monkland Friendly Society, Ayrshire, an association of local tenant farmers. His order included Knox's *History of the Reformation,* Watson's *Divinity, The Mirror, The Man of Feeling, The Man of the World,* Rae's *History of the Rebellion of 1715,* 'Any Good History of the Rebellion 1745', 'a

Display of the Secession Act and Testimony by Mr Gib,' Harvey's *Meditations*, Beveridge's *Thoughts* and another copy of Watson's *Body of Practical Divinity*, which was 'much admired'. Burns ordered for himself Otway's dramatic works, Ben Johnson, Dryden, Congreve, Wycherley, Sheridan, Molière in French, Racine, Corneille and Voltaire (Lindsay, 1968, p.247).

Burns wrote to Sir John Sinclair about this scheme in 1791, praising the local landowner, Robert Riddel, who had encouraged the idea. Burns believed that, 'to store the minds of the lower classes with useful knowledge is certainly of very great importance, both to them as individuals and to society at large. Giving them a turn for reading and reflection, is giving them a source of innocent and laudable amusement, and besides, raises them to a more dignified degree in the scale of rationality'. Riddel had got together a number of his own tenants and farming neighbours to form a library with a legal agreement to stay in the scheme for three years. Each member paid five shillings and sixpence more at their monthly meetings. This money was used for book purchase and all books had to be returned monthly. Amongst the books purchased were, 'Blair's *Sermons*, Robertson's *History of Scotland*, Hume's *History of the Stuarts*, *The Spectator, Idler, Adventurer, Mirror, Lounger, Observer, Man of Feeling, Man of the World, Chrysal, Don Quixote, Joseph Andrews* &c'. There is a strong emphasis on Enlightenment authors here. Signing himself 'A PEASANT', Burns concluded, 'A peasant who can read and enjoy such books, is certainly a much superior being to his neighbour, who perhaps stalks besides his team, very little removed, except in shape, from the brutes he drives'. A covering letter from Robert Riddel commended the scheme to Sinclair and praised the contribution Burns had made to its success. If adopted throughout Scotland, the scheme would, 'tend greatly to the speedy improvement of the tenantry, trades-people and work-people'. Burns had taken charge of the whole scheme and acted as, 'treasurer, librarian and censor, to this little society, who will long have a grateful sense of his public spirit and exertions for their improvement and information' (Burns, no date, pp.272–3).

Burns was also involved in an early mutual improvement activity in Ayrshire– the Tarbolton Bachelors' Club. This was an association of young farmers who met to debate such enlightenment-influenced topics as, 'Whether is the savage man or the peasant of a civilised country in the most happy situation' or 'Whether do we derive more happiness from Love or friendship?' The Club held its first meeting on 11 November 1780 with Burns in the Chair (Carruthers, 1998, p.265). Burns was an inveterate joiner of clubs and societies, including the Freemasons, which he joined in 1781, and the Crochallan Fencibles, an Edinburgh club which met in Dawney Douglas' Tavern, whose members included Adam Smith and Adam Ferguson, the philosopher, as well as Edinburgh lawyers. It was for this group that Burns wrote his collection of bawdy poetry, the *Merry Muses of Caledonia* (Lindsay, 1968, pp.49, 185).

Much reading material seems to have been made available in more informal ways, either in the home or through voluntary organisations such as churches. Writing from the parish of Dollar in Clackmannanshire in 1792, the Rev. Mr John Watson described under the heading, the 'Literary Shepherd', a man called John Christie, who was born locally in 1712 and lived with his unmarried brother and sister. Christie was:

> a man who was bred up and lived merely as a shepherd, and who received only a common education; and yet possesses a valuable library of books, consisting of upwards of 370 volumes; consisting of folios, quartos, octavos, duodecimos, and decimo-quartos. They are upon many different subjects, as divinity, history, travels, voyages &c besides magazines of various kinds such as the Scots, the Universal and the Christian magazines; a complete set of the spectator, Guardian, Tatler, Rambler &c. They are all of them of his own choosing and purchasing. They are neatly bound and lettered on the back. (*OSA*, 1978, IX, p.788)

In his *Rural Recollections*, published in 1829, George Robertson described the reading habits of the farmers he remembered, mainly in Ayrshire, Kincardineshire and the Lothians. Robertson claimed, 'the husbandmen of those days were a sober, a frugal and an industrious race'. In religious background 'they were nearly all the descendants of the more ancient covenanters' and their reading consisted of Sir David Lindsay, Buchanan, Knox, Rutherford, and Bunyan. They also read Robert Wodrow's *History of the Sufferings of the Church from the Restoration to the Revolution,* published in 1721. Their taste for ancient history included Abercrombie's *Martial Achievements of the Scottish Nation,* Blind Harry's *Wallace,* 'stories about Bruce and Bannockburn; and of Chevy Chase, and the Douglas; and of Roslin Moor, and Pentland Hills and Drumclog, and Bothwell Brig and Sheriffmuir; and of Culloden and Duke William and the Pretender. But no book was as familiar to them as the Scriptures' (Fyffe, 1942, pp.272–3).

This chimes with Burns' poem, *The Cottar's Saturday Night,* with its portrayal of the farm labourer's family gathering round in the home after a hard week's work to pray together and listen to the father read the Bible:

> The cheerfu' supper done, wi' serious face,
> They, round the ingle form a circle wide,
> The Sire turns o'er, with patriarchal grace
> The big ha' Bible, ance his Father's pride.

A similar popular culture existed in some Scottish burghs, particularly those with a large weaving population, such as Dunfermline or Paisley. In Paisley, for example, there was a long and skilled tradition of weaving fine linen, which eventually led on to fine muslin weaving and the Paisley pattern. The Paisley weavers were noted for their literary culture and love of discussion. It was reported:

> Books, then a rarer commodity than now, were scattered over every available spot in the kitchen, and in great demand after the day's labour. Milton, Burns, Shakespeare, and volumes of the Spectator might be found mixed in admirable confusion with Brown's Commentary and Concordance, Bunyan, Bibles and the Questions. Next to Joshua's Wars, Shakspeare was the book of books, however; and the attendance of the boys at the theatre in Bank Street was more frequent than at the Pen Kirk. (Gilmour, 1876, p.21)

In Perth, the weaver, journalist and local historian George Penny recalled that the minister of St Johns Parish Church, the Rev. James Scott, 'had classes that attended him in his own house in the evenings: always giving each a volume of a book home with them, and on their next visit he examined them on the subject they had been reading'. This cosy world was given a considerable jolt in Perth and many other places in Scotland with the outbreak of the revolution in France in 1789 and the publication of Tom Paine's *Rights of Man* in 1791. Penny reported, 'revolutionary doctrines began to be publicly lectured on; Paine's *Rights of Man* and *Common Sense* were read with avidity, and Political Societies were formed in every town and village in the kingdom'. In Perth, the Friends of the People set up a coffee room and 'in this room the party newspapers and pamphlets were read with extraordinary avidity' (Penny, 1986 edition, pp.169, 66–8).

The Scottish universities

At the beginning of the eighteenth century, there were five universities in Scotland, compared to two in England, one in Ireland (Trinity College, Dublin, founded 1592) and none in Wales. Three of them – St Andrews (1413), Glasgow (1451) and King's College, Aberdeen (1495) were pre-Reformation foundations. Edinburgh (1583) and Marischal College, Aberdeen (1593) were founded after the Reformation. Student numbers rose from approximately 1,200 in 1700 (Edinburgh and Glasgow, 300–400 each; Aberdeen, 290; St Andrews, 200) to nearly 3,000 in 1800 (Anderson, 2000, pp.154, 159). In the same period, the Scottish population rose from about one million to 1.6 million. During the eighteenth century, about 1.5–2 per cent of the relevant age group could have attended Scottish universities, a similar proportion to eighteenth-century Germany and probably Sweden, lower than Castile, but higher than

England or France (Houston, 1985, p.244). In Scotland, boys went to university young, perhaps at 15 or 16, although there was a developing tradition of men going later in life.

Compared to the Oxford and Cambridge colleges, Scottish universities were not well endowed and had to rely heavily on student fees for their income. Student fees were low in Scotland – Samuel Johnson visited St Andrews in 1773 and noted that, 'A student of the highest rank may keep his annual session, or as the English call it, his term, which lasts seven months, for about fifteen pounds, and one of lower rank for less than ten; in which board, lodging and instruction are all included' (Johnson, 1984 edition, p.38). A university educa-tion was available in Glasgow for as little as £5 a year, a fraction of the cost of attending Oxford or Cambridge and much cheaper than other universities else-where in Europe. Socially, this meant that Scottish universities were less dominated by those from aristocratic, professional, or official backgrounds than those in England, France or Germany. For example, when moves were made in Aberdeen in 1820 to stiffen up entry requirements in Latin and Greek and to extend the university terms (thus cutting down the opportunities of vacation employment), the Senate of King's College, Aberdeen declared this would deprive, 'the common people of Scotland of the privilege hitherto enjoyed by them of obtaining, for a considerable number of youths out of this class of society, a liberal education, with the various advantages accompanying it...(to rise) into the higher ranks of life than that in which they were born' (Withrington, 1987, p.74).

Because of the nature of matriculation records, it is difficult to establish the social composition of the student body with any degree of confidence. However, only 12 per cent of matriculands at St Andrews between 1750 and 1849 were from farming stock and 17 per cent at Glasgow between 1740 and 1839. Merchants and tradesmen made up 19 per cent of St Andrews entrants, with the remaining 69 per cent from the landowning and professional classes. Glasgow reflected its hinterland in that 44 per cent of its matriculands came from 'industry and commerce' but we do not know whether their parents were employers or employees (Houston, 1985, pp.245–6). Anderson concluded, 'few of the really poor, in town or country, ever reached a university' and that it was the middle ranks of society that mainly benefited from university expansion. It was estimated that the minister's son was a hundred times more likely to go to university than the son of the miner (Anderson, 2000, p.159). The 'lad o' pairts', while he certainly existed, was probably less prominent than popular myth sug-gests.

With the exception of St Andrews, Scottish universities were all in urban set-tings, and students could live and take part in the life of the city. Many students were drawn from their local area, although there were always a considerable number from outside Scotland at Edinburgh and Glasgow, who recruited from

England and, in the case of Glasgow, from Ulster. In the 1740s, 25 per cent of the 580 matriculated students at Glasgow University came from outside Scotland, which increased to 28 per cent of 1,070 in the period 1765–74, before falling to 17 per cent of 1,062 in the 1790s (Houston, 1985, p.245). English Dissenters could not enter Oxford or Cambridge because of having to testify to the Thirty-Nine Articles of the Church of England, hence the large numbers who came to study in Scotland, particularly medicine at Edinburgh or Glasgow. Students also came from the North American colonies and, after American Independence, from the USA.

During the eighteenth century, important changes took place in the Scottish universities. The common curriculum taught in Latin by generalist 'regents' was gradually replaced by a more specialised curriculum taught in English by professors who were specialists in their subject. Edinburgh and Glasgow, especially, began to offer professional training in law and medicine, to add to the preparation for the ministry they had always offered (Anderson, 2000, pp.157–8).

The Scottish Enlightenment flourished in an atmosphere of conviviality, and the links between town and gown included numerous clubs and societies of a literary and scientific nature. Edinburgh was famous for its clubs and societies, but Glasgow had a Literary Society, founded in 1752, which functioned as a faculty club for the presentation of papers and discussion. Its membership consisted mainly of the Glasgow professoriate, including Adam Smith, but it also included Presbyterian clergy and lawyers. Aberdeen had a similar organisation, the Aberdeen Philosophical Society or Wise Club, established in the 1750s and consisting mainly of academics. Each member presented a paper annually and was also supposed to introduce topics for discussion, with fines for those who failed to deliver (Sher, 1995, pp.335–6).

Scottish universities appear to have been more 'open' than in many other parts of Europe. Because the universities and their staff were so heavily dependent on student fee income, extra-mural lectures to the general public were a useful way of supplementing an academic income. It was said that Charles Hope, the Professor of Chemistry at Edinburgh University from 1799, recruited up to 500 regular students for his popular lectures to the general public and earned as much as £700 a year from outside lectures (Lenman, 1981, p.95).

At Glasgow University, a statute of 1727 stated that, 'Any person, not a student as said is, may attend the lessons in experimental philosophy without a gown' (Kelly, 1957, p.20). Dr Robert Dick, Professor of Natural Philosophy, offered, 'a course of philosophical lectures and experiments,' advertised in the local press in 1756. He also offered an astronomy course, illustrated by an orrery, and was sufficiently flexible to advise that, 'a sufficient number may have a separate hour, if they choose it' (*Glasgow Journal,* 22–29 November 1756). In the same year, John Anderson, then Professor of Oriental Languages at

Glasgow, was teaching French classes every evening at 6.30 p.m. from Monday to Thursday and, 'somethings relating to the English Tongue every Friday'. He also offered to adjust times to suit the needs of the students. The classes ran from 1 November to the end of May (*Glasgow Journal,* 18-25 October 1756). The timing of these classes suggests that they were aimed at those in employment. This formed part of a more general market for evening classes in Glasgow, which included courses in writing, arithmetic, bookkeeping, surveying, foreign languages, geography and navigation. A number of freelance teachers offered French language classes, 'to the younger sort of ladies and gentlemen', offered to ladies from 10–11 a.m. and from 7–8 p.m. Another teacher advertised classes in Latin, including one for 'young ladies' from 7–8 p.m. (*Glasgow Journal,* Oct./Nov. 1756).

Anderson succeeded Dick in the Chair of Natural Philosophy at Glasgow in 1757 and between then and 1796, turned his course of philosophical lectures into a course in applied science, 'for the benefit of the Manufacturers and Artificers in Glasgow'. The course met morning and evening on Tuesdays and Thursdays throughout the session at a fee of £1.11 shillings. Anderson claimed it was attended by, 'Town's people of almost every rank, age and employment' and he also claimed to have distributed free tickets to, 'gardeners, painters, shop-men, porters, founders, bookbinders, barbers, tailors, potters, glassblowers, gunsmiths, engravers, brewers and turners' (Kelly, 1992, p.102). John Anderson (1726–1796) was a strongly anti-Jacobite Whig, who had taken part in the defence of Stirling against the Jacobite army in 1745, and a radical, who trav-elled to France in 1791 to present a model of his 'Six Pounder Field Piece' to the French Convention (*Glasgow Mechanics' Magazine,* 1825, pp.vi-viii). He was a son of the manse 'raised on disputation' and spent a good deal of his career at Glasgow University quarrelling with his colleagues, who included Adam Smith. In his will, dated 7 May 1795, he provided for the foundation of the Andersonian University, the ancestor of Strathclyde University. Interestingly, the will provided for a Chair of Natural Philosophy to give a 'Mathematical Course' and, very significantly, a 'Ladies Course …with the idea of making the ladies of Glasgow the most accomplished...in Europe'. Admission to lectures was to be by ticket only and 'no men may be admitted who are disorderly, talk-ative, ill-bred or intoxicated; and no women that are giddy or incorrect in their manners' (Butt, 1996, p.22). These moves towards offering courses for skilled workers and women, the two groups either largely or completely excluded from Scottish universities, were a pointer to the future and will be more fully explored in the next chapter.

Chapter 2
Popular enlightenment: 1790–1850

It may be viewed as one of the noblest distinctions of the present enlightened age, that it has recognised as an incontrovertible principle, the propriety of educating all classes of society; and has established…that to raise any people in the scale of intelligence, is the best means of softening their barbarism, checking their tendency to misrule – increasing their powers of useful exertion – enlarging their means of happiness, - and promoting private good, social order and national prosperity. The more a people are enlightened the more access is there to their understanding and their conscience.

(Sir John Sinclair, *Analysis of the Statistical Account of Scotland,* 1826)

Population growth, urbanisation and industrialisation

From the late eighteenth century, Scotland experienced a period of rapid economic growth, combined with agricultural change, population movement and growing urbanisation and industrialisation. The Scottish population rose from 1.6 million in 1801 to 2.89 million in 1851 (Tranter, 1998, p.112). The population in the cities grew faster than the population in the country as a whole. Glasgow, which had overtaken Edinburgh as Scotland's largest city by 1801, grew from 83,700 in 1801 to 275,000 40 years later. Edinburgh grew more slowly, from 81,600 in 1801 to 138,000 in 1841 (Smout, 1969, p.261, 1986, p.8). By 1851, about one in five Scots lived in the 'big four' cities of Edinburgh, Glasgow, Dundee and Aberdeen (Devine, 1999, p.328). The proportion of Scots living in 'urbanised' areas (those in centres of 5,000 or more) rose from 21 per cent in 1801 to 35.9 per cent in 1851 and the proportion living in the Western Lowlands from 20.6 per cent in 1801 to 32.1 per cent in 1851 (Flinn, 1977, pp.306, 313). Even so, the majority of Scots still lived in rural areas and the 1851 census showed that the largest single occupational group was still employed in agriculture (316,257 people or 24 per cent of the working population), followed by textiles (257,127 people or 20 per cent of the working population) (Cooke and Donnachie, 1998, p.151). Using the 1851 census, Rodger has demonstrated the continuing importance of the small scale, traditional enterprise in the Scottish economy, 'the co-existence of small firms with their larger brethren' and the ways in which different sectors of the economy displayed widely differing degrees of modernity and traditionalism (Rodger, 1998, pp.82–113).

The *Rights of Man* and the French Revolution

Scotland was subject not only to rapid social and economic change in this period but to political and intellectual upheaval, with the impact of the War of American Independence and the French Revolution. Initially, both American Independence in 1784 and the outbreak of the French Revolution in 1789 were greeted with enthusiasm by the reform-minded section of the middle classes. In the summer of 1790, for example, the Whig Club of Dundee welcomed, 'the triumph of liberty and reason over despotism, ignorance and superstition' in an address to the National Assembly of France. Attitudes began to polarise with the publication of Tom Paine's *Rights of Man* in 1791 and the growing violence of events in France. The *Rights of Man* was designed as a riposte to Edmund Burke's *Reflections on the Revolution in France*, published in 1790. It was published in two parts in 1791 and 1792, the first part dedicated to George Washington, the Second to the Marquis de Lafayette. Paine called for universal suffrage, the redistribution of property, education for all, the abolition of titles, and of the monarchy, 'the master-fraud, which shelters all others' (Paine, 1995 edition, p.257). A royal proclamation was issued against the book in May 1792 but it had sold 200,000 copies in Scotland by the following year. The book met with a mixed reaction. There were protest riots against the book by the 'Langholm Patriots' in Eskdalemuir in the Borders, where Thomas Telford had sent a copy back to his birthplace. On the other hand, it was claimed that the local book-seller in a small town in the north of Scotland had sold 750 copies in three weeks. Extracts were sold as broadsheets and there was even said to be a Gaelic translation (Smout, 1969, p.442; Ferguson, 1978 edition, p.251).

Paine had suggested that the path to radical reform was by, 'a general convention elected for the purpose' and in July 1792 a reform society was founded in Edinburgh called the Friends of the People. Other branches soon sprang up throughout Scotland. Between December 1792 and October 1793, the Edinburgh Society hosted three conventions, the last one drawing delegates from England and Ireland as well as Scotland. As time went by, the reform-minded upper middle classes gradually deserted both the conventions and the Friends of the People. Historians have disagreed as to what extent the support for radical reform had a class basis but there is strong evidence that contemporaries were worried about the effect of these ideas on the lower classes. The leadership of the Friends tended to be middle class, such as Thomas Muir, a young Edinburgh advocate, or Thomas Fyshe Palmer, a Cambridge-educated old Etonian, who was a Unitarian minister in Dundee. Both these men were transported to Botany Bay in 1793 for making seditious speeches at the First and Second Conventions in Edinburgh. However, at the grass roots level, support for the Friends of the People was increasingly drawn from tradesmen, shopkeepers and weavers (Smout, 1969, pp.442–3; Whatley, 2000, pp.301–2).

In Perth, for example, estimates of membership of the Friends of the People varied from 100 to 1200 members. The leadership was largely middle class, consisting of merchants, a surgeon, a solicitor, a minister and 'other persons of some little respectability in the town,' but the bulk of the membership were 'operative weavers of which there are a vast number' and 'operative people in the various trades of Perth' (Fraser, 1988, pp.65–7). George Penny, the Perth weaver, journalist and local historian, claimed that the dissenting clergy had taken a prominent leadership role in Perth and had denounced reform and proclaimed revolution from the pulpit of the Relief Church. The entry of the French army into Brussels in November 1793 was celebrated by the erection of a liberty tree at the Perth Cross. Penny described the anti-aristocratic backlash that followed:

> The Perth Hunt, then newly instituted, having assembled at the races, the Friends of the People took the opportunity of displaying their sentiments in a way that could not be mistaken. The assemblies were then held in the Glovers' Hall and the ordinaries in the George Inn. At the time appointed for the meeting of the assembly, a numerous body of Friends ranged themselves in two compact lines, forming a lane betwixt the inn and the hall, along which the gentry had to pass...Every individual who was supposed to be a friend to the rotten constitution had a severe ordeal to undergo; even the best of them had to walk, hat in hand, and make obesience to the *Majesty of the People*. When the Duke of Athole appeared a terrible clamour was produced. The cry arose 'There comes citizen Murray, Black Jock who sold the Highlanders. To the guillotine with him that he may receive his deserts.' Mr. Dundas also received special notice. Many of the nobility came in chairs, but this did not save them; the occupant was examined: and even ladies were compelled to endure the insults of the rabble. (Penny, 1986 edition, pp.70–1)

Perth was also a stronghold of the United Scotsmen, a shadowy republican organisation modelled on the United Irishmen. Its membership was drawn largely from weavers and shoemakers, who 'had good wages at the time, and were able to sport away for a time, particularly the weavers, who in addition to high prices for their labour, had their time in a great measure at their command'. As a result, 'Their work was neglected, and much of their time occupied during the day with political pamphlets and discussion, and in the evenings their earnings were squandered at club meetings' (Penny, 1986 edition, p.69). The United Scotsmen were particularly strong in Tayside. Of some 26 societies in Scotland, half were in Tayside, drawing support from parishes with significant numbers of weavers and large Seceder congregations (Fraser, 1988, p.71).

Reports by parish ministers in the *(Old) Statistical Accounts* show the impact of these changes in some rather unlikely places and the unease or panic they caused. The Rev. William Cameron of Kirknewton in Midlothian pulled few punches in 1792 when he described the impact of the 'new' French doctrines on his parishioners:

> Some loose and libertine principles, the poisonous spawn of a false philosophy and false patriotism, have recently corrupted the minds of half-learned witlings and smatterers in science…From there, they have been catched out by many amongst the most ignorant, the obvious tendency of which is to destroy the foundations of all civil and ecclesiastical government. (*OSA*, 1975 edition, II, p.337)

In Auchterhouse, on the edge of the radical stronghold of Dundee, the Rev. James Scott boasted of his parishioners in 1793 that:

> In spite of the wicked arts employed by the seditious in a neighbouring town to disseminate French doctrines and to poison their honest minds, they remain unshaken in their loyalty and think not that they degrade themselves by paying honour to whom honour is due…The people of this country, in general, are happy, and will remain so, if they suffer not themselves to fall under the influence of ambitious, disappointed, turbulent and ill-designed demagogues. (*OSA*, 1976 edition, XIII, pp.49–50)

A similar reaction came from George Paterson of Castle Huntly in the rural parish of Longforgan in Perthshire, 'a Proprietor in the Parish, a Friend to Statistical Inquiries'. Paterson was a Dundee medical man who had made a fortune in the East India Company, and married the daughter of Lord John Gray on his return. He described in 1795 how:

> Some attempts have lately been made to introduce Jacobine principles into this parish; but by care, attention, and proper exertion of the heritors, in support of the country police, it is hoped that the idle, the unprincipled, and ill-disposed, will be effectually prevented from disturbing the public peace; and that the good sense of the inhabitants in general, who are loyal and well disposed, will teach others to put a proper value upon that most excellent Constitution, under which all enjoy many blessings. (*OSA*, 1976 edition, XI, p.346)

The Rev. Mr Graham of Fossaway and Tulliebole parish in Perthshire, on the Kinross boundary, believed that a change had taken place in the political climate since the publication of Paine's *Rights of Man*. Writing in 1796, he described how:

Few, except the gentlemen, conversed much about political affairs, till the works of Thomas Paine appeared. Since that time, however, the people converse more frequently on those topics. It is, however, but doing them justice to say, that they are firmly attached to the Constitution of this country, as established at the Accession of King William, and to the person and government of his present Majesty. (*OSA*, 1976 edition, XI, p.212)

In Perth, the Rev. James Scott expressed the belief that, 'the false philosophy, which, for above half a century, has prevailed much in France, and which was adopted by some writers in our own country, the effects of which, now appear, has made few or no converts in Perth'. Evidently, a good deal of radical reading material was available in Perth and Scott thought this should be countered by alternative reading. He had spoken to people who had read 'the visionary and irreligious writings of Thomas Paine' and felt that, 'If it be the fashion of the times, or has been the practice of some persons, to put into the hands of the poor people books of a dangerous tendency, surely the friends of our religion, and of our civil constitution, should endeavour to put into their hands, in as liberal a manner, books of a better kind' (*OSA*, 1976 edition, XI, pp.513–4).

These sorts of fears underlie a good deal of the writings on education in the *Statistical Accounts*. Education by the parish schools was seen, by most if not all, as a bulwark against revolutionary ideas, as was the established church in general. Similar attitudes were highly influential in the establishment of evening schools and other adult education activities, including the supply of books and other reading materials. William Barclay, the schoolmaster of Cadder in Lanarkshire, used these arguments to campaign for an increase in the salaries of Scottish schoolmasters. Contrasting the good behaviour of the lower ranks in Scotland with their English counterparts, Barclay attributed this to 'early education and proper instruction'. He reported that when an attempt was made to raise the salaries of Scottish schoolmasters, it was opposed by 'some gentlemen and lords' who complained that, 'they wished parish schools were suppressed altogether, because their servants were corrupted, by being taught to read and write. That they would be more obedient and dutiful, were they more ignorant and had no education'. Barclay added that no gentleman in Cadder parish believed this (*OSA*, 1973 edition, VII, p.77).

From the Gaelic speaking parish of Craignish, Argyllshire, the Rev. Mr Lachlan M'Lachlan also condemned the low salaries paid to Scottish schoolmasters as a national disgrace. In 1792, the Craignish schoolmaster was paid the equivalent of £20 a year, including all perquisites, compared to the minister's £66 a year in the same parish. M'Lachlan regarded this as 'a miserable allowance to a man of genius for employing his time and talents', and condemned those who had turned down the proposal for a modest increase in schoolmasters' salaries. He ended on an apocalyptic note, 'at this rate, the ages of darkness will again commence; and Scotland will, ere long, be as remarkable for wealth and ignorance as it was formerly for poverty and learning' (*OSA*, 1983, VIII, p.79).

Some responses

Sunday schools

It is usually claimed that the Sunday school movement originated in England through Robert Raikes, who began to provide Sunday classes for poor children in Gloucester in 1781 (Laqueur, 1976, p.23). However, at least two Church of Scotland ministers had made Sunday evening provision for destitute children before this, at Brechin in Angus in 1761 and at Calton parish in Glasgow in 1774–5 (Brown, 1981). The minister involved at Brechin was called Blair and, 'It is recorded on Blair's monument in the Church of Brechin, that to him belongs the honour of instituting Sabbath Schools, he having commenced one in my native town several years before any were opened in England by Raikes of Gloucester, to whom the honour is generally assigned' (Guthrie, 1877, p.14). Another early example was in the Highland parish of Banchory-Devenick, Aberdeenshire, where Robert Cormack, the parish schoolmaster, founded a Sunday school in 1782. Cormack, described as 'a most industrious and success-ful teacher', taught without fee, 'from six o'clock in the morning till late in the evening'. The Sunday school was popular and by 1798, 'Not fewer than 70, on an average, attend regularly in the course of the day; young men before public worship, and young women after it' (*OSA*, 1982, XIV, p.20).

Sunday schools were initially designed to provide basic education. The first Sunday school in Aberdeen was provided, 'for the instruction of poor children in reading English, learning the principles of the Christian religion and psalmody'. Their target audience was children whose parents could not afford school fees or for children and young adults working during the week. Another aim was, 'the reduction of lawlessness and Sabbath profanation' (Brown, 1981, pp.3–6). In November 1787, Glasgow town council, in cooperation with the General Session and private citizens, set up eight schools for over 400 boys. Within two years, the size of the project had doubled and girls were admitted. One historian has recently drawn an explicit link between popular unrest and the beginnings of the Sunday school movement in Glasgow, 'launched after the trauma of the Calton weavers' disturbances of 1787' (Whatley, 2000a, p.322). However, a Sunday school had already been established in Calton in 1774–5, some 13 years earlier.

By 1793, there were 1,200 children in Sunday schools in Glasgow. They were supported by voluntary subscriptions and 'were intended to preserve the edu-cation formerly given, to increase knowledge and to form good habits'. There was particular concern that children could easily lose the benefit of the modest schooling they had received through lack of practice – 'The only method, therefore, by which the education of the poor can be secured, is by giving it early and supporting the Sunday schools, which may prevent such education as they have got being lost' (*OSA*, 1973 edition, VII, pp.323–4).

By the late 1790s, Evangelicals in the Church of Scotland were coming under suspicion as a result of reactions to the French Revolution. In 1798, William Porteous, the founder of Sunday schools in Glasgow, complained of the impact of a Mr J. Haldane on the Glasgow Sunday school movement:

> Old and young, men and women, boys and girls, were invited to attend, they did attend in their multitudes, and in place of our simple exercises, a loquacious manufacturer from Glasgow preached and prayed with vehemence until a late hour. (Brown, 1981, p.10)

Porteous criticised the 'new' Sunday schools as 'attacking religious establishments' and circulating pamphlets, 'calculated to produce discontent, to foster an aversion to the present order of things and to increase that portentous fermentation in the minds of the people'. More calculated to appeal to middle-class support was a claim made in 1813 by the Scottish Sunday School Society that Sunday schools produced great benefits, 'from keeping the children from playing in the streets and fields on the Lord's Day, and committing depredations on people's property' (Brown, 1981, pp.6, 10).

Sir John Sinclair believed that Sunday schools were 'particularly necessary in manufacturing towns, where employment is found for children between seven and eight years of age, and when, even at that early period of their life, their work will bring from 1s to 1/6d per week'. He noted that they were concentrated in the manufacturing counties of Scotland. In 1819, there were 807 Sunday schools in Scotland with 53,449 scholars. Of these, 364 with 27,050 scholars were in the manufacturing counties of Ayr, Fife, Forfar, Lanark and Renfrew (Sinclair, 1826, pp.96–8). A great variety of organisations were involved in running them. A survey in 1819 of 452 Sunday Schools found that 181 were run by district or interdenominational societies, 133 by independents, 93 by the parish minister, 17 by gentry, nine each by Burgher and Methodist churches, three each by Anti-Burghers and groups of tradesmen, and two each by factory owners and day schools. By the late 1840s, the role of Sunday schools was diversifying, with more provided in the way of education for adults, particularly young adults. Spin-offs included, 'Bible classes, fellowship meetings, young men and women's institutes, mutual improvement societies, penny banks and libraries' (Brown, 1981, pp.12–18). However, they came under criticism in some quarters. In 1842, Hugh Franks remarked that, 'Sunday schools afford but an inadequate substitute for day teaching' (*Parliamentary Papers*, 1842, XVI, p.397).

By the 1840s, there were Sunday secular schools running in Glasgow, 'where the three Rs were taught free of charge, but no religious instruction given.' The Glasgow handloom weaver, William Hutton remembered that:

> Several leading citizens were supportive of these schools. My own voluntary work in connection with them was to induce young men and boys unable to read and write to attend the classes and get a little instruction. I have gathered in men over forty years old from Glasgow Green on a Sunday to the nearest secular school. The promoters believed that education would help greatly to elevate the masses, but there was keen opposition on account of not using the Bible as a class book, and after a good record for satisfactory work accomplished, the secular schools had to succumb for lack of public support. (Hutton, 1904, pp.29–30)

Towards the end of the nineteenth century, the Socialist Sunday School movement was established in the west of Scotland, modelled on its Christian counterparts, with Ten Precepts replacing the Ten Commandments (Fisher, 1999, pp.136–42).

George Miller and the Cheap Magazine

Sunday schools were largely, though not wholly, an urban phenomenon. By contrast, it was the rural and small town setting of Dunbar, East Lothian, which saw another related development. There, a bookseller, George Miller, opened the first circulating library in East Lothian on 20 November 1789, issued his first catalogue in October 1791 and set up the first printing press in the area in 1795. In 1802 and 1803, he published over 100,000 cheap tracts to counteract the effects of the popular chapbooks sold to the rural masses by travelling pedlars. Their titles suggest a high moral tone and an improving spirit, together with a dash of prurience – *The Magdalen, or the History of a Reformed Prostitute, Maria, or the Wanderer Reclaimed, and the Fatal Effects of Guilty Love, The Drunken Husband, The Slave Trade, The Honest Debtor* and so on (Miller, 1833, pp.44–9). In 1813 and 1814, Miller published the *Cheap Magazine* from the Haddington Press. The *Magazine* was explicit about its aims:

> Having for its object the Prevention of Crimes, and being calculated to ensure the Peace, Comfort and Security of Society by offering the Young and Thoughtless Taste for Reading Subjects of Real Utility. Having a Tendency to counteract the Baleful Influence of Depraved Habits in the interests of Religion, Virtue and Humility; Encourage a Spirit of Industry, Economy and Frugality and dispel the shades of Ignorance, Prejudice and Error, particularly among the lower orders of mankind.
> (*The Cheap Magazine,* 1813, Vol. I)

The *Cheap Magazine* consisted of improving tracts, such as *The History of an Irish Family* in Volume 2, January 1814, which showed 'The Difference in Human Characters the Result of Education.' Other features included helpful tips, such as a cure for cracked nipples, side by side with a cure for cancer. This was followed in 1815 by the *Monthly Monitor or Philanthropic Museum* at 6d an issue. The *Monitor* described itself as a 'Cheap Repository' for, 'Hints, Suggestions, Facts and Discoveries Relating to Humanity' and for, 'Papers of Every Description having a Tendency to Prevent THE COMMISSION OF CRIMES'. It hoped to 'encourage a spirit of industry, economy and frugality among the middling and laborious classes of man' (Miller, 1833, p.105). Alexander Somerville, who had started work as an agricultural labourer at the age of eight or nine, regarded Miller as 'the father of cheap reading' and described how he bought a book, Hutton's *Mensuration,* from him in Dunbar for the high price of four shillings (Somerville, 1967 edition, p.62). Miller's later publications, such as the *Book of Nature, or Popular Philosophy*, published in 1826, were often compilations of his earlier writing and attempted to reconcile religion with the new scientific discoveries taking place (Saunders, 1950, p.253; Smith, 1983a, pp.26, 32).

A major problem faced by Brown's scheme and other subsequent schemes for the supply of cheap reading material was the modest initial education received by most Scots and their enjoyment of literature that was less than improving. An Edinburgh investigator in 1819–20 reported that of those who could read, 'few had recourse to the books calculated to give them the most useful instruction, because they were unable to understand the language, while most resorted to work of a lighter and unfortunately less exceptionable kind, which they found not so difficult to comprehend' (Webb, 1955, pp.19–20). This is confirmed by other observers, such as Sir G.S. Mackenzie, of Coul in Ross Shire, who in 1836 noted the popular resistance to improving literature:

> the lowest class, and numbers, too, of that class immediately above, are exceedingly anxious to purchase things that are hawked about the streets, such as accounts of executions and last speeches, murders, shipwrecks and the like. The quantity of vice, trash, falsehood and mischief that gets thus into circulation is infinitely greater than is commonly imagined. (Webb, 1955, p.65)

Chapbooks have been briefly mentioned in Chapter 1. Dougal Graham, the 'Skellat' Bellman of Glasgow, was credited with the authorship of a number of popular chapbooks, including *The History of John Cheap, Chapman, Lothian Tam, The Whole Proceedings of Jockey and Maggy,* and *The Haverel Wives.* Graham, born in Raploch, Stirling in 1724, was 'lame of one leg and had a large hunch on his back and another protuberance on his breast'. He had served with the Jacobite army in 1745 and published a *History of the Rebellion* in verse. He ended his life as the town bellman in Glasgow and was championed by no less a literary figure than Sir Walter Scott (Macgregor (ed.), 1883, p.27). Chapbooks were aimed at the semi-literate or the barely literate, just as certain tabloid newspapers today are written for those with a reading age of ten. John Struthers, a shoemaker's son from East Kilbride, described working at Croftfoot Farm near Carmunnock on the outskirts of Glasgow, where the choice of reading material was limited:

Figure 1 Dougal Graham, 'Skellat' Bellman of Glasgow, 1774.
(Source: Macgregor, 1883)

> Books there were none, the Bible excepted, and it was but rarely opened; and though there had been books there was no desire and as little capacity to read them. The herd had a few stall ballads, the history of Bold Robin Hood, John Cheap the Chapman, the Twa Haveral Wives, Coal Sandy, Lothian Tam &c purchased out of hawkers' baskets with any odd pennies which were at rare times and occasions given to him, and to these, when read to them, they listened with great delight, but they could not read themselves so as to make sense of them. (Struthers, 1850, p.xxix)

However, sales of chapbooks were not confined to farmworkers and rural readers. John Mackinnon described how in the weavers' workshops in Calton, Glasgow:

> A considerable quantity of Chap Books were sold at that time, and ballads and penny histories were sold by almost every hawker. We had a bunch of chap books stitched together, and ballads innumerable. In fact, no ballad seller ever visited the weaver's shop without disposing of one or more of his ballads or histories. (Mitchell Library Mss., Mackinnon Correspondence)

Popular titles included prose works such as *John Cheap the Chapman, the History of Lothian Tam, Simple John and his Twelve Misfortunes, the King and the Cobbler, The History of George Buchanan, Sleeping Beauty,* and poetry such as *William and Nanny or the Yarmouth Tragedy, Babes in the Wood, the Tragedy of Douglas, Death and Dr Hornbrook* and *Watty and Meg.* However, the Calton weavers also bought other types of reading material, including newspapers, which they shared amongst themselves by rota (Mackinnon Mss.).

Samuel Brown and itinerating libraries

East Lothian was also the setting for another early experiment in adult education, the Itinerating Library Scheme of Samuel Brown of Haddington. Brown came from a family of autodidacts, with a religious background of Presbyterian dissent. His paternal grandfather, John Brown senior, was a weaver from Carpow, Perthshire, who was unable to read. Brown's father, also called John Brown, was orphaned at the age of ten and earned his living as a herd boy and shepherd, 'followed by a short trial at the pedlar life'. Although John Brown, 'had but very few quarters at school for reading, writing and arithmetic', he learned Latin and eventually became a student of Divinity, a minister, a Professor of Divinity and the author of 'The Self Interpreting Bible'. Brown's mother, Violet, was 'a voracious reader' and other members of her family were said to be 'addicted to Natural Science'. Brown was their eighth son and his father died when he was seven. He was taken under the protection of his mother's family and apprenticed at the age of 11 to his mother's brother, John Croumbie, an ironmonger and drysalter in Edinburgh (Brown, 1856, pp.3–18).

Samuel Brown took an active part in the Haddington Tract Society and distributed the London Society's tracts amongst the four-shilling subscribers in the area. They in turn passed them on to others, including, 'Highland and Irish reapers, who annually resort to East Lothian'. For the itinerating library scheme, which began in 1817, Brown bought 200 books, 'about two thirds of which were of a moral and religious tendency, while the remainder comprised books of travel, agriculture, the mechanical arts and popular science'. He divided them into four sets, exchanged at intervals, and stationed each set in the villages of Aberlady, Salton, Tyninghame and Garvald, supervised by volunteer librarians, often the parish schoolmaster. The scheme met with considerable resistance at first, but Brown pressed ahead, in spite of poor health, and by 1836, there were 36 libraries, with 2,380 volumes (Brown, 1856, pp.20–65). Oberlin attempted something similar in the Alps at about the same time and in the early years of the eighteenth century the SSPCK had established libraries in the Scottish Highlands, as outlined in Chapter 1. In the 1730s, a similar idea lay behind the Circulating Welsh Charity Schools, founded by Griffith Jones for teaching children and adults to read the Bible in Welsh. Like the SSPCK scheme, it was claimed, 'the primary object of the East Lothian libraries is to promote the interests of religion' (Brown, 1830, p.4).

Brown's scheme was praised by Henry Brougham in his *Practical Observations on the Education of the People*, published in 1825. After criticising the tax on paper as a tax on knowledge, Brougham went on to say that circulating libraries were of little use to the working classes – book clubs or reading societies being far more useful. He commended the East Lothian scheme, which by 1825 had expanded to 19 libraries, and reported that a similar scheme was being proposed by Mr Buchan of Kelloe, Berwickshire (Brougham, 1825, pp.2–3). Alexander Somerville was aware of the existence of the East Lothian scheme, although he did not benefit from it personally. After borrowing books from a fellow agricultural worker, Somerville used the Innerwick Library in Berwickshire, although he complained that many of the books there were, 'silly stories, of that silliest kind of literature, religious novels' (Somerville, 1967 edition, p.60).

Thomas Dick and adult education institutes

The third member of Saunders's triumvirate of early adult educators was Thomas Dick, who was born in 1774 in the Hilltown, Dundee. His father was a small linen manufacturer and member of the Secession Church. Dick showed an early interest in astronomy and attended Edinburgh University but left without graduating, like most Scottish students at the time. He was ordained as assistant of Viewfield Anti-Burgher Church in Stirling in 1803 but was dismissed in 1805 for 'flagrant immorality'. He then taught a school in Methven,

Perthshire for ten years and towards the end of his tenure there, in 1814–5, published articles in the *London Monthly Magazine,* in which he called for, 'the establishment of literary and philosophical societies among the middling and lower ranks of the community in every town and prosperous village'. Dick believed that, 'the period is fast approaching when the ignorance and superstition of former ages shall be dispelled and the gates of the temple of science thrown open to all'. He moved on to teach at Stewart's Free Trade school in 1817, and in 1823 published the *Christian Philosopher,* which was an immediate success and allowed him to leave teaching in 1827 and build a house with an observatory in Hill Street, Broughty Ferry, near Dundee (Smith, 1983a, p.27, 1983b, pp.255–70).

The main object of the *Christian Philosopher* was to demonstrate the links between science, religion, morality and politics and the compatibility of religion and science. This theme continued in Dick's essay, *On the Improvement of Society by the Diffusion of Knowledge,* published in 1833, which argued with true Enlightenment logic, 'ignorance is one principle cause of the want of virtue, and of the immoralities that abound in the world' (Dick, 1833, p.199). Dick served as a Director of the Watt Institution, the Mechanics' Institute in Dundee, from 1830 to 1831 and lectured there frequently. He was critical of the narrow curriculum of the Institution, which he believed should include, 'not only the whole of moral and political science but those fundamental principles of religion in the belief of which all mankind concur' (Smith, 1983b, p.264).

The *Christian Philosopher* is mentioned by a number of autobiographers, particularly those from a Secession Church background, where there was conflict between a literal interpretation of the Bible and the findings of modern science. David Livingstone's father, Neil, for example, had left the Church of Scotland and become deacon of an independent church in Hamilton, Lanarkshire. David started his working life in 1823 at the age of ten as a piecer in the Blantyre cotton mills. The boy developed an interest in nature and science, which aroused the anger of his father, and the disagreement was only resolved when David discovered Thomas Dick's books, which were concerned with the reconciliation of science and religion (NLS, Mss. 10767; Ross, 2002, pp.4–6). John Muir, the founder of the American National Parks movement, was born in Dunbar, East Lothian, where he attended the local grammar school, the family eventually emigrating to the USA. At the age of 15 or 16, Muir, by now working on his father's Wisconsin farm, began to hanker after knowledge. He borrowed books from his neighbours, including Scott's novels, but took care to hide them from his father, who, 'had brought only a few religious books from Scotland'. When Muir borrowed Dick's *Christian Philosopher,* his father objected to the 'Philosophy' in the title (Muir, 1913, pp.240–1).

James Smith studied this trio of early adult educators, Samuel Brown, George Miller and Thomas Dick and others such as Rev. Henry Duncan of Ruthwell in Dumfrieshire, the originator of popular savings banks, who tried to organise adult classes in scientific subjects, particularly astronomy, in his parish. Duncan was also the co-founder of the *Dumfries and Galloway Courier* (1809), which he used to promote reformist causes. All these men combined a background in evangelical Christianity with the scientific interests of the Enlightenment. Smith argued that terms like 'benevolent' and 'philanthropic' were not neutral; they implied, 'a clearly demarcated "map" of society' and could not be taken wholly at face value (Smith, 1983a, p.25–7).

Industrialisation and urbanisation on the one hand and the spread of radical ideas from France on the other had created great anxieties amongst many. The response of many evangelical churchmen, including prominent figures like the Rev. Thomas Chalmers, was to try to turn back the clock by creating the idealised small town or rural parish in the much less promising environment of the industrial city or manufacturing town. George Miller, Samuel Brown and Henry Duncan actually came from the kind of small town or rural background that was deemed to be under threat, as did Thomas Chalmers, who was raised in Fife. A historian of the English adult education movement has argued that:

> The development of a literate section of the working classes opened the way to the spread of radical and unorthodox opinions, and a good deal of adult educational effort stemmed from the middle-class desire to check this. So patently was education used as an instrument for social control that it became suspect. (Harrison, 1961, p.43)

A more recent historian has pointed out that the outcomes of education are unpredictable and that working-class adults did not always draw the conclusions they were supposed to from the educational experiences provided by their social betters, however slanted these were in terms of curriculum or reading material (Rose, 2002).

Robert Owen, New Lanark, Orbiston and the Owenites

A more radical critique of society was offered by Robert Owen of New Lanark (1771–1858). Owen was born in Newtown in Montgomeryshire, Wales, but moved at an early age to work as an assistant in haberdashery shops in Stamford, Lincolnshire, London and Manchester. In the early 1790s, he went into partnership in the Manchester cotton industry and founded his own cotton spinning business a few years later. In 1800, Owen moved to Scotland when he and his partners bought the New Lanark cotton mills from David Dale, Owen having married Dale's daughter, Caroline, the previous year (Donnachie, 2000, pp.1–71).

Owen ran the New Lanark mills as a highly successful and profitable cotton spinning business for a number of years before branching out with the publication of his *New View of Society* in 1813 and his *An Address to the Inhabitants of New Lanark* in 1816. In these, and in subsequent works, Owen developed a critique of contemporary society and a series of ambitious solutions, which he tried to get adopted by government. He differed from the social reformers discussed earlier in his complete rejection of all forms of religion as a solution to social problems, which did not endear him to many of the governing classes. The *New View of Society* was subtitled 'Essays on the Principle of the Formation of the Human Character' and Owen displayed a strong belief in the ability of both the environment and of education to shape human character and behaviour.

Owen's ideas owed a good deal to the Scottish Enlightenment, particularly the concept of enlightened self-interest developed by Adam Smith in his *Wealth of Nations*. In the *First Essay* of *A New View of Society,* Owen claimed that the guiding principle behind his views was, 'the happiness of self, clearly understood and uniformly practised; which can only be attained by conduct that must promote the happiness of the community' (Owen, 1966 edition, p.17). In the *Third Essay,* Owen spelled out this principle more clearly and, in the process, revealed his close links with utilitarian thinking:

> That man is born with a desire to obtain happiness, which desire is the primary cause of all his actions, continues through life, and in popular language, is called self interest. (Owen, 1966 edition, p.54)

He also displayed a healthy scepticism as to the value of organised religion, believing that religious teachings, 'generate superstitions, bigotry, hypocrisy, hatred, revenge, wars and all their evil consequences'. In the *Third Essay*, he took delight in pointing out that, 'The Sabbath, in many parts of Scotland, is not a day of innocent and cheerful recreation to the labouring man' (Owen, 1966 edition, pp.52, 42).

However, in spite of these radical differences from many of his contemporaries, Owen resembled them in wanting to create a sober, obedient and industrious working population. In his *New View of Society,* he claimed to have found the population of New Lanark, 'in idleness, in poverty, in almost every kind of crime; consequently in debt, out of health and in misery.' As a result of the reforms he carried out, 'Those employed became industrious, temperate, healthy, faithful to their employers and kind to each other; while the proprietors were deriving services from their attachment far beyond those which could be obtained by any other means than those of confidence and kindness' (Owen, 1966 edition, pp.27, 33).

Owen's views on education were largely shaped by the concept of what nowadays would be called Human Capital. In an address to 'Superintendents of

Manufactories' at the beginning of his *Third Essay,* he compared the attention given to machinery in factories with the lack of attention given to the human beings who operated the machinery:

> If then, due care as to the state of your inanimate machines can produce such beneficial results, what may not be expected if you devote equal attention to your vital machines, which are far more wonderfully constructed? (Owen, 1966 edition, p.8)

Owen viewed education as a lifelong activity, from the children, who were to be admitted to school 'almost as soon as they can walk', to the adults, who were to be instructed, 'particularly in the proper method of training their children to become rational beings' and encouraged to save. In *An Address to the Inhabitants of New Lanark,* delivered on 1 January 1816 on the opening of the Institution for the Formation of Character, he spelled out his ideas on schooling for children before they entered the mills at the age of ten and on evening classes for the older children who were working in the mills. In addition, three lower rooms were to be set aside for:

> the use of the adult part of the population, who are to be provided with every accommodation requisite to enable them to read, write, account, sew, or play, converse, or walk about....Strict order and attention to the happiness of every one of the party will be enforced, until such habits shall be acquired as will render any formal restriction unnecessary. (Owen, 1966 edition, p.99)

Owen's son, Robert Dale Owen, described how at New Lanark, 'the school is open in the evening to the children and young persons, from 10 to 20 years of age' who pursued the same system of education, founded on kindness and the absence of corporal punishment, that was used for the younger children (Owen, 1824, p.33). Another observer noted there were, 'weekly lectures on chemistry and mechanism, for the benefit of old and young of the community,' in addition to facilities for adult recreation, including music and dancing (Silver, 1965, p.125). Owen ceased to be managing partner at New Lanark in 1825 and devoted the rest of his life to lecturing, writing, travel and the creation of model communities in line with his ideas. These communities also had an adult education agenda. Orbiston, near Motherwell in Lanarkshire offered debating as well as lectures for the adult population and at New Harmony in Indiana, lectures were delivered by outside speakers, often on a weekly basis (Donnachie, forthcoming).

Amongst the numerous visitors to New Lanark, not all were won over completely, or wholly impressed by Owen's long-term impact on the community.

Thomas Malthus visited New Lanark in 1810, ten years after Owen had taken over. He reported:

> About 15 hundred people are employed at the cotton mill, and great debauchery prevails among them. The hours of work are from 6 in the morning to 7 in the evening. A good school is established in the village, but the spinners cannot have much leisure to attend it, as after their day's work, they naturally want some recreation. Sunday is therefore the only day on which they can be expected to give much attention to reading. (James, (ed.), 1966, p.223)

Some seven years after Owen's departure, in November 1832, William Cobbett visited New Lanark. He described it as, 'the most interesting spot on earth that I ever set my foot upon in the course of my long and rambling life' and was 'rather curious to know whether there was any reality in what we had heard about the effects of the Owen "feelosophy"' (Cobbett, 1984 edition, pp.81, 100). The Owenite legacy left Cobbett distinctly unimpressed:

> It is difficult to determine, whether, when people are huddled together in this unnatural state, this sort of soldiership discipline may or may not be necessary to effect the purpose of schooling; but I should think it a very strange thing if a man...could ever come to perfection from a beginning like this. (Cobbett, 1984 edition, p.101)

Of course, Cobbett had his ready-made prejudices, and a different light on the effects of the education provided at New Lanark is provided by other sources. For example, the mother of the Glasgow radical, James Mackinnon, had worked as a child at New Lanark, under David Dale's regime and Mackinnon claimed, 'the knowledge she acquired here was of use to her afterwards' (Mitchell Library, Mackinnon Mss.). Lanark Provident Society, a Cooperative Society, was founded in 1861 and it was reported that, 'Some of the men, we believe, who were early members of Lanark Society had as children been in Owen's school' (Maxwell, 1910, p.183). Similarly, two prominent Scottish Cooperators, who subsequently became Labour MPs, Robert Murray (1869–1950) and Neil Maclean (1873–1953), both had mothers who had been educated at New Lanark school (Knox, 1984, pp.192, 222–3).

Mechanics' Institutes

The pre-history of Mechanics' Institutes in Scotland lies in the extra-mural activities of Scottish universities discussed in Chapter 1. In both Edinburgh and Glasgow Universities, some professors augmented their income by giving public lecture courses, the audiences at various times including middle-class women and male artisans. From its foundation in 1795, the Andersonian Institution in Glasgow had a mission to link with its local community. It was governed by 81 trustees representing, 'nine classes of citizens, viz. tradesmen, agriculturalists, artists, manufacturers, physicians and surgeons, lawyers, divines, philosophers and lastly, kinsmen or namesakes'. The opening ceremony, on 21 September 1796, took the form of, 'Dr. Garnet's readings in the Trades Hall to persons of both sexes popular and scientific lectures on natural philosophy and chemistry, illustrated by experiments' (*New Statistical Account,* hereafter *NSA,* 1845, VI, pp.179–180).

Dr Thomas Garnet (1766–1802) was appointed the first Professor of Natural Philosophy in the new institution. He held the Chair from 1796 to 1799 and claimed that the Andersonian, 'was the first regular institution in which the fair sex have been admitted… on the same footing as men'. Garnet left Glasgow to become Professor of Experimental Philosophy and Chemistry at the Royal Institution in London. His successor was George Birkbeck (1776–1841), a Yorkshire Quaker, who was appointed Professor of Natural Philosophy on 18 October 1799. Like Garnet, he had been educated at Sedburgh School in Yorkshire and Edinburgh University (Butt, 1996, p.29). Both men were part of a tradition of English Non-Conformists, excluded from Oxford or Cambridge, who attended Scottish universities in this period, often settling either temporarily or permanently in Scotland after graduation.

Birkbeck began a free course of lectures for mechanics on popular science, which recruited an audience of 500 for what became a three-month course. His interest in popular science had been stimulated by the interest shown by workers in the Glasgow workshops where his scientific apparatus was being made, in particular a centrifugal pump manufactured at a tinsmith's workshop on Glassford Street (Kelly, 1957, p.28). The courses ran annually until Birkbeck's departure for London in 1804. His successor, Dr Andrew Ure (1778–1857), the author of the *Philosophy of Manufactures* (1835) (Thompson, 1968b, pp.395–8) was an inveterate proponent of laissez-faire, who showed little interest in the mechanics' class and wished to target the university's offerings towards the middle classes. Ure's cavalier treatment of the mechanics caused great resentment and in 1823 the class split, with one half staying with the Andersonian, the other setting up the Glasgow Mechanics' Institution (Butt, 1996, p.35).

However, the first Mechanics' Institute proper in Britain was the Edinburgh School of Arts, founded in April 1821 by Leonard Horner, who was part of a Whig circle based on the *Edinburgh Review*. The catalyst was said to have been a conversation between Horner and Robert Bryson, a Princess Street watchmaker, about the lack of any scientific or technical education for working men (Marwick, 1932, p.390). Horner was allegedly aware of, and influenced by, developments in Glasgow. The aim of the Edinburgh School of Arts was to provide

Figure 2 George Birkbeck in the tinsmith's shop in Glasgow, c.1800
(Source: Claxton, 1839)

systematic courses of lectures for working men, 'in such branches of physical sciences as are of practical advantage in their several trades' (Kelly, 1992, p.119). It enrolled 482 members who paid 15 shillings a year membership and membership lists closed within a month. The educational programme was closely geared to the Edinburgh economy. For example, a course of lectures on the 'Veterinary Arts' attracted 20 people while a free course on farriery enrolled 65. The lectures on Mechanics led to a self-help group on mathematics under the direction of a joiner, who taught the basics of geometry and arithmetic free of charge. Membership was limited to 30 and the group split into five, 'with the best scholar as monitor'. The Directors of the School of Arts were said to have given 'little encouragement' to these attempts at self-help (Hudson, 1851, pp.39–40).

Mechanics' Institutes were a characteristic response to industrialisation and urbanisation. They targeted skilled artisans, who were increasing in numbers as a result of the growth and diversification of the Scottish economy. The Institutes had a clearly defined scientific mission and were careful to steer clear of controversial political and economic topics. A key issue was the management of the Institutes, their funding and control. The Edinburgh School of Arts took care to invest its management in the upper classes. Its patron was the King and it had six noblemen as Presidents. Its Directors were selected from the annual subscribers or donors, 'securing to the non-participating class the entire management of the society'. Great care was taken to confine teaching to scientific topics and exclude anything of a controversial nature. Lectures were limited to, 'such objects of science as would be useful to workmen in their several trades' and book purchases for the library were restricted to science or art (Hudson, 1851, p.4; Marwick, 1932, p.390).

There was continuing criticism that Mechanics' Institutes in Britain failed to reach their target audience of skilled workers, attracting instead a lower middle class clientele of clerks, shop assistants and similar occupations. This does not seem to have been true of many Scottish Institutes, at least in their early days. In Edinburgh, for example, in 1823–4, out of a total of 317 members, almost half, 144 or 45 per cent, were skilled artisans and craftsmen. They included 91 joiners, carpenters and cabinet makers, 24 masons and marble cutters, 13 smiths, engineers and iron founders and 16 clock and watch makers. The lower middle classes were represented by 54 shopmen and merchants' clerks, amounting to 17 per cent of the total. Miscellaneous occupations included two of each of the following occupations – architects, hatters, hairdressers, plumbers, flax dressers, farmers and brewers (*Glasgow Mechanics' Magazine*, 7 May 1825, pp.214–5).

Lower middle class groups did feature prominently in another venture to promote popular scientific or quasi-scientific lectures, the Edinburgh Association for Procuring Instruction in Useful and Entertaining Science. This was the brainchild of the phrenologist, George Combe, who seems to have made a comfortable living out of it. Combe published the *Phrenological Magazine* to advocate his views and established the Phrenological Lecture Hall and Museum, 'where he collected an immense number of busts of distinguished and notorious characters' (Smiles, 1878, p.47). Coincidentally, Combe's brother, Abram, who died in 1827, had been a leading light in the development of the Owenite community of Orbiston in Lanarkshire (Combe, 1824, 1825; Maxwell, 1910, p.38; Donnachie, 2000, pp.227–8). Henry Cockburn described the Edinburgh Association as, 'a sort of popular unendowed college, where lectures are given to all, male or female, who choose to pay either for all the lectures or a single one'. Subjects included botany, geology, chemistry, astronomy, physiology, natural philosophy, phrenology and education. The first session in 1832 proved a profitable one. The promoters drew about £720 from 400 to 500 regular pupils and had nearly 3,000 visitors at 6d each night. On the whole, Cockburn approved of the new venture:

It is a very useful establishment, giving respectable discourses very cheaply to a class of persons for whose scientific instruction and amusement there is no other provision. They are of course contumelious of colleges, and are rather more conceited of their knowledge than humble of their ignorance. George Combe is their genius, and consequently phrenology is a favourite and most productive branch. The poor classics are held in utter scorn. In spite of these follies, it is gratifying to see hundreds of clerks and shopkeepers, with their wives and daughters, nibbling at the teats of science anyhow. (Cockburn, 1874, I, pp.73–4)

Cockburn returned to the same themes in December 1836, when he reported on 'soirees' in Edinburgh:

Being cheap evening public meetings, attended by crowds, male and female, who get tea and speeches for a shilling or sixpence or even for twopence…they are the familiar conventicles of the Radicals, of the Dissenters, of several classes of the benevolent and religious, of the patrons of unendowed institutions of science, of temperance societies, and in general of all those who want to hear or make speeches, to excite or be excited at a cheap rate, and without the labour and risks of open public meetings. (Cockburn, 1874, I, pp.75–6)

Phrenology was a pseudo-scientific subject, popular with advanced Owenite thinkers. Indeed, George Combe examined Robert Owen's head and was amazed by the size of Owen's 'bump of benevolence' (Donnachie, 2000, p.190). Another pseudo-scientific subject popular at the time was mesmerism, which also featured in commercial adult education ventures. James Paterson, the Editor of the *Ayr Observer,* described how:

The town (Ayr) was inundated with lecturers, chiefly from Glasgow, and they came generally prepared with adepts, who professed to be physically overcome by their illustrations. Among other subjects, that of mesmerism was much run upon by a certain class of enthusiasts, who went so far as to profess an entire belief in all the extravagances attributed to the science … Spirit rapping, and all the other array of natural impossibilities were essayed. Whether the people of the county town were not superstitious enough, I could not say; but the adventurers, who plied them strongly, generally had to decamp without any success to boast of. (Paterson, 1871, p.215)

It was this type of pseudo-scientific venture, and the bogus trappings that went with it, that a recent historian of American adult education had in mind when he commented:

Exploring the history of continuing and adult education entails making sense of astounding statistics, frustratingly loose terminology, lofty idealism and base hucksterism. (Kett, 1994, p.xi)

However, the Mechanics' Institute movement in Scotland was generally free of the worst excesses of hucksterism, although phrenology was not unknown on the curriculum and George Combe lectured at Anderson's Institution, Glasgow. In Glasgow, about half the members of the mechanics' class in Anderson's Institution broke away in 1823 to form their own Mechanics' Institution for the Promotion of Arts and Science. It was founded, 'by the mechanics of Glasgow, with the view of disseminating mechanical and scientific knowledge among their fellow operatives, particularly those branches more immediately connected with their daily occupations' (*NSA*, 1845, VI, p.180).

Unlike Edinburgh, the Glasgow Institute was under the control of the artisans who used its facilities. It had what has been described as 'an ultra democratic constitution' and its teachers were appointed and paid by the students, sometimes after a competitive trial lecture (Marwick, 1931, p.91). Lectures were given on natural philosophy and chemistry and the initial annual fee of three shillings was increased to ten shillings, a substantial sum. Numbers averaged about 500 and free annual admission to lectures and the library was given to, 'poor apprentices, one being admitted for every 20 tickets sold'. In 1835, it was reported that 220 apprentices had been granted free admission since the scheme started in 1823. At the close of the 1834–5 session, the President reported that students were drawn from about 40 different trades but unfortunately did not specify the trades. In addition to the Glasgow Institute, there were others in the Glasgow industrial suburbs, with some 1,200 students. In Calton, for example, there were 450 attending classes in natural philosophy, 'of whom nine tenths were operatives: 200 females attend the astronomy and geography classes, seven tenths of whom were mill girls' *(NSA*, 1845, VI, pp.180–2). Elsewhere in the Glasgow area, the Gorbals Popular Institute was founded in 1833, 'for the diffusion of science by means of public lectures and a library'. It was managed by the magistrates, councillors and clergy of the Barony of the Gorbals, together with twenty directors chosen from those who had class tickets (Marwick, 1931, p.91).

In Aberdeen, a Mechanics' Institute was founded in 1824 but struggled to survive. Its original aim was to provide cheap lectures on science to mechanics but attendance fell off and lectures were discontinued in 1830. The Institute continued as a library of 1,100 volumes 'on practical and scientific subjects'. Lectures were revived in 1835 with cheap classes in various branches of science and literature. The most striking development was the Mutual Instruction Class, a self-help group drawing attendances of 100–120. There were no restrictions on subjects for discussion, 'except that controversial theology and politics are peremptorily excluded' (*NSA*, 1845, XII, pp.47–8).

Alexander Bain left a brief record of his membership of the Aberdeen Institute. Bain, the son of a former soldier and handloom weaver, was born in Aberdeenshire in 1819. He left the parish school at 11, having learned some Latin, but carried on reading his father's small collection of books, including *Pilgrims' Progress*, *Scots Worthies* and Watson's *Body of Divinity*. At the age 13, he became a handloom weaver and later became friendly with brothers called Stewart, the sons of a blacksmith. They were self-taught mathematicians and introduced Bain to, 'the Library of the Mechanics' Institution, then in existence about ten years, and at a somewhat low ebb, after a flourishing commencement'. Together, they attempted to revive the Institute and Bain became its Secretary. He described the development of a Mutual Instruction Class out of the Mechanics' Institute. The class opened in May 1835 and had a vigorous life for two or three years. Bain was friendly with George Innes, a mathematically minded watchmaker and with Peter Gray, a bookseller and fellow member of the Mechanics' class. It was through Gray that Bain met the Rev. John Murray, the minister of the North parish in Aberdeen, who encouraged him to go to university by preparing for the bursary competition. This was the start of a successful academic career for Bain, who went on to become Professor of Logic at Aberdeen. Bain was very conscious of being one of the elect. His parents had eight children, three of whom died in infancy and he was the only one to reach 40. Of his surviving siblings, he remarked, 'Of the other four, I may say, that they were all failures in life; every one of them had, at some time or other, to be assisted by me' (Bain, 1904, pp.4–29).

The Watt Institution in Dundee was founded on 10 November 1824, with the encouragement of Provost Patrick Anderson, a Tory. It commanded all party support from the Radical *Dundee Advertiser* and the Tory *Courier*. The leading light behind the Dundee scheme was James Brown, a Dundee flaxspinner, who argued in the prospectus, 'It would be expected that the Watt Institution would be the means of promoting virtuous and industrious habits amongst the working classes by furnishing them with an agreeable and rational mode of employing their spare time'. Although aimed at skilled artisans, the Watt Institution was controlled by the Dundee middle class. Voting power was determined by the amount of money subscribed – a vote for every pound subscribed (Smith, 1977).

The teaching staff at the Watt Institution tended to be part-time and peripatetic, with a high degree of geographical mobility. This mirrored experience elsewhere in Scotland. Early full-time lecturers included a Mr Macvicar and Andrew Roy. Macvicar resigned after a year to apply for the post of chemistry lecturer at the Glasgow Mechanics' Institute. He was unsuccessful and continued to work for the Watt Institute on a part-time basis, his successor being the

Rev. William Dow from Dumfries and Maxwelltown Institute. Andrew Roy stayed until 1828, when he became a mathematics teacher at the Academy in Cupar, Fife. The last full-time teacher at the Watt Institute was James Bowman Lindsay, a remarkable autodidact from Carmyllie in Angus. Born in 1799, Lindsay began working life as a weaver, spending his spare time in self-improvement. In 1821, he entered St Andrews University and taught the children of crofters and farmers during the vacation 'for nominal fees' (Smith, 1977, pp.13–14). In 1835, Lindsay carried out a demonstration of 'sustained electric light' in Dundee (Macdonald, 2000a, p.135).

Like the Aberdeen Institute, the Watt Institution fell on hard times and opted for the same solution of mutual instruction. This followed a fall in membership in 1829 to a record low of 81, which led to a nine-year period of mutual instruction, to save expenditure on teaching fees. Both membership numbers and the social composition of the membership fluctuated with the slump and boom in Dundee's industrial fortunes and with the impact of other social and political movements, such as Chartism. After the depression of 1839–43, the proportion of working class members fell. In 1841, the directors complained that political meetings were poaching their membership, Chartist meetings, 'being more temporary and very exciting monopolised almost all the spare time at the command of those for whose benefit the mechanics' institutes were established' (Smith, 1977, p.30). Women also used the Watt Institution and the *Annual Report* for 1840 boasted, 'It is one of the best features of this Institution that Ladies are invited and encouraged to avail themselves of all its benefits'. However, women only amounted to some 4 per cent of library users in the period 1842–46.

The Mechanics' Institute in Haddington, East Lothian was formed in 1823, when the local Mutual Improvement Society transformed itself into the Haddington School of Arts. Its founding father was Samuel Brown, who had started the East Lothian Itinerating Library Scheme in 1817, described earlier. Samuel Smiles, who had just graduated in medicine from Edinburgh University, gave lectures on chemistry to the School of Arts, which was held in the parish school. He recalled:

> The lectures were well attended by the leading mechanics of the town. I remember three of them who worked as carpenters for Messrs. Scoular of Sunnybank...Two of these men saved money enough during the summer to pay for their class instruction at Edinburgh University during the winter. One became the minister of a Presbyterian congregation at Blackburn; another became master of a large public school at Hull; and the one who remained a mechanic rose higher than the others. (He became General Manager of the P. and O. Company.) (Smiles, 1905, p.31)

This reflects the strongly utilitarian character of Mechanics' Institutes, with their ethos of self-improvement and self-help.

The movement grew rapidly north and south of the border. By 1851, Scotland supported 55 Mechanics' Institutes with 12,500 members and 59,661 volumes in their libraries, compared with 610 Institutes, 102,000 members and 691,500 volumes in England. A contemporary historian of the movement complained that the Scottish Institutes were, 'less numerous and less effective than similar societies in England, owing to the practice of closing them entirely during the summer and autumn' (Hudson, 1851, p.vi). However, a modern historian has argued that the Scottish Institutes were better able to maintain systematic science courses because of the superiority of the Scottish parochial school system and the Presbyterian tradition of rigorous theological discourse (Kelly, 1992, p.114).

Peter Carmichael, a Dundee textile manufacturer who had been a director of the Watt Institution in Dundee, was less sanguine about the Scottish educational system. He wrote in 1853:

> My decided opinion is that the failure of the Mechanics Institutions generally has arisen from a mistaken idea that mechanics were better educated than they really are. Taking the young men in Dundee engaged in the mechanical trades, say from fourteen to twenty four years of age, it will be found that most of them have not received an education beyond reading, writing and the simple rules of arithmetic, or if in the course of their school training some may have advanced further, it has been acquired, as too much school learning is by boys, with such a dim perception of its uses to them in after life that it is allowed to rust out for want of cultivation. Now the benevolent promoters of Mechanics Institutions, forming their opinions from the higher standpoint of their own education, think what a fine thing it would be for mechanics to attend a course of lectures on the philosophy of mechanics, and be able to read from the library choice works on such subjects, not seeing that their previous education unfits them for appreciating or apprehending such higher culture.
> (Gauldie, (ed.), 1969, pp.142–3)

How effective were Mechanics' Institutes in Scotland? A contemporary historian of adult education, J.W. Hudson, Secretary of the Manchester Athenaeum and Founder of the Scottish and Northern Union of Literary and Mechanics' Institutes, admitted that across Britain as a whole, they had often failed to recruit the very people they were set up to reach, the skilled male artisans. He acknowledged the 'universal complaint that Mechanics' Institutes are attended by persons of a higher rank than those for whom they were designed, applies with equal force to the Athenaeums and Literary Institutes of the country'.

Hudson attributed this to social unease at being in the company of those of a higher social status. He reported that just as the clerk would leave the Athenaeum when he found 'the governor', his boss, present and join the Mechanics' Institute, so, 'the warehouseman, the packer, the carter and the mill-hand shun the society of the clerk and the foreman' and either did not join or left the Institutes (Hudson, 1851, p.vii). Others gave different explanations. A letter from 'an Oppressed Workman' in the Glasgow *Herald to the Trades Advocate*, for example, dated October 1830, claimed that popular schools and Mechanics' Institutes started their meetings too early for many workmen to attend. Most meetings started at 8.15 p.m., whereas many working men only finished work at 8.00 p.m., so that, 'no workman of that class, already alluded to, can be forward at any public lecture before a quarter to nine o'clock' (*Herald to the Trades Advocate*, 1831, p.57).

In Scotland, the Mechanics' Institutes were a fairly mixed bag, in terms of their geographical location, their size, their management structure and the social composition of their membership. To take one example – there was huge variation in management structures. Edinburgh was under upper-class patronage, Glasgow democratic. At Barrhead, the management committee, 'consisted almost entirely of intelligent artisans', whilst Brechin was controlled by local dignitaries and financed by Lord Panmure. Hawick was under the patronage of the local landowner and Dunfermline was chaired by the Earl of Elgin. In Lanarkshire, Coatbridge was promoted by local lairds and industrialists, including John McKenzie, manager of Dundyvan Ironworks and Archibald Reid, manager of Bredisholm Colliery (Marwick, 1933b, pp.300–1; Campbell, 1979, p.224). The management of the Watt Institution was dominated by the Dundee merchant and manufacturer class, whilst clergymen played a major role in places like Stirling or the Gorbals in Glasgow.

Generally speaking, the Scottish Mechanics' Institutes had a strong establishment aura about them. Their ostensible purpose was to teach science and technology to the working man, particularly the skilled worker, but there was also a not-so-hidden curriculum concerned with individual social and economic advancement and the reconciliation of workers to industrial society. The address at the opening of the Stirling School of Arts in 1825 by the Rev. Mr Bennie neatly sums this up, 'such institutions as we now propose, will have a very powerful effect in arming the minds of the young against the seductions of unholy speculations' (*Glasgow Mechanics' Magazine*, 7 May 1825, p.408).

Many Radicals believed that Mechanics' Institutes were part of a middle-class conspiracy to brainwash the working classes. William Cobbett voiced these fears when sending a donation of £5 to the London Mechanics' Institute. He added:

I gave my £5 as a mark of my respect for and my attachment to the working classes of the community…But I was not without my fears that this
institution may be turned to purposes extremely injurious to the mechanics themselves. I cannot but know what sort of people are likely to get
amongst them…Mechanics, I most heartily wish you well, but I also most
heartily wish you not to be humbugged, which you certainly will be if you
suffer anybody but REAL MECHANICS to have anything to do in managing the concern. You will mean well; but many a cunning scoundrel will
get place or pension as the price of you. (quoted in McIlroy and
Westwood, (eds.), 1993, p.257)

The *Herald to the Trades Advocate,* published by the Trades Committee of
Glasgow, welcomed the Mechanics' Institutes in 1830, but criticised their
socially and economically conservative analysis of society, offering advice:

to the managers of such Institutions to direct the energy of the professors
to the most important subject viz. That the scientific and mechanical
power now brought into existence in Britain…be distributed for the benefit of the working classes. (*Herald to the Trades Advocate*, 6 November 1830)

A contributor to *Chambers's Papers for the People* believed that working men,
'would sooner attend a political meeting, to demand what they consider their
"rights", than a scientific lecture; that they would rather read a party newspaper
than a calm historical narrative; and that they would sooner invest money in a
benefit club or a building society than in a mechanics' institute' (Altick, 1957,
p.193). By contrast, the Glasgow-based *Chartist Circular* welcomed all educational initiatives, regardless of the motives of their sponsors, 'All that tends to
spread information advances our cause…every Mechanics' Institute reared
paves the way for fresh converts' (*Chartist Circular*, 18 September 1841, p.433).

The Whig view was generally that offered by the Rev. Bennie of Stirling, that
education could be used to guide working-class opinion in a favourable direction, away from radical politics towards moderate reform. Many Tories feared
the opposite, that too much education would give people ideas beyond their station and cause them to question the existing social and economic order. These
controversies found expression in the activities of Henry Brougham and the
Society for the Diffusion of Useful Knowledge (SDUK).

Henry Brougham and the Society for the Diffusion of Useful Knowledge

Henry Brougham (1778–1868) was born in Edinburgh, the son of a
Westmorland squire and a Scottish mother who was the niece of William

Robertson, the Principal of Edinburgh University. He entered Edinburgh University at the age of 14 and did a general arts course. George Birkbeck was a fellow student and Brougham attended classes by Joseph Black and Dugald Stewart. In 1796 he began to study law and a year later, was elected to the Speculative Society, becoming one of its four Presidents two years later. In 1801, Brougham, together with Sydney Smith, Francis Horner and Francis Jeffrey, launched the *Edinburgh Review*, a reformist Whig publication, with Smith as its first Editor. The *Review* championed the cause of peaceful parliamentary reform and Brougham came to see education, including adult education, as a concomitant of political reform. He entered Parliament in 1812 and served as an MP for 54 years, first for Winchelsea, then Knaresborough and finally, and briefly, for the County of Yorkshire, eventually becoming Lord Chancellor (Brougham, 1871, Vol. II, p.65; New, 1961, pp.1–51; Herman, 2003, pp.255–277).

Brougham used his seat in Parliament to call for the improvement of education and the establishment of a national system of education, along Scottish lines. The *Edinburgh Review* commented (with misplaced optimism) in 1818:

> Nobody can have forgotten the murmurs and dissonant clamours with which the first proposal for communicating the blessings of Education to the great body of the people was lately received. Already, however, that disgraceful opposition is extinct. (Silver, 1965, p.19)

In 1825, Brougham published a pamphlet entitled *Practical Observations on the Education of the People,* which became the Bible of the Mechanics' Institutes and of the SDUK. He divided popular education into three branches – infant schools, elementary schools (for reading and writing) and adult education. Only with elementary schools could the state 'safely interfere', whereas meddling with adult education would be 'perilous to civil and religious liberty'. Brougham saw the principle obstacles to adult education as lack of money and lack of time. He stressed the central importance of reading and assumed that all social classes could spare an hour or two each day for reading and could contribute something financially towards this. The pamphlet criticised taxes on paper as a tax on knowledge and commended Samuel Brown's East Lothian Itinerating Library Scheme. Brougham spelled out various ways in which adult education could be progressed. He commended the practice of one worker reading to others in the workplace, the growth of mutual instruction societies, the provision of elementary textbooks in subjects such as mathematics, chemistry, natural philosophy etc., and above all, the provision of lectures in the larger towns; 'the institution of Lectures is, of all the help that can be given, the most valuable'. Brougham saw clearly that financial and managerial control by artisans of the Mechanics' Institutes was crucial to their success, 'it is a fundamental principle to make the expenses be mainly defrayed by the mechanics themselves; it is another principle, in my opinion equally essential, that they should have the principle share in the management' (Brougham, 1825, pp.11, 15). The pamphlet sold well and went through 20 editions in six months (Stewart, 1985, p.186).

The SDUK was founded in 1826. Its committee consisted of the great and the good drawn from the Whig elite, who played a prominent role in the passing of the Reform Act of 1832. Its Chairman was Henry Brougham, its Vice-Chairman Lord John Russell, MP and its Treasurer William Tooke. Members included Rowland Hill, Leonard Horner, James Mill and Henry Parnell, MP. Its aim was to produce, 'useful information to all classes of the community, particularly such as are unable to avail themselves of experienced teachers, or may prefer learning by themselves' (Silver, 1965, p.211). It produced the Library of Useful Knowledge, the *Penny Magazine,* the *Penny Cyclopedia,* booklets for farmers, a series of maps and another of almanacs. The Library of Useful Knowledge consisted of a series of specially commissioned booklets – 66 on scientific topics, 92 on other subjects, including history, philosophy and art (New, 1961, pp.348–9).

In 1830, the SDUK published G.L. Craik's *The Pursuit of Knowledge under Difficulties,* an early self-improvement tract that pre-dated Samuel Smiles' better-known *Self Help* by some years (Craik, 1830). The models for much of this activity were the experiments in popular enlightenment pioneered by George Miller and Samuel Brown in East Lothian. The SDUK, caricatured as the Steam Intellect Society, met with initial success. Brougham's own *Discourse on the Objects, Pleasures and Advantages of Science* ran through eight editions in its first year and sold 39,000 copies. Sales of other publications were similarly encouraging at first but then fell away. The *Penny Cyclopedia,* issued monthly, saw its circulation fall from 75,000 to 20,000 in 1844. The *Penny Magazine* had a circulation of 200,000 at its height but ceased publication in 1845 when the Society was wound up because of mounting debts and falling membership (Webb, 1955, p.68; Stewart, 1985, pp.188–194).

Brougham brushed aside objections to his educational plans as evidence of obsolete and out-of-date thinking. He saw little need to counter, 'objections to the diffusion of science amongst the working classes, arising from objections of a political nature. Happily, the time is past and gone when bigots could persuade mankind that the lights of philosophy were to be extinguished as dangerous to religion' (Brougham, 1825, p.31). However, this was overly optimistic. Heated opposition to Brougham's plans came from two quarters – the Tories and the Church of England, who feared almost any reform, and the Radicals, who believed that the reforms proposed by Brougham and his fellow Whigs did not go far enough. For example, the Tory *Blackwood's Edinburgh Magazine* fulminated in 1825:

We cannot be ignorant that the educating of the working adults of a great nation is a thing entirely without precedent…We cannot be ignorant that hitherto, whenever the lower orders of any great state have attained a smattering of knowledge, they have generally used it to produce national ruin. (Silver, 1965, p.212)

The Radicals had different reservations about Brougham's proposals. William Cobbett, for example, had a deep-rooted dislike of Brougham and his fellow Whig reformers. In his *Tour in Scotland* (1833) he denounced, 'the gabbling, hair-brained, feelosofizing BROUGHAM and all his crew' and 'BROUGHAM and all his puffing tribe,' for their plans to reform the English Poor Law. In particular, Cobbett challenged Whig assertions, 'that the misery and crimes of the working people of England arose, not from their hard lives and ill-treatment, but from their *want of education*; and that it was the *better education* of the Scotch that made them *more prudent and more moral*. I always denied… that the Scotch were more prudent and more moral' (Cobbett, 1833, pp.48, 91, 140). In his *Political Register*, Cobbett mocked the 'brilliant enterprise to make us "a' enlightened" and to fill us with "antellect, brought, ready bottled up, from the north of the Tweed"' (quoted in Altick, 1957, p.191).

Cobbett, with all his prejudices, was noting an important trend. Whereas Davie and others have mourned the increasing Anglicisation of Scottish education in the nineteenth century (Davie, 1964 edition), the 'Scottish invasion' of the English education system in the same period was arguably more important. Many of Brougham's colleagues in the education reform movement, in the Mechanics' Institute movement, in the SDUK and in the launch of the University of London, were either Scots or had received their education in Scotland and brought the ideas of the Scottish Enlightenment into the different culture of England. Indeed, its influence went further afield than England. In 1832, Brougham's *Practical Observations on the Education of the People* was published in Sweden. A year later, the Society for the Diffusion of Useful Knowledge among the Peasantry and Working Classes was founded (Rubenson, 1992, p.317).

Chartism

The Chartists made education an important plank in their reform programme. They campaigned for a free press and the removal of the tax on newspapers and for secular education for children and adults. Rather like the Whigs in an earlier period, they saw effective popular education as a necessary concomitant of widening the franchise. The *Chartist Circular*, printed in Glasgow, published a number of articles detailing the failures of the existing education system. In 1839, it claimed that, 'Parochial schools have failed to accomplish the education of the people', contrasting Scotland with countries where educational opportunities had expanded such as Prussia, Holland, Germany, Switzerland and France. It estimated that only a fourteenth of Scotland's population was at school, compared with a fifth in Holland, a sixth in Prussia and an eighth in Bavaria (*Chartist Circular,* 28 September 1839, pp.18–9). These figures have been challenged by a modern historian, who has claimed that the figures for those learning to read and write in Scotland in 1834 were closer to the Prussian figures of one in six (Withrington, 1988, p.184). The *Circular* deplored the predominance of private as opposed to parochial schools in Scotland, particularly in industrial areas such as Lanarkshire. One solution to the problems of Scottish education was seen to be better training for teachers and the *Circular* called for the establishment of normal schools for teacher training.

Another plank in the Chartist programme was better female education. The *Circular* complained that in the parish schools, women were not taught, 'any other maxims than to 'Fear God and honour the King – to revere Aristocrats and their satellites – and not to meddle with any of those God has placed in authority'. Women were seen to have an important role in the political education of their children, 'I wish you still to be religious and virtuous, but I also wish you to understand philosophical and political sciences, and to be able to teach them to your children' (*Chartist Circular,* 28 September 1839, p.35). However, not all women were content to remain in such a passive and supportive role. In Glasgow, it was claimed that Chartist women had moved from an auxiliary to a more active role in the movement and had 'improved their habits of thought' by reading and by writing essays on various topics (Clark, 1995, pp.229–30).

The Chartist message was easier to convey to areas with an existing culture of popular radicalism, often linked to an earlier history of religious dissent. The *Circular* described some of these links between adult education, radical politics and religion in Scotland:

> The people have acquired a taste for general literature and cheap periodicals have found their way into every poor man's cottage. In many towns and villages, philosophical and political institutions are established, where the masses congregate on Saturday nights to hear philosophical and political lectures, and to witness experiments on natural sciences; Pneumatics, Geology, Animal and Vegetable Physiology, Chemistry, Phrenology, Mechanics, Astronomy, Hydro-statics are now as accurately known and remembered as the Shorter Catechism was in the days of our great-grandfathers. (*Chartist Circular,* 4 January 1840)

Against this background, middle-class lecturers in the Mechanics' Institutes and elsewhere could struggle to make headway. Dr Thomas Murray lectured in the years 1836–39 in Hawick, Montrose, Falkirk, Dunfermline and Glasgow 'on a

Whiggish curriculum' and was said to have encountered a rising tide of Chartist feeling (Tyrell, 1969, p.160). In Ayrshire, the Rev. Norman Macleod reported similar feelings amongst the weavers of Newmills, who had formed a Philosophical Institution in 1842:

> There has always been a set of shrewd, well-read, philosophical weavers here – vain, but marvellously well informed and half infidel – who were very civil when I went to see them, but would never come to church. They were generally Chartists, and talked very big about the 'priests' not wishing the people to become well informed. (Boyd, 1961, p.126)

Macleod offered to lecture to them on geology, the offer was taken up, and a class of 150 turned up, with a further 50 outside. The dissenting church was hired, with audiences of 600–700 (Boyd, 1961, p.126).

In the Ayrshire village of Fenwick, the Fenwick Improvement of Knowledge Society was founded by a group of weavers in 1834. It met every second Friday night in a member's home, 'when a Question on any subject shall be proposed (Doctrines of Religion excluded)'. Like Robert Burns' earlier Tarbolton Bachelors' Club, the presidency of the Society went by rotation, and when discussion began, 'those who have written Essays shall have the precedence' (*SHR*, 1920, pp.119–20). An article by Samuel Kydd in the *Northern Star* in 1847 waxed lyrical about his experiences in Ayrshire:

> The inhabitants of the weaving villages are the most intelligent men with whom I have ever conversed; they are readers and thinkers. In those districts is many a well-thumbed pile of pamphlets – Cobbett's *Register*, the *Black Dwarf* and two penny *Dispatch* being the textbooks of the old politicians; the *Northern Star* the book of political life read by the younger of the schools of political and social regeneration. Literature, too, is a favourite pursuit with the weaving population …Those who speak of the ignorance of the working classes would do well to visit Ayrshire. (Simon, 1960, p.257)

There were communities like this in other parts of Scotland, often in burghs with long-established weaving populations, such as Dunfermline in Fife or Paisley in Renfrewshire. They were noted for political activism and for a tradition of popular and often radical literature, particularly poetry. For example, Tom Leonard has identified 68 poets who were born or lived in Renfrewshire, mainly in Paisley, during the period from the French Revolution to the First World War. Of these, no less than 20 (29 per cent) had worked as a weaver or a weavers' drawboy (assistant). This radical literary culture was sustained by a network of clubs and societies such as the Literary and Political Club founded in

1803 by a group including the weaver-poet Robert Tannahill, or the Paisley Literary and Convivial Club of 1814, its founders including James Yool, a radical weaver, poet and trade unionist (Leonard, 1990, pp.38, 63; Murray, 1978, pp.168–172).

In the East of Scotland, Dr Harding reported in 1839 that the handloom weavers:

> show a remarkable desire for intellectual improvement; lectures delivered on subjects of any interest to them (eg. on political economy) are generally very fully attended; books and periodicals are obtained by means of subscription amongst themselves, the latter to a great extent; most of them read the newspapers which accord with their political opinions. It may perhaps afford some indication of their literary tastes, to state that, next to the newspapers, 'Chambers' Edinburgh Journal' and 'Wilsons' Tales of the Borders', were almost universally popular...On the whole, however, the superiority of their intellectual condition to that of the generality of the labouring classes in England is very striking. (*Parliamentary Papers*, 1839, Vol. XLII, p.190)

In Dunfermline, 'the public and circulating libraries' contained upwards of 5,100 volumes and about 450 weavers were regular readers at these libraries, out of an estimated weaving population of 3,700. Favourite reading in 1837 included *Chambers Edinburgh Journal,* the *Scotsman* and *Tait's Magazine (op. cit.,* p.202).

With the introduction of the power loom, the earnings and living standards of handloom weavers went into a long and painful decline, and this type of culture came under severe pressure. In the west of Scotland, it was reported in 1838 that amongst handloom weavers, 'Book societies, formerly supported by themselves alone, are either extinct, or in the last stages of existence. Newspapers, magazines, reviews, histories, travels and books on science and philosophy, are well nigh excluded from their dwellings, where, of all others, they were the most frequently found'. Weavers' reading was now confined to newspapers, *Chambers Edinburgh Journal, Tait's Magazine* and Scott's novels. In Govan, J.C. Symons lamented the decline of the local library, 'the poor weaver, though the ticket for it were presented to him gratis, has little time to spare for reading, and that little he prefers to spend in perusing the newspapers and periodicals in search of some panacea for the accumulating calamities of his hard lot'. Symons concluded sadly, 'Poverty is a great barrier to enlightenment' (*Parliamentary Papers,* 1970 edition, Industrial Revolution, textiles, Vol. 9, pp.37, 56–7).

James Stuart (1843–1913), who played a pioneering role in University Extension at Cambridge, noted a similar culture of radical politics and self-improvement amongst the workers at his father's flax mill in Balgonie, Fife. Stuart described how the workers were, 'extreme Radicals, Chartists in those days to a man' and how they organised reading in the workshop, with one man reading aloud to the others while they worked (Stuart, 1911, p.58). In Scotland, the Chartists tried to create this culture across the country. In 1838, there were about 200 local associations in Scotland, which had declined to 125 by 1840. As well as engaging in political activities, the associations offered social, cultural and educational activities, sometimes linked with fundraising. Soirees and concerts were held to raise funds in Dalkeith, Montrose, Stirling, Saltcoats and Dunfermline. In Glagow, Greenock and Cumnock, there were social meetings and concerts held on a weekly or monthly basis. Saturday evening concerts were held in the Glasgow Lyceum, and the Lanarkshire Universal Suffrage Association attempted to bring more women into the movement by organising a dancing class in Glasgow throughout the winter. The same organisation also ran a weekly lecture series in the winter months in Glasgow (Wilson, 1970, p.123).

In 1843, the Rev. William Hill, recently deposed as editor of the *Northern Star*, and Julian Harney, its future editor, visited Scotland. Hill reported that in Glasgow, the Gorbals, Anderston, Hamilton, Aberdeen, Dundee and the Vale of Leven, 'the strength and power of Chartism' lay in its Christian Chartist churches and schools. Chartist schools were often attached to Chartist churches in places like Alexandria, Arbroath, Greenock, the Gorbals, Strathaven and Hamilton. The meeting places served as, 'church, day school, evening school, committee room, concert hall and public meeting place'. From 1849 to 1852, Chartist figures such as Feargus O'Connor, Samuel Kydd, Julian Harney, Bronterre O'Brien, G.W.M. Reynolds, Ernest Jones, George Jacob Holyoake and Thomas Cooper all carried out lecture tours in Scotland (Wilson, 1970, pp.149, 199–200, 245).

The feelings of the Chartists for the Whigs are summed up by a satirical, if slightly ambivalent, poem in the *Chartist Circular*.

Harry Brougham

Britain's now astir all over
All complaining and conspiring
And from John o' Groats to Dover
Democrats all souls are firing
Ask you whence arose the storm?
All is owing to 'Reform';
If the people rage and fume
'Tis the fault of Harry Brougham
Education, education

Free from articles and creed
Agitation, agitation
Schoolmasters abroad, indeed;
Ask you why all hearts so warm
All is owing to 'Reform';
If knowledge reaches e'en the loom,
'Tis the fault of Harry Brougham

Whigs, you give not half enough
All soft sawdor words and blarney
Let's have men of sterner stuff
Will not our wide grumbling warn ye?
Thus it is the people bore 'em,
And all owing to 'Reform',
When they cry, 'make room, make room',
'Tis the fault of Harry Brougham
(*Chartist Circular*, 1840)

It was against this background that the Glasgow Athenaeum opened in October 1847, enrolling 1,600 men and women at a guinea a year for courses in Business Studies and the Arts (Butt, 2000, p.183). It was modelled on the Manchester Athenaeum and was designed, 'to fill the educational vacuum between the Mechanics' Institution and Glasgow University...combining with its classes... the advantages of a newsroom, a reading room, a library, a gymnasium and a coffee room, all in one central building'. Charles Dickens presided at the formal inauguration on 28 December 1847 and Ralph Waldo Emerson delivered a lecture on 15 February 1848, which drew some bile from the conservative *Glasgow Courier*. Emerson gave lectures on 'New England' and 'The Genius of the Present Age', which were received with great enthusiasm by his Glasgow audience. Not so the Rev. Jamieson of St Pauls, who gave a lecture on 'Natural History', which many of his youthful audience walked out of (Marwick, 1930, pp.92–4).

In 1848, the same year as the *Communist Manifesto* was published and a year of revolutions across Europe, John Stuart Mill summarised the impact of social movements such as Chartism:

The working classes have taken their interests into their own hands, and are perpetually showing that they think the interests of their employers not identical with their own, but opposite to them. Some among the higher classes flatter themselves that these tendencies may be counteracted by moral and religious education; but they have let the time go by for giving an education which can serve their purpose. (J. S. Mill, *Principles of Political Economy*, 1848)

However, in the 1850s and 1860s, there were strenuous attempts made in Britain to play down class differences, which met with a fair degree of success. Antonio Gramsci (1891–1937), the Italian political activist, developed a theory of hegemony to describe the ways in which the dominant classes tried to keep power by persuading the mass of the population to accept their political and moral values. He argued that the State was not a purely coercive power but relied on, 'a balance between political and civil society, by which I mean the hegemony of one social group over the entire nation, exercised by so-called private organisations like the Church, trade unions, or schools. For it is above all in civil society that intellectuals exert their influence' (Gramsci, 1973, p.204). Much of the adult education provision described so far in this book, mainly carried out by private organisations, had a strongly ideological flavour to it, although there is evidence that its working-class recipients did not always respond in predictable ways, and also developed their own ideologies and systems of self-education. The next chapter examines this distinctive culture of artisan self-improvement.

Chapter 3
Self-improvement

Knowledge is no exclusive inheritance of the rich and the leisure classes but may be attained by all.

(Samuel Smiles, *Autobiography*, 1905)

Popular culture – the rough and the respectable

At first glance, there would seem to have been little space for popular culture to exist in eighteenth-century Scotland. In a country with no religious holidays – no Saints days, little observance of Christmas or Easter and with the Kirk policing people's behaviour on the Sabbath – the opportunities for popular leisure time activities seem limited, to say the least. However, most early modern economies had a considerable amount of built-in unemployment or underemployment and Scotland was no exception. Outside observers frequently commented on this. The energetic Celia Fiennes, for example, made a brief foray across the Scottish border into Dumfriesshire in 1698 and was struck by, 'seeing two or three great wenches as tall and bigg as any women sat hovering between their bed and the chimney corner all idle doing nothing, or at least was not settled to any work, tho' it was nine of the clock when I came thither, having gone nine long miles that morning' (Fiennes, 1982 edition, p.173).

The Highlands were a particular target for these kinds of observations. Captain Edmund Burt, writing about Inverness in the 1720s, commented that, 'the working tradesman, for the most part, are indolent' and that, 'the fishermen would not be mentioned, but for their remarkable laziness' (Burt, 1998 edition, pp.59–60). In the early 1790s, cotton mills were established at Spinningdale in Sutherland on the Skibo estate of George Dempster, MP for the Perth burghs. The partners were a group of Glasgow merchants and manufacturers, including the Ross-shire-born George MacIntosh (Cooke, 1995a). Writing in 1795, MacIntosh complained that the Sutherland people were, 'by no means industrious or fond of work, in so much that the manager finds difficulty in getting apprentices for the weaving or spinning – especially since the recruiting became so universal'. Later that year, he blamed 'our good indolent country people' as the main source of the company's problems (Gilchrist of Ospidale Mss., MacIntosh to unnamed correspondent, 31 March 1795 and MacIntosh to Dr

Scorza, 10 July 1795). In the same period, the more censorious Highland ministers complained about such phenomena as 'tipling huts' in their parishes, 'where young and idle people convene and get drunk' (*OSA*, XVII, p.682).

In the eighteenth century, the two main holidays in Scotland were Handsel Monday, which was held on the first Monday after New Year, and the King's Birthday on 4 June. In Edinburgh, the King's Birthday was celebrated by, 'the lower orders and the boys having a long day of idleness and fireworks, and by the upper classes going to the Parliament House, and drinking the royal health in the evening, at the expense of public funds' (Cockburn, 1856, p.69). In Perth, there was an appropriate military feel to the occasion, with bells ringing, fireworks and a military salute. One historian has described these occasions as a 'safety valve' and a 'ritual of revolt' (Whatley, 2000a, p.161). The outbreak of the French Revolution and the impact of the *Rights of Man* brought about important changes. George Penny, a weaver, journalist and local historian, recalled that in Perth, 'Democrats began to make their appearance; dead cats and basses were hurled about and dirt thrown; and the birthday fell into great disrepute' (Penny, 1836, pp.38–9). In Glasgow, the night of George III's birthday in June 1792 saw, 'a loose disorderly rabble throwing brickbats, dead dogs and cats, by which several of the military were severely cut' (Whatley, 1995, p.383). There were also local holidays or fairs, often pre-dating the Reformation. In Glasgow, for example, the Glasgow Fair, established in mediaeval times, was held in mid-July at the feast of St Peter and Paul and has continued down to the present day as a holiday (King, 1987, p.157). The Lammas Fair in St Andrews and the Links Fair in Kirkcaldy are examples of mediaeval street fairs that have survived the Reformation.

The work patterns in some occupations in eighteenth and nineteenth-century Scotland often allowed workers spare time for recreation or self-improvement, depending on their temperament. Groups such as handloom weavers, shoemakers, tailors, carpenters, masons and other craftsmen and artisans were often self-employed or had some degree of control over their working lives. William Thom, for example, described the life of the (factory-based) Scottish handloom weaver in the early years of the nineteenth century, before the introduction of the power loom:

This was the daisy portion of weaving – the bright and mid-day period of all who pitched a shuttle, and of the happy one whose luck it was to win a weaver's smile. Four days did the weaver work – for then four days was a week, as far as working went – and such a week to a skilful workman brought forty shillings. Sunday, Monday and Tuesday were of course jubilee. Lawn frills gorged freely from under the wrists of his fine blue, buttoned coat. He dusted his head with white flour on Sunday, smirked and wore a cane. Walked in clean slippers on Monday, Tuesday heard him talk war bravado, quote Volnay and get drunk. Weaving commenced gradually on Wednesday; then were little children pirn fillers, and such were taught to steal warily past the gate-keeper, concealing the bottle. (Thom, 1880, p.3)

Many occupations had their own customary or local holidays. Bob Smillie noted that, 'Thursday was the weekly holiday' in the Lanarkshire coalfields in the late nineteenth century (Smillie, 1924, p.40) and many workers observed 'St Monday', the unofficial day off taken at the beginning of the working week. In Dundee, for example, it was reported in 1838 that for handloom weavers, 'Saturday afternoon, Monday, and often Tuesday, are considered holidays, or rather idle days, during which little, if any, work is done' (*Parliamentary Papers,* 1970 edition, Vol. 9, p.187).

Social divisions seem to have widened from the 1790s, both between middle and working-class groups and within the working class itself. This relates to many of the changes discussed in Chapter 2, such as growing urbanisation, industrialisation and the spread of radical ideas from America and France. The growth of towns, cities and industrial villages led to increasing social segregation in housing. Within the workplace, there was a growth in the size of the average workforce, although Rodger has emphasised the continuing importance of the small-scale traditional employer in Scotland, at least until 1850 (Rodger, 1998). By the 1850s, at least three distinctive popular cultures were to be found in urban Scotland – Lowland Scots, Gaelic speaking Highlanders and Irish Catholics, together with smaller groups such as Ulster Protestants (Walker, 1979; Devine, (ed.), 1991; Withers, 1998). These groups tended to follow a distinctive form of worship at separate churches, to live in geographically-defined parts of the town or city and often to follow certain occupations. They had their own music, songs, dances, poetry and literature. Tensions existed between them, particularly along religious lines and in the competition for jobs. The distinctiveness of the Gaelic speaking Highlanders and the Irish Catholics was reinforced by continuing migration from the 'homeland'.

Handsel Monday was a traditional holiday held on the first Monday in January. In the cotton manufacturing village of Stanley in Perthshire, for example, the holiday was celebrated by races and a flute band of ploughmen paraded through the streets. In 1836, a group of workers formed a Singing Club and, with the Stanley Instrumental Band, gave a concert on Handsel Monday for the benefit of the poor, with an audience of three to four hundred. The local newspaper was pleased to report that whereas the day had, 'commonly been set apart for the degrading purpose of intoxication' it was hoped 'the day is not far distant when people, instead of spending their holidays in riotous drinking and other bacchanalian festivities, will employ them in rational and praiseworthy amusements' (*Perthshire Courier*, 28 January 1836, p.3).

A modern historian has described a popular culture, 'in which noise was enormously important; in "rough music", rhythmic drum beating, bell ringing, rhyming doggerel, verse and song' (Whatley, 2000a, p.12). This is confirmed by accounts such as that for Perth by George Penny, who described football on the Inch, the cause of numerous broken limbs, curling, quoits, hand ball and the ball and nine holes. As regards music, 'a great many of our old Scotch songs were sung, chiefly picked up by the ear from the maids at the wheel'. Storytelling was another popular pastime and Penny mentions a chapbook *Satan's Invisible World Discovered*, which was popular in the 1780s (Penny, 1986 edition, pp.111–8).

Rougher amusements included 'Riding the Stang', a charivari-type of activity found in Lowland Scotland and the north of England. Here, adulterers or hen-pecked husbands were humiliated by being forced to ride a rail and carried round the town before being pitched into a dung heap or a pond (Thompson, 1991, pp.472–9). 'Riding the Stang' took place in burghs like Edinburgh and Perth, and in Glasgow, where a strike-breaker was forced to 'ride the stang' when the Calton weavers went on strike in 1787 against a reduction in earnings (Penny, op. cit.; Cockburn, 1856, p.70; Clark, 1995, p.128).

Many social activities, such as heavy drinking or cockfighting, were found across the social spectrum and only came in for condemnation if the lower classes were involved. Houston quotes indulgent references to heavy drinking by Edinburgh noblemen, for example, compared to condemnation of similar activities by lower-class women (Houston, 1994, pp.221–2). Music forms an interesting case study, as it could be seen as a display of 'superior' culture when performed in an upper-class household but as a potential threat to law and order when played at a penny wedding or while begging in the street. The survival of Scots traditional music and dance seems particularly remarkable, in the face of disapproval by powerful religious groups.

In his *Life of Robert Burns,* Dr Currie explained that dancing was hugely pop-ular amongst the Scottish peasantry, in spite of the disapproval of the Kirk. It usually took place in a barn, during the winter months and 'reels, strathspeys, country dances and horn-pipes are here practised'. Currie commented:

> the prevalence of this taste, or rather passion for dancing, among a peo-ple so deeply tinctured with the spirit and doctrines of Calvin is one of those contradictions which the philosophic observer so often finds in national character and manners. It is probably to be ascribed to the Scottish music, which, throughout all its varieties, is so full of sensibility; and which, in its livelier strains, awakes those vivid emotions that find in dancing their natural solace and relief...the numerous sectaries who dis-sent from the establishment...universally condemn the practice of dancing, and the schools where it is taught. (Burns, no date, pp.149–50)

The Rev. Andrew Murray, a Moderate Presbyterian clergyman of Auchterderran parish in Fife, observed in the 1790s:

> Among the infinite advantages of the Reformation, this seems to have been one disadvantage attending it, that, owing to the gloomy rigour of some of the leading actors, mirth, sport and cheerfulness, were decried among a people already by nature rather phlegmatic. Since that time, mirth and vice have in their apprehension, been confounded together. Some of the sectaries punish attendance on penny weddings, and public dancing, with a reproof from the pulpit, in the presence of the congregation: so that the people must either dance by themselves, or let it alone. (*OSA*, 1978 edition, p.X)

This is confirmed by the Rev. Thomas Guthrie, who remembered that the Secession churches in his native burgh of Brechin 'disapproved of promiscuous dancing', where the sexes danced together, but sanctioned the 'separate system', where men danced with men, women with women (Guthrie, 1877, p.24).

The world of working-class respectability and self-improvement was paralleled by a competing, sometimes overlapping, world based on drink and linked to rougher forms of amusement such as cockfighting, bare-knuckle boxing, traditional football games, racing and gambling. In the mining village of Larkhall, Lanarkshire, for example, older colliers would meet up at the pit-head, 'for a social glass', while, 'the younger ones were in the nearest field, jumping, running, putting the stone, throwing the hammer etc'. In the Lanarkshire coalfields, it was claimed, 'a collier's coat o' arms was "a fighting dog and no male i' the house"' (Stewart, 1893, pp.4, 18).

At times, 'rough' and 'respectable' forms of behaviour could coexist in some unexpected settings. For example, cockfighting contests were an established feature of Scottish school life in the late eighteenth and early nineteenth century. At Cromarty, Hugh Miller recalled, 'The school, like all the other grammar schools of the period in Scotland, had its yearly cockfight, preceded by two holidays and a half, during which the boys occupied themselves in collecting and bringing up their cocks'. Miller and his uncles regarded this as, 'a relic of a barbarous age' and he described how the school floor was stained red with blood afterwards (Miller, 1874, pp.45–9). Donald Sage was born at Kildonan manse in Sutherland in 1789, the son of a minister. At his school in Dornoch, cockfighting contests were held in the Sheriff Court Room on Shrove Tuesday and on 13 February. Crowns were made for the king and queen, who were the two boys whose birds had gained the greatest victories, and the winners were addressed by the schoolmaster in Latin (Fyfe, (ed.), 1942, p.447). Cock fighting contests were also held on Shrove Tuesday in Kirkmichael in Highland Perthshire and in the West Highland parish of Applecross, where the dues for cockfighting formed part of the schoolmaster's salary, 'equal to one quarter's payment for each scholar' (*OSA*, XII, p.678, XVII, p.293). Donald Sage claimed, 'About the beginning of this century there was perhaps not a single school in Scotland in which at its season the "cock fight" was not strictly observed' (Fyfe, (ed.), op. cit.).

Similar claims were made by William Myles, born in 1819 in Liff parish, on the edge of Dundee. Myles described how there was a cockfight, 'at almost every school in the country' on the morning of Shrove Tuesday, or Candlemas, old style. Each boy arrived at school, 'with a cock under his arm', and the contest was supervised by the master to see fair play. The winning bird was crowned 'king' and a blue ribbon and a bell was tied round his neck. The runner-up was styled 'prince' and received a blue ribbon. Myles observed, 'This barbarous custom ceased to be practised about the end of the last century' (Myles, 1850, p.22). Shrove Tuesday also saw other activities, such as the ball game played in Scone, Perthshire from 2 o'clock until sunset between married men and bachelors. There were few rules, except that no one was allowed to kick the ball and the object was to 'drown' the ball on the bachelors' side, i.e. dip it three times in the river, or to 'hang' it on the married men's side, i.e. put it three times into a small hole in the moor. Every man in the parish, 'the gentry not excepted', had to turn out and play the game, on pain of a fine, but 'the custom being attended with certain inconveniences', it was abolished a few years before 1796 (*OSA*, XI, 1976 edition, pp.585–6).

Fairs, circuses, and public theatres met with the disapproval not only of many of the middle classes and certain church groups, but of some radical and working-class groups as well. Certainly, many socialist leaders were distinctly lukewarm about many aspects of popular culture in the late nineteenth and early twentieth centuries. An article dated July 1913 in *The Vanguard*, for example, published by John Maclean and John Macdougall, appealed to young workers to give up their usual leisure time activities:

> Your recreation and amusements today are not creditable to your knowledge and intelligence and energy. You crowd to football matches and the cinema, you spread yourselves over Antonio's bar and fried fish counters, you tell silly, soppy jokes and dirty stories, and loaf and horse play about the street corners in a way you think is manly, but is not. (Young, 1992, p.69)

John Maclean, it was claimed, 'had one dissipation, every Christmas Day along with Harry Ross, he went to see Third Lanark play football and after the match, they had tea and then went to the theatre' (Young, 1992, p.68).

Temperance was crucial to the cult of respectability and Total Abstinence Societies flourished in Lowland Scotland in the 1830s and 1840s. Prior to this, working-class organisations in Scotland had shown a more relaxed attitude to the consumption of alcohol by their members. For example, William Hammond, a Glasgow handloom weaver and secularist, claimed that, 'Book clubs and sub-scription libraries were first started in Glasgow about 1795, and afterwards spread throughout Scotland and into many English towns. These clubs generally met in taverns'. Hammond cited as an example a book club, which met in a Paisley tavern in the early 1830s. The President was a blacksmith and other mem-bers included weavers, a barber and a tailor. The meeting place was a tavern and each member ordered, 'a gill and a bottle of sma' yill'. Books and politics were discussed and the general character of the meeting was that of a debating soci-ety (Hammond, 1904, pp.87–8). Similarly, the Larkhall Victualling Society, an early cooperative society, resolved in 1821, 'that half a gallon of aqua (whisky) be presented to every member to assist them in keeping the festive season,' in this case Handsel Monday (Maxwell, 1910, p.56).

As early as 1792, the local minister praised the lead miners of Leadhills in Lanarkshire, who, he claimed, within the last 30 years, had given up drinking cheap spirits at work in favour of 'pure water' and had improved their health and prolonged their lives as a result (*OSA*, 1973, VII, p.216). However, it was from the late 1820s and early 1830s that cooperative societies and radical organisa-tions, such as the Owenites and the Chartists, began to embrace temperance in a wholehearted manner. In the Ayrshire village of Fenwick, for example, the Improvement of Knowledge Society, founded in 1834 by local weavers, solemnly debated the virtues of temperance on several occasions. On 5 September 1836, the Society carried a motion that, more than war, 'Intemperance has been most hurtfull to the human race for 100 years past', and other motions were carried on the utility of abstinence societies and the value of abstinence over 'a temperate use of ardent spirits' (*SHR*, 1920, p.121–4). With the slow and painful decline in earnings and living standards amongst handloom weavers, this kind of culture came under severe pressure. In Dundee in the late 1830s, for example, it was claimed that handloom weavers of heavy linen goods pawned their clothes on a weekly basis to buy whisky (*Parliamentary Papers*, 1970 edition, Industrial Revolution, Textiles, Vol. 9, p.187).

In Aberdeen, the Total Abstinence Society had a membership of 3,000, made up 'almost entirely' of Chartists and other radicals (Knox, 1999, p.43). This tradition continued into the Scottish Labour movement later in the cen-tury. Disproportionate numbers of Labour activists had a temperance background, often based on hard experience of the devastating effects of drink on tight family budgets and family life. Out of a sample of 76 Scottish Labour Leaders active between 1918 and 1939, 48 (63.1 per cent) were known abstain-ers, only 3 (3.9 per cent) were known non-abstainers and the remaining 25 (33 per cent) were not known. One historian has suggested that this temperance background distanced the Labour movement from the mass of the working class, particularly unskilled workers (Knox, 1984, pp.23, 113–21).

Amongst the 62 Scots-born autobiographers studied, there were significant numbers of teetotallers, who had often arrived at temperance either from harsh family experience, or from a family background of temperance. Temperance was not simply, or even mainly, a case of the working class embracing middle-class values; it was as much to do with economic survival and the dignity of the artisan. An anonymous baker, born in Dysart, Fife in 1804, described how his joiner father passed his leisure time, 'in the public house along with bacchanalian companions,' whilst his mother worked long hours on the spinning wheel to support her family (*The Commonwealth,* 13 December 1856). Both Mary Slessor and Willie Gallacher had alcoholic fathers, while Walter Freer had an alcoholic stepmother. Born in 1846, Freer, the son of a radical Glasgow hand-loom weaver, joined the Band of Hope, and became a member of the Glasgow Abstinence Union, which organised concerts, 'to wean folks from the unhealthy atmosphere of the squalid public house and the low down music hall' (Freer, 1929, p.34). Freer made a career in entertainment and in 1890 became manager of the Glasgow Corporation Halls (King, 1987, p.160). Another example was Keir Hardie, born in 1856, who started his working life as an underground trapper in the Lanarkshire coalfield. His stepfather was a heavy drinker and Hardie reacted by becoming a temperance organiser and leading member of the Band of Hope and the Good Templars. The Good Templars, an American organisation, arrived in Scotland in 1869 and grew rapidly, with a mainly working-class membership of 62,000 by 1876 (Fraser, 2000, p.93). Hardie blamed the poverty of the miners on their addiction to drink, commenting in 1884, 'To my mind, the answer is as clear as the noonday sun; the people are pouring it down their throats in intoxicating drinks' (McLean, 1975, p.6).

William Hammond, a Glasgow handloom weaver and active secularist, had similar attitudes, reflecting his Calvinistic upbringing, with its emphasis on the elect versus the others. A strong believer in temperance, he considered that, 'education will not lift a drinking man' and believed there were, 'too many working men of the low class living like dogs to enable them to save every possible copper for drink' (Hammond, 1904, p.30). Similarly, Willie Gallacher, the son of an Irish Catholic father and a Presbyterian Highland mother, confessed, 'I had a terrible hatred of pubs and strong drink. My father drank too much and my mother had to slave to keep a home for the family. My older brother started drinking when young and that almost broke my mother's heart' (Gallacher, 1966, p.25). Other Labour leaders and socialist activists such as John Maclean, Patrick Dollan, David Kirkwood and John Wheatley were all teetotallers or active in the temperance movement. Wheatley (born 1869) was a total abstainer, although he worked as a publican for a time (Knox, 1984, p.275). Another advocate of temperance was the Dundee weaver/poet, William McGonagall, who appealed to his readers, 'to abstain from all kinds of intoxicating liquor, because seldom any good emanates from it' and wrote poems on temperance themes, including *The Demon Drink* and *The Destroying Angel,* an apocalyptic poem, which described the street by street destruction of Dundee pubs (McGonagall, 1969 edition, pp.11–12, 17, 35–8).

Given low wages, the widespread availability of alcohol did create major social problems. J.C. Symons claimed in 1838 that the annual average consumption of spirits in Scotland was 23 pints a head, compared to seven pints a head in England and 13 pints in Ireland (*Parliamentary Papers,* 1839, 1970 edition, p.51) In the 1840s, Edinburgh had 555 pubs, one for every 30 families, Dundee one for every 24 families and Glasgow 2,300 pubs, one for every 150 inhabitants (Fraser, 1990, p.241). Drink was part of the workplace culture, including not only manual trades but also middle-class groups, such as lawyers. Hugh Miller, who was born in 1802, described how, when he became a stonemason, he discovered the delights of the dram shop:

> when a foundation was laid, the workmen were treated to drink; they were treated to drink when the walls were levelled for laying the joists; they were treated to drink when the building was finished; they were treated to drink when an apprentice joined the squad; treated to drink when 'his apron was washed'; treated to drink when 'his time was out'; and occasionally, they learned to treat one another to drink. (Miller, 1874, p.158)

A similar workplace culture of drink existed among groups such as cotton spinners, calico printers, iron founders and labourers in iron works, shipbuilders and colliers. It predated industrialisation – drink was used to strike a bargain in agricultural auctions, at feeing fairs and by cattle dealers and drovers. It was also in widespread use in transactions by blacksmiths, wheelwrights, millers etc. (Donnachie, 1979, pp.12–13; Whatley, 1988, p.229; Knox, 1990, pp.146–7). Women workers experienced similar pressures. Janet Bathgate, for example, described how when she began work as a servant in an Edinburgh household, she was told by the cook that new arrivals were expected to treat the other servants to a bottle of whisky (Bathgate, 1895, p.140). As well as personal and family tragedy, alcoholism or heavy drinking by workers could represent a threat to industrial discipline and considerable loss of income to employers. In the Lanarkshire ironworks, excessive drinking among workers was noted in a report of 1844 and the same problem was reported five years later amongst the 800 workers at Houldsworth's Coltness ironworks where, 'Much loss and annoyance had frequently been occasioned by the negligent conduct of workmen under the influence of this habit' (*Parliamentary Papers,* 1849, XXII, p.14).

Sometimes, the connection between temperance and self-improvement was made quite explicit. In Edinburgh, for example, the British League Evening Classes were established in 1847 to provide instruction for apprentices, combined with a temperance message. Classes began with a prayer and the sexes were segregated. The fees were sixpence a month and the classes finished at 9.45 p.m. to allow young people time to get back to their homes before ten o' clock (Hope, 1851).

A particular problem associated with many occupations was the custom of paying wages in a public house at the end of the week. The anonymous autobiographer 'Jacques', described how, when he was a young apprentice, 'my wages were invariably paid in a public house and the scenes of debauchery I there witnessed, the conversation, chiefly characterised by lewdness and profanity, I there heard, were too shocking to prove – to one brought up as I had been – corrupting, or to induce approval or imitation' (*The Commonwealth*, 1 November 1856). Pat Dollan, born into an Irish Catholic family in Baillieston, Lanarkshire, described a similar custom in his home village, where the miners, 'who worked in groups of three or four with one man as a paymaster always met in the pub on Friday evenings to cut up the swag. Youths did not like these arrangements; although they were teetotallers, they were always expected to pay their share of drinks they did not consume' (Mitchell Library, Glasgow, Dollan Mss. Autobiography, p.12).

In Glasgow, David Kirkwood remembered that, 'the drink habit was very strong amongst artisans in those days, and youths were started off drinking with a sort of initiation ceremony'. Kirkwood reacted by joining a temperance group called 'The T.T. Youths', whose distinguishing feature was a strong desire for self-improvement. The group used, 'a Temperance Hall, where we met for lectures, concerts, socials and the rest of it. We also went to night school'. Another group from his school formed a hard-drinking alternative group called 'The Jolly Twelve'. Kirkwood claimed that of the 11 members of 'The Jolly Twelve' he had been able to trace, eight had committed suicide and none had lived beyond the age of 36. By contrast, of 'The T. T. Youths', all except one were living in 1935 and most had done well in life (Kirkwood, 1935, pp.57–9).

Another badge of respectability was church attendance. A study of church attendance in nineteenth-century Aberdeen noted factors deterring the working classes from attending church, including pew rents, the need for decent clothes, the segregation of the social classes between pews and a general patronising attitude (Maclaren, 1967, pp.115–39). Similar attitudes existed in Glasgow, where it was reported in 1838 that, 'Attendance on places of worship is unhappily on the decline, even among the older class (of weavers), at least in Glasgow, where the influence of their poverty, owing to the higher rents, rates etc., is more pressing than in the country. Want of decent clothing is almost invariably assigned as the cause of non-attendance, and by some of the witnesses in Glasgow, inability to pay for sittings in the churches, and dislike to accept them gratuitously as paupers' (*Parliamentary Papers*, 1838, 1970 edition, p.44). These cultural norms also seem to have affected immigrant groups such as Irish Catholics. An Ayrshire priest noted in the 1830s that, 'The Irish will not come out on Sunday and go to chapel unless they can be clothed and appear like natives. They will not go in ragged clothes as they went in Ireland' (Brown, 1998a, p.83).

Some of the autobiographies confirm these descriptions. For example, the Roxburghshire shoemaker John Younger described how his family fell on hard times after they were evicted from their small Borders farm and his mother died shortly afterwards. In spite of this and the hardships of the famine year of 1799, 'I even went to church, at two miles distant, in whatever garb I might happen to get invested'. He also attended a Sabbath evening school (Younger, 1849, p.29). Another autodidact who went to church in spite of poverty and a shabby appearance was John Duncan, the Stonehaven weaver, whose, 'poor attire did not keep him from attending public worship, though submitting him to public remark' (Jolly, 1883, p.41). David Livingstone grew up in the mill village of Blantyre, in Lanarkshire. His family had little money but the mother was a skilled needlewoman and dressed both her sons with 'frills round their necks', so they could attend church (NLS, Janet Livingstone's Notes for Dr Blaikie). In Glasgow, in the later part of the nineteenth century, David Kirkwood remembered, 'It was unusual in my young days for those of the labouring class to go to church. The church was regarded as a place for "the well off folk wi' guid clothes"'. Kirkwood's parents were an exception. On a weekly wage of 20 shillings, they were regular church attenders and wore good Sunday clothes, the father, 'in a good suit of clothes and a silk hat, with my mother in a black dress and bonnet and an umbrella' (Kirkwood, 1935, p.23).

By contrast, the weaver poet, William Thom, who was brought up in poverty by a widowed mother, went to work as a weaver in the School Hill Factory in Aberdeen, 'a prime nursery of vice and sorrow'. He claimed: 'had one of us been bold enough to enter a church, he must have been ejected for the sake of decency. His forlorn and curiously patched habiliments would have contended the point of attraction with the eloquence of that period'. As a result, 'church bells rang not for us. Poets were indeed our priests' (Thom, 1880, pp.1, 8).

The division between the 'rough' and the 'respectable' working class was marked by other signals, such as the use of 'correct' speech or swearing. David Livingstone's sister, Janet, recalled that her father 'could not bear slang' and disliked 'Trashy Novels' in the Blantyre village library (NLS, Janet Livingstone's Notes). Arthur Anderson started life as a beach boy curing fish in Gremista, Shetland and finished up as Chairman of the Peninsula and Oriental Company. He endowed £8,000 for the first secondary school in Shetland, the Anderson Educational Institute. When the school opened in 1862 with an English

Principal, Anderson observed, 'a training of our youth to English habits and a correct pronunciation of the English language, will be of no inconsiderable advantage to them' (Nicholson, 1932, p.103). John Muir, who attended the grammar school in Dunbar, East Lothian, claimed that, 'In Scotch schools only pure English was taught, although not a word of English was spoken out of school' (Muir, 1913, p.57). However, a modern historian has challenged this view, claiming that Scots was, 'the normal medium of instruction in many schools' until well into the nineteenth century (Donaldson, 1986, p.36). There was clearly great variation between different areas and different schools. Thomas Guthrie, for example, minister of Greyfriars and founder of the Ragged School Movement in Edinburgh, grew up in Brechin, Angus, the son of a substantial merchant who became Lord Provost of the burgh. At the age of four, he was sent to an infant school taught by an old weaver, an elder of the Burgher Church. Guthrie recalled, 'The mode of pronunciation we were taught was very primitive...Ours was the broadest Doric'. However, the next local school he attended taught standard English (Guthrie, 1877, p.23).

The opposite to this was the use of swear words and foul language, usually associated with pubs, the male workplace and 'rough' culture. A report on the mining areas of Lanarkshire commented on the widespread improvement in behaviour since Baird and Company built a school for the children of their workers, 'emulation is excited among the parents by seeing their neighbour's children improved by the school, better clothed and kept more clean and decent; swearing and the use of improper language has been greatly checked; and the parents themselves, are in many instances, led insensibly to better habits by observing the effects of the school upon their children' (*Parliamentary Papers*, 1849, XXII, p.12). By contrast, in the booming textile centre of Dundee in the late 1850s, it was claimed, 'The social evil was then pretty pronounced. Big-breasted, sturdy, short-petticoated strumpets walked about the streets quite unashamed and the language heard in such avenues as the Overgate on a Saturday night was quite appalling' (Fleming, 1922, p.28).

Many working-class organisations took strong action against the use of this type of language by their members. The articles of an early cooperative society, the Larkhall Victualling Society, dated March 1821, provided that members, 'shall on no account be guilty of cursing, swearing, using intemperate or offensive language of any kind' on pain of fines or as a last resort, removal from the meeting. This type of prohibition was widespread. An early historian of the cooperative movement commented, 'in almost all the old rules they take power for penalising persons who may be guilty of using bad language or who may take drink to excess' (Maxwell, 1910, pp.55, 96). Another example is given by the Articles of Association of the Fenwick Improvement of Knowledge Society, founded by Ayrshire handloom weavers in 1834. Article 6 provided that, 'all profane and abusive language shall be reproved by the president and if persevered in shall exclude the offender from the Membership of the society' (*SHR*, 1920, p.120). A later example, this time of behaviour by trade unionists, is provided by David Kirkwood, who worked in D.Y. Stewart's Works at St Rollox in Glasgow. He claimed that the workers were 'the roughest crowd of labourers in Glasgow and the workshop was 'riddled with sectarian controversies'. The workforce was mainly Irish, both Catholic and Protestant, and stand-up fights between Orange and Green were commonplace. However, when a trade unionist came from Falkirk to address the men, having heard they were:

> a rough, swearing crowd, he thought the right way to address them was to use their own workshop language. He began with the ungrammatical tongue, common among us. 'Ach, he's nae guid,' a man muttered behind me. 'He's nae eddication.' After a few sentences, the man began to use swear words. Immediately, there was an uproar. 'Awa wi' him!' shouted the men. 'We're no here to be insulted.' He could not go on. The meeting ended. (Kirkwood, 1935, p.77)

Adult education played an important part in this culture of respectability, in terms of self-improvement or 'getting on' in life. Sometimes, women could act as enforcers, or reinforcers, of 'respectability'. David Kirkwood had a friend, William Harvie, a talented footballer who played for the Scotland Junior team. When Harvie was 23, he came to Kirkwood to tell him that his girlfriend refused to marry him unless he gave up football and educated himself, 'she says it wud be a disgrace to mairry a fitballer, and says I'll no get her unless I gae to the evening classes an' read books' (Kirkwood, 1935, p.75).

Autodidacts – autobiographies, diaries, memoirs

The learners' experience – narratives of self-education

Almost all the autobiographers in this book described their educational experiences, from their schooling, often shortened by poverty, to attempts at self-education and the support, or lack of support, they received from family and community. A rare example of an autobiographer who did not sign up for the Smilesian project of thrift, temperance and self-education was John Macdonald, a member of a Highland family from Keppoch, Inverness, who left behind a memoir, published as *Memoirs of an Eighteenth Century Footman*. Born in 1741, he lost his mother two years later and his Jacobite father disappeared after Culloden. The children were taken under the charge of his elder sister and travelled to Edinburgh to search for their father, without success. They had to live off their wits and Macdonald recounted, 'My sister and two brothers were always in town. We saw one another frequently and wanted for nothing. All the others had education. I had none, but learned wickedness'. Macdonald was good at handling horses and became a groom, then a postilion and finally a footman, travelling around Europe with various employers and being present at Laurence Sterne's deathbed in London (Macdonald, 1927 edition, pp.1–18).

The majority of the autobiographers, however, came from a different tradition. They represent the earnest minority who have left a record behind them, although the attitudes and behaviour of the majority can sometimes be glimpsed in comments in these memoirs. Hugh Miller, the Cromarty stonemason, for example, grew up in an artisan family where reading was commonplace. However, when he went to live in a masons' bothy on the banks of the River Conan, Invernessshire, he was shocked to find that, 'During the whole season a newspaper never once entered the barrack door'. The older men spoke about the state of the markets, in particular, the price of oatmeal, the young apprentices 'talked about lasses' and 'politics proper I never heard'. However, there was

Figure 3 Hugh Miller c.1854 by David Octavius
Hill and Robert Adamson
(Source: The Scottish National Photography
Collection, The Scottish National Portrait Gallery)

one Highlander who told stories, mostly about himself. Later, Miller described a masons' strike in Edinburgh, when after attending a strike meeting on the Links, he and his workmates adjourned to a tavern in the Canongate, where badger baiting was taking place. Miller recalled, 'The scene which followed was exceedingly repulsive and brutal' and after much hard drinking by his workmates, 'I stole out to the King's Park, and passed an hour to better purpose among the trap rocks than I could possibly have spent it beside the trap door'. He claimed, 'Of that tavern party, I am not aware that a single individual save the writer is now alive' (Miller, 1874, pp.208–9, 333–4). Another example is that of John Paton, born in 1824 on a farm at Braehead, Dumfriesshire, into a Secession Church family of small stocking makers. He got work as a young man with the Sappers and Miners, who were carrying out work for the Ordnance Survey. The working hours were 9 a.m. till 4 p.m. but, 'Instead of spending the mid-day hour with the rest, at football and other games, I stole away to a quiet spot on the banks of the Nith, and there pored over my book, all alone' (Paton, 1889, p.22).

Many autobiographers, like these two examples, give the impression of learning as a somewhat isolated activity that could alienate them from their workmates and friends. Others, however, grew up in families that were supportive of reading and education or in communities where there was a tradition of popular libraries and self-improvement. Alexander Sommerville's family, for example, were agricultural labourers from a strict religious background. His father's favourite reading was the *Marrow of Modern Divinity* and Sommerville borrowed books from another worker at the Skateraw limestone quarries in East Lothian where he worked. Another worker in the quarry was Robert Wallace, 'whose wife taught him to read' – he became an amateur astronomer (Sommerville, 1848).

Sometimes, these mutual improvement activities were linked to radical politics and social action. For example, the Glasgow born shoemaker, John McAdam, who took part in the agitation leading to the 1832 Reform Act and was later an active Chartist, described how after a short-lived period of school, he joined a book club, 'common in those days of dear literature. The members, chiefly Calton weavers and warpers, were very indulgent, giving me often first choice of books. If since, then, I have been of service to working struggles, I owe it much to their kindly counsels' (Fyffe, (ed.), 1980, p.3). In Kilmarnock, the 13-year-old printer's apprentice, James Paterson, joined Willie Semple's Club during the Radical Years of 1819–20. Willie Semple was a married cobbler, noted for 'habits of industry and sobriety'. Paterson recalled:

The Club met three times a week – upon the nights of Monday, Wednesday and Friday. It consisted of about ten members, all weavers, save Willie himself. One or two had been in the army, but enjoyed no pension, perhaps from limited service, or some other cause of which we knew nothing. The stock of newspapers consisted of the *Black Dwarf*, published in London by Wooller, and the *Glasgow Chronicle*, at that time a keen radical, printed three times a week. The Club, when assembled, completely filled the little apartment, which served Willie for workshop and bedroom...There sat Willie, who might be styled the speaker of the house, with spectacles on nose and an ample Kilmarnock red cowl on his head, busy, over the oil lamp which burned before him, with his awl and hammer; he whose duty it was to read aloud to his fellows, had the use of a candle, contributed from the general fund. The audience were intense listeners, and generally all remark was suspended until the news of the day had been exhausted. Then the more important topics were taken up and discussed. All were keen Reformers; some carried their notions so far, as to come under the denominations of Blacknebs, which latter were understood to stop at nothing less than an absolute and bona fide division of property. (Paterson, 1871, p.66)

Hugh Miller's father was a Cromarty shipmaster, who drowned at sea in 1807. As a child, encouraged by his uncles, Miller, 'began to collect a library in a box of birch bark about nine inches square'. From children's stories, he moved on seamlessly to Homer's *Odyssey* and the *Iliad*. His uncle, James, was a harness maker, who worked from six in the morning till ten at night. He often found someone to read to him in his workshop during the day, and at night, his brother Alexander, 'whose occupation left his evenings free, would read aloud from some interesting volume for the general benefit'. Occasionally, the family circle would be widened by the arrival of neighbours, 'and then the book, after a space, would be laid aside, in order that its contents might be discussed in conversation' (Miller, 1874, p.35).

Reading aloud was a widespread phenomenon. Initially, it was a way of passing on news and events from the literate minority to the less literate majority. William Chambers, for example, used to earn a penny roll by going to read to an Edinburgh baker and his sons when they started work at 5.00 a.m. Roderick Random was a great favourite and this was followed by other works of Smollett, the works of Fielding and Gil Blas, 'the tricks and grotesque rogueries in the last mentioned work of fiction giving the baker and his two sons unqualified satisfaction' (Chambers, 1967 edition, p.24).

However, reading aloud was also a way both of easing the monotony of long working hours and of circumventing the 'taxes on knowledge' that made newspapers so expensive. As James Paterson, the Kilmarnock printer and journalist, explained:

Newspapers, as the saying is, were newspapers in those days; that is every stamped broadsheet cost at least seven-pence. "What a tax upon knowledge!" we of present times may exclaim, when as large a sheet may be had for a penny! It was out of the question for a tradesman to buy a paper for his own use, hence the people formed themselves into reading clubs. (Paterson, 1871, p.65)

This is confirmed by the Glaswegian, John Mackinnon, who explained how the high cost of newspapers (7d, including a stamp duty of 4.5d) meant that, 'working men were unable to buy papers themselves and they Clubbed together and got them that way, every one being allowed a certain time to read them'. His father was a good reader, who, 'often got his paper at 10 at night and he had it till eight the next morning. On the paper nights, three or four of the neighbours would gather in, and my father being an excellent reader, he generally read the news with an audible voice' (Mitchell Library, Mackinnon Mss.).

David Kirkwood's grandfather belonged to the same tradition as a member of a readers' club in Parkhead, Glasgow. Members paid a halfpenny a fortnight subscription, which was used to buy a weekly newspaper and, 'they appointed a reader, an excellent exercise in articulation. When the newspaper arrived, the club met in an eicht-loom shop. The news was read and discussed' (Kirkwood, 1935, p.9). There were similar organisations in the East of Scotland. In the 1840s, the flax heckling workshops in Dundee had 'one local newspaper, and one Edinburgh, Glasgow or London newspaper' delivered to each workshop, paid for by subscription. The workmen took it in turns to read out loud to each other:

> By this means, the flax-dressers, as a body, have become much better informed than any other class of working men, and as a natural consequence, become more intelligent. Many who have learned the flax dressing business and could neither read nor write when they commenced have, by means of reading aloud – that is hearing others read – have actually been forced through chance to learn what they might in all probability have remained ignorant of. (*Chambers Edinburgh Journal,* November 1844, pp.335–6)

This spirit of mutuality is found in many of the autobiographies. Charles Campbell, for example, was born in 1793 in Tarbert, Argyllshire. His family moved to Johnstone in Renfrewshire, where his father worked in the warehouse of a cotton mill. Campbell was sent to school at an early age and could read and write by the age of six or seven. His family then sent him back to Argyll to learn Gaelic at the village school. When his father fell sick with asthma, Campbell had to return to Johnstone and go to work in the cotton mill. He joined a subscription library in a neighbouring town and read, 'History, Biography, Voyages, Travels, almost all the old dramatic Poets, of whom I was passionately fond, and the majority of the English classics'. He became a member of a literary debating society with a membership of 12. They met once a week and religion and politics were 'absolutely excluded'. The constitution was similar to Burns' Mauchline Club. The Presidency went by rotation and as they only met in a public house once or twice a year, they never developed 'habits of irregularity or dissipation'. Campbell reported that the club, 'experienced a good deal of opposition at its first outset in the village but gradually won minds over'. Membership, 'consisted chiefly of artisans and mechanics, such as had a taste for reading and literary pursuits' and he boasted that one of its members, 'is at present a Lecturer in Philosophy and Editor of a reputable Medical Journal'. Campbell's later life was eventful. For a time, he was a slave overseer on a West Indian plantation and he wrote his account of his life in 1826, while on trial for the murder of his wife at a dance in M'Gowans public house in Glasgow. He was found guilty but insane and sentenced to life imprisonment (Campbell, 1828, pp.1–4). In 1831, a radical newspaper in Glasgow launched an appeal for a subscription fund of £200 as security for Campbell's release, saying that he wished to make a new life in America (*Herald to the Trades Advocate*, 16 April 1831).

Another example is that of William Chambers, who was the founder of *Chambers's Edinburgh Journal,* the first title in what became an empire of self-improvement publications. Born in 1800 in Peebles, his father's drapery business failed in 1813 and William and his brother Robert had to move to Edinburgh to seek work. William found work as an apprentice in a bookseller's, working in the shop and delivering books for circulating libraries and flyers for state lottery tickets. Reading in the shop was not allowed but William got up at five and made some progress in French. He also read Smith's *Wealth of Nations*, Locke's *Human Understanding,* Paley's *Moral Philosophy* and Blair's *Belles-Lettres*. Shop hours were from 7.30 a.m. to 9.00 p.m., including Saturdays, so there was little time for self-improvement. Chambers reported, 'At that period there were no public institutions of a popular kind to stimulate and regulate plans of self-culture. The School of Arts, the precursor of mechanics' institutions, was not set on foot until 1821. Young persons in humble circumstances were still left to grope their way'. He became friendly with James King, apprenticed to a seedsman next door. King and his brother, an apprentice dyer, 'were great upon chemistry. Their talk was of retorts, alkalies, acids, conduction and oxygen gas'. On Sundays, Chambers and his brother went for walks along the Firth of Forth, often including a visit to Inveresk Church. He, 'usually carried a French new Testament in my pocket for lingual exercise' (Chambers, 1967 edition, pp.6–27).

Born in Aberdeen in 1798, William Thom was the son of a merchant or contractor/architect who died young. Thom was brought up in poverty by his widowed mother and crippled by being run over by a nobleman's carriage while a child. He attended a dame school and at the age of ten was apprenticed to a cotton manufacturer in Aberdeen. In 1814, Thom entered the School Hill weaving factory of Gordon, Barron and Co. in Aberdeen, a 'prime nursery of vice and sorrow' (Thom, 1880, pp.i-v, 1) The only form of escape was offered by the nearby gardens of Gordon's Hospital, where cotton weavers of a literary disposition met for discussion during the summer months:

> Then came glimpses – the only glimpses afforded us – of true, and natural, and rational existence...The Wizard of Waverley had roused the world to wonders, and we wondered too. Byron was flinging around the terrible and beautiful of a distracted greatness. Moore was doing all he could for lovesick boys and girls – yet they never had enough! Nearer and dearer to hearts like ours was the Ettrick Shepherd, then in his full tide of song and story; but nearer and dearer to us still than he, or any living songster – to us dearer – was our ill-fated fellow craftsman, Tannahill. (Thom, 1880, pp.7–8)

Many autobiographers had faced family break-up through death or disease. Robert Smillie was born into a working-class family in Belfast in 1857. He was orphaned at an early age and brought up by his Scottish grandmother, who taught him to read and used to recite poetry, especially ballads in Scots, such as the 'Sir James the Rose' ballad. He left school at nine to become an errand boy and then worked as a 'half timer' in a spinning mill. His brother was a keen reader and encouraged him to read, too. They read *The Boys of England* and *The Young Men of Great Britain, Dick Turpin, Tom King* and *Three-Fingered Jack*. Smillie remembered:

> We managed to borrow, or pick up from a bookstall, and at a small price, two or three of the Waverley novels, and one or two of the works of Charles Dickens. At the age of fourteen, I knew something of Burns, and had read some of Shakespeare's plays and some of his sonnets. At this age, too, I had seen Barry Sullivan in Richard the Third and J.L. Toole in the part of the Artful Dodger. (Smillie, 1924, p.15)

Not all autobiographers came from such impoverished backgrounds Tom Bell's father was a stonemason, who lived in Parkhead in the east end of Glasgow, then a semi-rural village with coal mines and handloom weaving. When Bell's parents got married, they were driven in a coach and four with postilions and, 'as a symbol of affluence, my father wore a suit of white moleskins, while my mother wore a brand new Paisley shawl'. His father belonged to a lending library in the village, set up by weavers and for a shilling a year took out two books a fortnight, paying 2d a week for each book. Bell (born 1882) went to the local school, where his parents had to buy all the books and pay 7d a week for teaching. Bell left school at 11 and eventually got a job in Beardmore's Foundry, the main local employer. As a teenager, he attended meetings of the Secular Society in Glasgow and began to read Darwin's *Ascent of Man* and *Origins of Species*. He also read an early sex education manual called *Dr. Foster's Plain Home Talk and Cyclopedia,* which was passed around amongst his workmates, 'until it became as black as coal, and the batters torn' (Bell, 1941, pp.14, 33).

Many of those who later became active in the Labour movement describe similar experiences in the late nineteenth and early twentieth centuries Harry McShane remembered a string of second-hand bookstalls along the Clyde in Glasgow, where he bought Macaulay's essays for the relatively expensive sum of 1/8d (McShane, 1978, p.6). Willie Gallacher became apprenticed as a brass finisher and began to read voraciously – Burns, Scott, the Brontes and Mrs Gaskell. Dickens was his favourite and he, 'bought – always very cheaply – all of his works. From Dickens, it was an easy transition, a few years later, to socialist literature' (Gallacher, 1966, p.25). Manny Shinwell began to buy second-hand books in his teens and read Dickens, Thackeray, Walter Scott, Thomas Hardy, and French and Russian authors, such as Emile Zola, Victor Hugo, Guy de Maupassant, Tolstoy, Gogol and Gorky. He then discovered Glasgow Public Library and read Darwin's *Origins of Species* and *Descent of Man*, plus books on geology, zoology and palaeontology. However, the main influence on his political development was the writings of Robert Blatchford, whose book *Britain for the British* sold a million copies (Shinwell, 1955, p.23, 1981, p.25). Blatchford was also an important influence on John Maclean, who was converted to socialism not by Marx, but by Blatchford's *Merrie England*. Maclean commented, '*Merrie England* is the primary school of socialism but *Das Kapital* is the university' (Knox, 1984, pp.180–1).

This tradition persisted into the 1930s and 1940s. For example, Jimmy Reid, born in 1932 into a Catholic family in Govan, found secondary school, 'an almost complete waste of time'. In spite of this, he became 'hooked on reading' and in the evenings, 'After school, there would be the obligatory game of street football, dinner, and then I went into the bedroom I shared with my brother John and read for hours. Stevenson, Scott, Shaw, Dickens, My mother thought I was sickening for something'. By the age of fifteen, at work in the shipyards, he had read everything of Shaw and 'the Govan library became a home from home' (Reid, 1976, pp.4–6). Pat Lally had a similar experience. He was born into an Irish Catholic family in the Gorbals in 1926 and found his secondary school experience less than satisfactory. His father was a casual labourer who died when Lally was ten. However, he had a profound effect on his son, as Lally explained, 'Dad was an avid reader. Virtually as soon as I could read he introduced me to Gorbals Library' and his son became an avid reader as well, devouring books by H.G. Wells, Jules Verne, Charles Dickens and Jack London (Lally, pp.1–6).

Mutual improvement societies

Mutual improvement societies functioned as a sort of halfway house between self-education for the individual learner and the more formal evening class with a recognised teacher. A recent historian has noted, 'Unsurprisingly, mutual improvement was Scottish in origin' (Rose, 2002, p.59). The phrase was adopted by the Easy Club, which Allan Ramsay founded in 1712, and the idea underlay many of the societies of the Edinburgh Enlightenment. For example, after James Hogg had published the *Forest Minstrel* in 1810, he moved to Edinburgh, where he joined the Forum Club, a debating society. He became secretary of the club, with a salary of £20 a year, 'which was never paid'. Meetings were open to the public, who paid 6d per session and large crowds attended for three years running (Hogg, 1972 edition, p.23). As we have seen, there was a strong element of mutuality in self-education, in the form of support by friends and family, membership of libraries and mutual support groups such as Robert Burns' Mauchline Club or Charles Campbell's literary society. By 1796–7, there were said to be 35 reading societies around Glasgow and Paisley, mostly based in weaving communities. They usually had from 30 to 40 members and charged a monthly subscription of 6d or 9d. Acquisitions were decided democratically and most libraries had holdings of around 1,000 volumes, including histories and travels, along with the *Spectator* and other periodicals (Rose, 2002, pp.59–60). The tradition of reading aloud was another example of this element of mutual support. Mutual improvement elements were also important in the Mechanics' Institute movement, sometimes as a way of reducing costs, as in the case of the Aberdeen Institute or the Watt Institution, Dundee, sometimes not fully supported by middle-class patrons, as in the case of the Edinburgh School of Arts.

There were strong links between popular journalism and mutual improvement. *The Buteman*, for example, was founded by the Rothesay Young Men's Literary Association, a mutual improvement society, who selected one of their members, a cotton spinner called Robert McFie, as editor-elect and persuaded Blackies of Glasgow to employ him while he learned the newspaper business (Donaldson, 1986, p.4). Mutual improvement was a Scottish-wide phenomenon and could be found in some surprising settings. The Dundee Royal Asylum had its own mutual improvement society, which discussed literary, scientific and philosophical subjects. Its meetings were called 'cookie shines', as coffee and cookies were served afterwards, part of a more humane treatment for those with mental illness. The proceedings started with a temperance song composed by one of the members, a poet who had tried to murder his wife:

> Come, let us join wi' heart and mind,
> Sweet friendship's board to grace –
> For daftness of the social kind
> Is never 'oot o' place
> Oh! Some get fou wi' barley bree,

And some get fou wi' wine;
But we'll get fou wi' friendship's glee,
And haud oor cookie shine.
(*Dundee Year Book*, 1902, p.167)

There were numerous mutual improvement societies in the Edinburgh area. The Haddington Society of Arts was formed in 1823 out of the local mutual improvement society. In Edinburgh itself, the Bristo Yong Men's Mutual Improvement Association held an annual soiree in December, with addresses by the members and musical intervals. There was a strong social element to these occasions, as well as an educational one. On 19 December 1856, the Queen Street soiree saw tea and fruit served to the membership, together with addresses on 'The Poetry of Astronomy' and 'The Influence of Knowledge'. One of its members, David Pae, who later became the editor of the Dundee-based *People's Friend*, took part in a dialogue on 'A Day in Edinburgh' (Pae Mss.). In some cases, mutual improvement was encouraged by employers. At Calder in Lanarkshire, a mutual improvement society was formed for ironworkers, whilst at the giant Gartsherrie Ironworks near Coatbridge, Baird and Company arranged popular lectures on topics such as, 'The triumph of perseverance – a story for working men' (Campbell, 1979, p.224).

In the rural areas around Aberdeen there were 19 mutual improvement societies in 1851, which had grown to between 35 and 50 by 1897. Many had their own libraries and they served as a stronghold of radical Liberalism, closely linked with the Free Church of Scotland. Membership was drawn mainly from the lower middle and upper working class. At Rhynie, Aberdeenshire, in 1846, members included five farmers, two merchants, a baker, a soldier, a contractor, a miller, a salesman, three estate workers, and five students. Missing, however, were the backbone of rural society, the agricultural labourers (Carter, 1976, pp.383–92). An exception to this general rule was William Milne, who was born at Greyrigg, near Forfar in Angus and raised by an elderly female relative. He became an agricultural labourer and when he moved to a farm near Laurencekirk, Kincardineshire, joined the local mutual improvement society. The society held lectures in the Town Hall, given free and the public paid 3d a head. Lectures were on topics such as the River Jordan by the local minister, a tour of Germany by a local farmer, an account of celebrated battles by the Rector of Montrose Academy, another on reading by a divinity student and one on experimental chemistry by the local doctor. Milne was the only agricultural labourer in the society. He took his four unmarried workmates and one of the married cottars along to the meetings, 'but I never got a man of them to join our membership or take any part in the useful and entertaining proceedings' (Milne, 1901, pp.237–8).

Other accounts of mutual improvement societies are given by William Alexander and Robert Barclay. Barclay, the son of a handloom weaver and crofter, worked in a variety of jobs, including farm servant, tailor and postman. He was a strict teetotaller and a Good Templar and submitted a poem to the *People's Journal*. He joined a mutual improvement class in Ythanwells, Aberdeenshire, whose members gave papers to each other, in his case on temperance and a trip to Shetland (Barclay, 1985 edition, pp.11–46). William Alexander was the third child of a blacksmith from the Garioch in rural Aberdeenshire, a stronghold of the movement. He remembered how, 'the Garioch swarmed with earnest autodidacts in the 1840s, all writing politico-philosophical essays and reading them to each other'. Alexander lost a leg in an accident when young and could not work on the family farm. He became active in the mutual improvement movement. The President of the Aberdeenshire and Banffshire Mutual Instruction Union was William McCombie of Alford, a small farmer, a fervent Baptist, a Radical Liberal and part-proprietor of the *North of Scotland Gazette*. He offered Alexander a job on the *Gazette* as a reporter in 1852. A year later, the *Gazette* merged into the *Aberdeen Free Press* and after McCombie's death in 1870, Alexander became its editor. He became an elder of the East Free Church, a member of the Aberdeen Public Library Committee, and of the governing bodies of the Aberdeen Philosophical Society and the Spalding Club. He published many articles in the *Free Press*, including the serial novel *Johnny Gibb of Gushetneuk* (Alexander, 1992 edition, pp.7–8; Donaldson, 1986, pp.101–44).

Another North-East figure who came to journalism via the route of self-education and mutual improvement was James Annand. He was born in 1843 on a croft at Nether Kinmundy, near Peterhead. His father was a blacksmith and elder of the Church of Scotland. James left school at 12 to work on the croft. He had access to only two books at first – the Bible and *Pilgrim's Progress*. He began to attend evening school at Longside, a three-mile walk from his home. In 1863, he joined a mutual improvement society in Longside and made his first attempts at public speaking there. Annand began to write articles for the *Peterhead Sentinel* and then for the Dundee-based *People's Journal*. He became Editor of the *Buchan Observer* and moved on to the *Newcastle Chronicle*. In 1906, he was elected Liberal MP for East Aberdeenshire against a sitting Tory but died shortly after the election (Hodgson, 1908, pp.8–171).

Perhaps the best-known name associated with mutual improvement was Ramsay MacDonald, the first Labour Prime Minister, born in Lossiemouth in 1866 to a single mother who had been deserted by his ploughman father. The family background was Free Kirk and MacDonald attended the Free Kirk school, which he disliked, and then the parish school, where he came under the influence of an outstanding schoolmaster, James Macdonald. He became a pupil teacher at the parish school and joined the mutual improvement society, becoming its secretary and taking part in its debates (Marquand, 1977, p.13).

Evening schools

Evening schools were part of a Scottish educational tradition stretching back at least as far as the late eighteenth century, as described in Chapter 1. They relied on a combination of the Scots' enthusiasm for learning and self-improvement and the poverty of the schoolmasters, who augmented their meagre salaries by teaching evening classes and Sunday schools. In 1830, there were 3,000 people of different ages attending evening schools on Sundays in the Highlands, of whom 800 were adults learning to read the Scriptures in Gaelic. By 1849 there were 60 Gaelic schools in the Highlands and Islands, giving instruction in reading to 2,280 pupils, of whom 242 were over 20. The oldest student was a man of 70 in Creich, Sutherland, who was learning to read St John's Gospel, along with 19 others over 20. In the evening school at Evanton, Rossshire, there was one 50-year-old and seven others over 20 (Hudson, 1851, pp.21–2). Despite these efforts, the Highlands and Islands maintained a reputation for educational backwardness well into the nineteenth century. As late as 1867, a report on the Hebrides and Western Islands concluded that despite the efforts of benevolent societies and individuals, 'the adult population, and especially the women, are still, to an extent not generally known, unable to read or write' (*Parliamentary Papers,* 1867, XXV, p.lxxxi).

In Scotland as a whole, there were 438 night schools in 1851 with an enrolment of 15,071 – 9,500 men and 5,571 women. Proportionately, the enrolments in England and Wales were much smaller – 1,545 schools with an enrolment of 39,783. The occupational breakdown in Scotland was 4,386 artisans, 2,397 factory workers, 561 agricultural labourers and 553 servants. Writing and arithmetic were the main subjects studied and the schools were heavily concentrated in the west of Scotland, with Lanarkshire accounting for 40 per cent of enrolments (Kelly, 1992, pp.155–6).

There were limits to self-improvement, however. In Glasgow, it was reported in 1866 that, 'the principal months when these schools are in their strength are September, October, November and December. At the New Year they collapse. The customs of the people make it imperative that this session be given up to merrymaking'. The evening schools started again in February but with attendances greatly reduced. The education offered in the Glasgow evening schools was at a very basic level. At the Martyrs Evening School Classes, 230 young men and women attended, aged from 18 upwards, most (75 per cent) between 18 and 25. Of these, 25 per cent came to learn the alphabet, 45 per cent, 'have very imperfectly acquired the elements of reading, with scarcely any writing and no arithmetic'. The rest had some skills in reading, writing and arithmetic. At Bridgeton Evening School, in the heart of the factory district, of 150 attending, 'not above twenty could do more than read the New Testament. They could not read a book or a newspaper, and to speak of reading as a pleasure was not to be thought of'. These were institutions catering almost exclusively for young working-class adults. At the Martyrs School, 'The male portion is employed as mechanics, engineers, warehousemen, carters and labourers, and the female portion is employed in various capacities in factories, warehouses, shops and domestic service'. Their previous education had been extremely limited, 'It can hardly be said of any, indeed, that they possess a good general education' (*Parliamentary Papers*, 1867, XXV, pp.108, 145).

Many autobiographers kept in touch with learning by attending evening school. David Livingstone, for example, left school at the age of ten and went to work in the Blantyre cotton mills. He attended the factory evening school from eight to ten o'clock at night and when he was 13, the village schoolmaster started a Latin class in the evenings. Livingstone described how:

> With a part of my first week's wages, I purchased Ruddiman's *Rudiments of Latin* and pursued the study of that language for many years afterward, with unabashed ardour, at an evening school, which met between the hours of eight and ten. The dictionary part of my labours was followed up till twelve o' clock, or later, if my mother did not interfere by jumping up and snatching the book out of my hands. I had to be back in the factory by six in the morning and continued my work, with intervals for breakfast and dinner, till eight o' clock. I read in this manner many of the classical authors, and knew Virgil and Horace better at sixteen than I do now. (Livingstone, 1857, p.13)

Born in 1786 on the Carse of Gowrie, Alex Moncur, the son of a ploughman, had a brief schooling. He was apprenticed as a weaver in Dundee and continued his education later in life with, '3 months I got of an Evening School in Mid Wynd (Scotts) shortly after I was married' (Dundee City Archives, GD/X99/10). Another example of a later education is that of two Fife brothers, Alexander Bethune (born 1804) and his brother John (born 1811), the sons of farm servants. They received virtually no schooling, due to the poverty of their parents. At the age of 21, while working as a handloom weaver, Alexander became friendly with a student from St Andrews University, who was running evening classes in the parish of Abdie, Fife (Bethune, 1884, pp.11–13). Another handloom weaver, Alexander Bain, was active in the Aberdeen Mechanics' Institute and enrolled in 1834, 'for the evening hours of a mathematical school' in Aberdeen, run by a dwarf called Elgin (Bain, 1904, pp.19–20). Andrew Carnegie grew up in a family of radical weavers in Dunfermline, Fife. In 1848, when Carnegie was 13, the family emigrated to Pittsburgh, USA, where both he and his father got jobs in a cotton mill, with Andrew working as a bobbin boy. Because he could write, Andrew got a job as a clerk and began to attend night school to learn double-entry bookkeeping (Carnegie, 1920, pp.25–36).

Many autobiographers took part in a wide range of learning activities. The anonymous 'Jacques' was born in 1803 in the east of Scotland and in the course of 'a chequered life' worked as a flax dresser in Dundee and later as a clerk. He was a classic autodidact, who boasted, 'I was a member of a society for mutual improvement, of a vocal music society, attended popular lectures on science, public meetings of various kinds'. He also took 'a subordinate role' in agitation for, 'Reform, the Corn Laws and Temperance' (*The Commonwealth*, 1 November 1856). The Glasgow radical Charles Hutcheson took part in similar activities. He attended sermons by the Rev. Thomas Chalmers in St John's, Glasgow and on 13 May 1822 went to an evening lecture by William Hazlitt. Hutcheson was distinctly unimpressed by Hazlitt, 'He appears to me very much of the Cockney School...The shabby appearance of the man, his slovenly reading and the little enthusiasm he seemed to feel for his subject disgusted me' (NLS, Mss 2773, f.34). Another inveterate attender of evening and Sabbath lectures was the Dundee millwright, John Sturrock. On 2 October 1864, aged 24, he attended a lecture by the Rev. George Gilfillan and on 11 October 1865 paid four shillings for a course of six lectures in the newly inaugurated Young Men's Christian Association in Dundee. He also heard a lecture by, 'the great Italian patriot, the Rev. Alexander Gavazzi, who delivered a lecture today in the Corn Exchange on "Italy – Past, Present and Future" and which was one of the most powerful pieces of eloquence that ever I had the pleasure to hear' (Whatley, (ed.), 1996, p.98).

Many Scottish radicals and self-improvers, whether Owenites, Chartists, radical Liberals or socialists, were internationalist in their outlook. John McAdam, the Glasgow Chartist, for example, was a staunch supporter of European nationalist causes, particularly Mazzini in Italy and Kossuth in Hungary, and corresponded with both men (Fyffe, (ed.), 1980). Similarly, a number of working-class poets, such as William McGonagall, Ellen Johnston and Janet Hamilton, wrote poems in support of Italian, Polish or Hungarian independence, sometimes making a link with the Scottish patriot, William Wallace.

Many activists in the labour movement in Scotland made up for a truncated early education by attending evening schools. Both of Keir Hardie's stepbrothers left school early to work in the Lanarkshire coal mines but continued their education by attending evening classes. Born in 1870, David Hardie left school at 11 but received enough education through evening classes to eventually leave the pits and get work as a bookkeeper, then as a salesman. In 1906, he became manager of the Reformers' Bookstall, Glasgow's leading radical bookshop. He moved into advertising and after a period in local government, was elected Labour MP for Rutherglen in 1931. His brother George left school in 1885 at 12 but followed the same ladder of social mobility through evening classes and the Labour movement, qualifying as a mining engineer and being elected ILP MP for Springburn in 1921 (Knox, 1984, pp.139–42).

Others had similar experiences. Robert Smillie left school in 1868 at the age of 11 to work as a 'half-timer' in a spinning mill. After working in a boiler shop in Glasgow, he went to work in the Larkhall Colliery, Lanarkshire. At 17, he was earning 42 shillings a week, a good wage for a young working-class man. He attended night school at Muir Street Board School, where arithmetic was taught 'rather indifferently'. Smillie became active in the miners' union and contrasted his position with that of Dicky Rundell, his close friend in Larkhall, who refused to become involved either with evening classes or with the union. Whilst Smillie moved on, Rundell, 'continued as a miner in Larkhall, spending his whole life in the employment of the Summerlee Iron Company at the pit where I made a start as a pumper' (Smillie, 1924, p.28). Other Labour leaders who 'got on' through education at evening classes and involvement in the Labour movement include James Brown, the Ayrshire miners' leader and Labour MP for South Ayrshire from 1918, who left school at 12 and continued at night school until he was 16 and George Buchanan, born in the Gorbals in Glasgow in 1890 to parents of Highland origins. Buchanan, who became Labour MP for the Gorbals in 1922, attended evening classes and learned the pattern-making trade in a foundry. Another Labour MP, Thomas Scott Dickson, born in 1885 in Cleland, Lanarkshire, left school at 11 to work as a shop boy. He drifted in and out of various jobs, but continued his education in evening classes and became a journalist. He wrote articles for *The Scotsman* and eventually was elected Labour MP for Lanark in 1923 (Knox, 1984, pp.70–92).

There are many more narratives like these, where men who had largely missed out on their school education through poverty, were self-denying and ambitious enough to make up for it by going to classes in the evenings after a long working day. Viewed in this light, the Scottish Labour movement can be seen as a ladder of social mobility for its more prominent and ambitious members and as a vehicle of self-improvement. The titles of memoirs and biographies of successful Labour activists suggest the same thing. Such titles as *From Pit to Parliament* (Keir Hardie by David Lowe), *From Workshop to War Cabinet* (George Barnes), *From Miners' Row to Lord Provost's Room* (Patrick Dollan) and (best of all) *From Workman's Cottage to Windsor Castle* (John Hodge) are revealing in their assumptions. Similarly, the title of David Kirkwood's autobiography, *My Life of Revolt*, is tempered by the knowledge that he eventually became Baron Kirkwood of Bearsden. The autobiographies also reflect a male world, where women could find it much harder to get a foothold.

Women's experiences

On the evidence of the autobiographies alone, self-education in Scotland would appear to have been a largely male, Lowland, Presbyterian preserve. However, other sources, such as the 1851 census, which showed that large numbers of

Scottish women enrolled for evening schools (5,571 women compared to 9,500 men) suggest a different, more inclusive picture. Literacy levels for women in Scotland were generally lower than for men, a trend found in other European countries such as Sweden. A survey of factory workers in Bridgeton, Glasgow, in the 1860s, found that out of a total sample of 4,978, 3,159 (63 per cent) were female, 1,819 male. Reading levels were relatively high amongst this group, with 1,938 (61 per cent) of the 3,159 women being able to read well, as opposed to 1,343 (73 per cent) of the 1,819 men. It was a very different story when it came to writing. The sample here was slightly smaller – 3,145 women and 1,817 men, a total of 4,962. Of the women, only 1,035 (33 per cent) could write well and a staggering 1,323 (42 per cent) could not write at all, with the remainder being able to write indifferently. The figures for men were very different, with 1,113 (61 per cent) being able to write well and only 208 (11 per cent) being unable to write at all (*Parliamentary Papers*, 1867, XXV, p.109). The Bridgeton figures may also reflect the high proportion of Irish–born workers amongst Glasgow factory workers in this period.

Women faced particular difficulties in the pursuit of education. Married women especially were seen as having few legitimate roles outside those of housework and childcare, sometimes on top of paid outside work. There are fleeting glimpses of women's educational experience in male-generated sources, referred to in Chapter 2, such as Violet Croumbie, the mother of Samuel Brown, who came from an East Lothian pedlar family and was said to have been 'a voracious reader' who read the Haddington Library dry. Similarly, one of Alexander Sommerville's workmates at the limestone quarries in Skateraw, East Lothian had been taught to read by his wife. The single mother of John Duncan, the Stonehaven weaver and self-taught botanist, could neither read nor write. He became a weaver in Drumlithie, where his employer's wife was described as 'a terrible scholar.' She was a farmer's daughter, a great reader who had received a good education and encouraged Duncan in his education. He was taught to read, however, by the wife of another local weaver (Jolly, 1883, p.35).

Women also featured largely in the early education of another autobiographer, John Struthers. Born into a shoemaker's family in East Kilbride in 1776, he was taught to read by his mother from the Shorter Catechism and went on to read the Proverbs of Solomon. His mother had not been taught to write properly but amused him by writing the letters of the alphabet on an old slate, which he copied. He also benefited from the encouragement of a neighbour, the widow of, 'a Professor of theology in the College of Glasgow' and her two daughters. At a very early age, he was sent to work as a herd on his grandfather's farm, where his grandmother read to him from his grandfather's library, which, 'contained almost all the controversial works connected with the Scottish Reformation' (Struthers, 1850, pp.ix-xvi). Many autobiographers were taught to read by their mothers or by other female relatives, or neighbours. Others attended dame schools, which, however, often functioned as a rather basic form of childminding, with a very limited educational input.

Later in the nineteenth century, David Kirkwood had a friend, a talented footballer in Glasgow, who was given an ultimatum by his girlfriend, to give up football and go to evening classes to improve himself, or else she would call off the marriage. Generally, however, women appear in the guise of mothers and wives, usually described as supportive 'angels', except for William Milne's mother, who abandoned him to an elderly female relative until he was seven, or the alcoholic stepmother of Walter Freer. Stepmothers were generally suspect, in life as in popular fiction. When the father of the St Boswells shoemaker, James Younger, remarried after the death of his wife, his sisters disliked the idea of a new mother, and they and their brother moved into a new house, away from the stepmother (Younger, 1848, pp.34–5). Similarly, the self-taught botanist and geologist, Robert Dick of Thurso, had a stepmother who regularly beat both him and his brother, and when his brother hit back, he was, 'pommelled so hard he could barely stand'. Dick, his brother and sister all left home at an early age as a result (Smiles, 1878, p.14).

There are very few autobiographies by working-class women in Scotland. I have managed to track down five – by Janet Hamilton, Ellen Johnston, Christian Watt, Janet Bathgate, author of *Aunt Janet's Legacy*, and Barbara Farquhar, the author of *The Pearl of Days* (1848), who described herself as 'A Labourer's Daughter'. To these five, I have added Janet Little, the Ayrshire-born 'Scotch Milkmaid' and Mary Slessor, the Dundee factory worker who became a missionary in Calabar, West Africa.

Janet Little, the 'Scotch Milkmaid,' published a book of poetry in 1792, dedicated to Flora, Countess of Loudon. Although she left no autobiography behind, there are hints of Little's life in her poems. For example, she visited Robert Burns and contrasted his position as a 'ploughman chiel' with the fate of his female equivalent. While it was difficult enough for a ploughman to be accepted as a poet, it was harder for a milkmaid:

> But then a rustic country quean
> To write – was e'er the like o't seen?
> A milk maid poem-books to print;
> Mair fit the wad for dairy tent
> Or labour at her spinning wheel
> All this and more, a critic said;
> I heard and slink behind the shade
> So much I dread their cruel spite,
> My hand still trembles when I write.
> (Little, 1792, pp.115–6)

The earliest of the autobiographers, Janet Hamilton, was born in Shotts, Lanarkshire in October 1795, the daughter of a shoemaker. The family were of Covenanter stock and her parents moved to Langloan near Hamilton, where they worked as agricultural labourers. Janet was taught by her mother to spin and to work the tambour frame. When she was eight, Janet found, 'upon the loom of an intellectual weaver, a copy of *Paradise Lost* and Alan Ramsay's poems'. She became a reader in the village library, 'devouring, instead of novels, of which she met few, Rollin, Plutarch's *Lives*, Ancient Universal history, Raynal's *India* and Pitscottie's *Scotland*, besides the *Spectator, Rambler*, Fergusson, Burns and McNeill, as titbits,' all the time working at spinning or tambouring. Janet Hamilton married her father's assistant in 1809 and they had ten children. In spite of these pressures, she continued to read, often surreptitiously, because of prejudices against mothers reading:

> She often tells how for years she got the loan of *Blackwoods* and whilst nursing her child, she would take the magazine out of a sort of hole in the wall and if any one unexpectedly entered the house, she quickly replaced it, as if afraid of it being known. She did the same with Shakespeare and other noted authors, against whom in Scottish country circles there lingered a prejudice which it was wiser to evade than to defy. (Hamilton, 1868, p.xxvi)

Janet Hamilton began composing verse at the age of 17 or 19. When she was 54 and had just learned to write, some of her poems were published in Cassell's *Working Man's Friend*. A year later, she went blind. Her *Poems and Ballads,* published when she was 72, were dedicated, ' To Her Brothers. The Men of the Working Classes' (Hamilton, 1868, p.xxvii). Her subjects included temperance poems and support for European nationalist causes, such as *The Spanish Revolution, Pray for Poland* and *Freedom for Italy – 1867*. These were common themes amongst autodidact poets, male and female.

Another female autobiographer, Christian Watt, was born into a fishing family in 1833 in the village of Broadsea, near Fraserburgh in north-east Scotland. She started work as a domestic servant at the age of eight and a half, then from the age of ten learned to gut fish and spent many years selling fish in the landward areas of Aberdeenshire. Like Janet Hamilton, she also encountered prejudice against women receiving education or appearing to enjoy reading. She attended Broadsea School with her two young brothers and her cousin, Annie. They 'had to take a bawbee, a lump of coal or peat each day'. After three years, 'I could read, write and spell according to the standard. I left Broadsea school to help mother with the fish'. She then went to another school 'in the dead of winter', which cost a penny a day. She reported, 'We were both good at the English and we learned the stops and interrogations in writing, every odd moment, I could never get enough to read, I read anything I could get my hands on'. The teacher encouraged Christian Watt to continue her studies, 'but we had no money to do so, but in the winter I went to school as often as I could, right till I was 20 years old'. She vented her frustration at her poverty and her sex:

> I was always furious that girls were not allowed to be educated. It was assumed a man must work for a wife and needed learning, a lot of men I would not have seen in my way – I would have worked any of them blind. (Fraser, (ed.), 1988, p.31)

Christian Watt went to work as a maid at Philoth, for Lady Saltoun, in 1843 and astonished her employer by asking for a dictionary as a gift, instead of the dress length offered, 'She thought this a strange request, but gave me one from the library. It opened up new realms in my life, for my nose was never out of it'. She married in 1859 but the pressures of poverty and family life eventually led to a mental breakdown and her admission to Cornhill Infirmary in Aberdeen in 1880, where she spent much of the next 43 years as a patient. She died in 1923 aged 90 (Fraser, (ed.), 1988, pp.x, 14–22).

Janet Bathgate, author of *Aunt Janet's Legacy*, was born Janet Greenfield, 'of poor but pious parents' in Sunderland, a hamlet two miles south of Selkirk in the Scottish Borders. She was sent out to work at the age of eight, looking after the elderly mother of a shepherd on a remote farm. She taught herself to write by copying out a letter from her father, and the problems she had in getting hold of writing materials reveal the difficulties learners faced, particularly in remote rural communities:

> She considers the letters and thinks she should copy them, but then she has neither pen, paper, nor ink; and more than that, though she could make out the sense of her father's writing, there were some of the letters she was not very sure about. For instance, she could not distinguish very well T from F. At last she notices that there is a little bit of blank paper on her father's letter. This she cuts off, takes the Question book out of her pocket, looks carefully how the letters in it are formed, then takes a pin, and on the blank piece of paper pricks with the point of the pin their forms, and thus 'writes' a letter to her father. (Bathgate, 1895, pp.109–10)

As a result of this letter, Janet Bathgate was sent briefly to the parish school and then to a sewing school at Peebles run by Lady Hay, ' for teaching little girls reading, writing and sewing'. However, after six weeks, the sewing school closed down, due to the illness of the teacher. Bathgate went into domestic service and had a variety of employers, including a Mrs Smith, the widow of an English clergyman, who gave her, 'some good books to read'. While in service, 'much of her spare time was spent in reading good books and committing to memory psalms and hymns and portions of the Bible'. She married James Kemp, an autodidact saddler, but he died after only four years of marriage and she went back into domestic service and became a nursemaid (Bathgate, 1895, pp.114–67). Eventually, she got a job teaching in a small school in Dalkeith and on the basis of good reports from this school, was employed by the Penicuik Paper Mills to teach their workers' children. As Janet Kemp, she started a school in the late 1830s, 'on the Sabbath afternoon' for the religious teaching of the children, but found that it was popular with their parents as well. However, she supported the Evangelical camp in the Church of Scotland and was eventually removed from her teaching post. She married James Bathgate later in life (Lewis, 1902).

Ellen Johnston was born in Hamilton in the 1830s, the daughter of James Johnston, a mason on the Duke of Hamilton's estate, who was a poet, called 'Lord Byron' by the Duke. Her mother was Mary Bilsland, the daughter of a dyer from Bridgeton, Glasgow. The father emigrated to America, but at the last minute her mother refused to go and stayed in Scotland, supporting herself and her daughter by dressmaking and millinery. When Ellen was eight, her father died in America and her mother married a power loom tenter. Mother and daughter moved from the happy home of her grandfather's house into the step-father's house next to the Cross Keys Tavern, London Road, Glasgow. At the age of 11, the stepfather took Ellen into a power loom factory in Bishop Street, Anderston, Glasgow to learn weaving. Before she was 13 she had read Walter Scott and was, 'a self taught scholar'. After nine months at school, she claimed, 'I could read the English language and Scottish dialect with almost any classic scholar'. In her memoirs, Ellen hinted at sexual abuse by her stepfather and described how she fled from home and considered suicide in the Paisley Canal. Eventually, she got work in Brown and McNee's factory in Commercial Road. Here, she claimed, her refusal to conform to female stereotypes got her into trouble with other women workers. She talked to, 'the most intelligent of the factory workers…about poets and poetry', which created jealousy among other women workers (Johnston, 1867, pp.4–9).

Ellen Johnston had a child out of marriage in 1852. She put it into the care of her mother and lived an itinerant life, writing poetry and working in factories in Glasgow, Belfast and Manchester. On her mother's death in 1861, she moved to Dundee where her father's sister lived. She worked at Verdant Works, Dundee (now an industrial museum) but was discharged in 1863 and, 'my poor ignorant deluded sister sex went so far as to assault me on the streets, spit in my face, and even several times dragged the skirts from my dress'. Eventually, she got a job in Chapelshade Factory in the east end of Dundee and her poems were accepted in the *Penny Post*. They were dedicated, 'To all men and women of every class, sect and party, who by their skill, labour, science, art, literature and poetry, promote the moral and social elevation of humanity, by their obedient servant, Ellen Johnston, the Factory Girl'. The tone of the poems was generally deferential and consensual. Her *Lines on the Opening of the Baxter Park,* (1863) for example, rivals William McGonagall in its social deference and celebration of Victorian consensus:

> The ninth day of September
> The sun arose in splendour
> His glory to surrender
> To Sir David of Dundee
> The Trades came forth in grandeur
> Each led by a commander
> Bold as an Alexander
> Of eighteen sixty three
>
> Our Queen, peace rest upon her!
> Her noble Lord of honour
> Came here to greet the Donor
> Of our park, and get the key
> To open for our pleasure
> That lovely flower-gemmed treasure,
> Where we may sport at leisure
> When from our toil set free
> (Johnston, 1867, pp.102–3)

However, not all Johnston's poems were as deferential as this. In her *Lines on Behalf of the Boilermakers of Great Britain and Ireland* she criticised the 'selfish souls' of the rich and exhorted the workers, 'Be your watchword – Union for Ever'. Other poems, like those of Janet Hamilton, dealt with temperance issues, such as the *Drunkard's Wife,* or with European nationalism, such as *The Exile of Poland* or *Welcome-Garibaldi,* which drew a parallel with William Wallace (Johnston, 1867).

Another female writer who faced discrimination because of her sex was Barbara Farquhar, the author of the *Pearl of Days* (1848), who described herself as 'A Labourers Daughter'. Her father was a gardener, who worked for a landed family in Strathmore, Angus near the River South Esk. Her formal schooling was minimal, 'I am one of those who never enjoyed the advantages of attending school in early days, except for two years, or rather for one; for it was but for two years that my sister and myself attended a sewing school alternately'. As a result, what education she received was at home, at the hands of her mother, 'at the fireside of hard working parents'. She was a precocious child and claimed, 'I have no remembrance of ever learning, or having any difficulty with common books'. The children were taught reading by their mother, 'Four times a day, usually, each of us had our short lesson', which nothing was allowed to interrupt. In the mornings, the mother read the Bible, but they had a wide range of reading in the afternoon and the mother read aloud during meal times. The family lived too far from church to attend regularly but Sundays began with family prayers in the home and the rest of the day was spent learning a passage from the Scriptures, to be recited to the parents. After six years in Strathmore, the landowner died and the father got a job on the east coast. His daughter worked as a servant but her mother's health began to fail and she went back home to look after her ten brothers and sisters (*The Pearl of Days*, 1848, pp.xiv, 5–14).

Her essay the *Pearl of Days* was written for the Working Man's Sabbath Prize Essay, a competition held in 1847 to choose the three best essays by 'labouring men' on the subject 'The Advantages of the Sabbath'. The prize giver was motivated by, 'the fearful increase in Sabbath desecration by railways, steamboats and other travelling facilities'. The prizes were £25 for first prize, £15 for second and £10 for third. The competition came under the patronage of Queen Victoria and Prince Albert and Albert donated ten additional prizes of £5 each. Within three months, more than 950 entries had been received, only one of which (*The Pearl of Days*) was from a woman. Its author, Barbara Farquhar, 'The Labourer's Daughter' enclosed a letter stating, 'The subject of the essay is of equal interest to woman as to man'. In an interesting sidelight on the superiority of popular education in Scotland, although the First Prize was awarded to an Ipswich printer, the other two winners were both from Scotland – John Younger, a shoemaker from St Boswells, Roxburghshire and David Farquhar, a Dundee machinist. Inevitably, one of the London-based judges was a Scot, David Thomson, from Younger's home town of St Boswells. The *Pearl of Days* caught the spirit of the times and 16,000 copies were sold in three months (*The Pearl of Days*, 1848; Younger, 1849, pp.v–vii).

While Mary Slessor did not leave an autobiography, her transformation from Dundee mill girl to African missionary is a classic narrative of self-help. She was born in Aberdeen in 1848, the second of seven children, her father a shoemaker, her mother a weaver. The father became an alcoholic and lost his job in 1859 and the family were forced to move south to Dundee to find work. Mary began to work in a jute mill as a 'half timer' and spent the next 16 years in the mills. The family attended the Wishart Memorial Church and Mary, who had been somewhat wild as a child, began to read the New Testament and to borrow books from the church library. She had difficulty understanding the books and enrolled for evening classes two nights a week. She was inspired by the story of David Livingstone, who had been a mill worker like herself. Like him, she read books at her loom, having applied for permission from her employers. She became friendly with a new minister, James Logie and taught Sunday school.

After attending missionary school, she was recruited to work as a missionary in Calabar, West Africa (Buchan, 1980, pp.7–13).

Women often found it hard to be taken seriously as learners. The Labour movement in general and Scottish trade unions in particular were notoriously chauvinistic and found it hard to accept women on equal terms. An exception was John Maclean, whose friend, Tom Anderson, explained:

> The Co-operative Society found in John a teacher and a friend, and I have heard many a woman speak of his class and his teaching in very moving terms. Up till John's time, the woman was never considered, to have suggested the asking of her to come to an economics class, you would have been laughed at, the women then of course had no vote, she was also outside the pale of the men's organisations. In a word, she did not count. John was the means towards the end of breaking that barrier down. (Young, 1992, p.71)

Teachers

The teachers that feature in the autobiographies, both schoolteachers and evening and Sunday school teachers, are a very mixed bunch, some barely literate, others outstanding scholars. What they had in common with each other was usually their poverty. At the top end of the educational spectrum were teachers like Robert Cormack, who was the parish schoolmaster in Banchory-Devenick, Aberdeenshire and founded a Sunday school there for young men and women in 1782. Cormack, 'had his education at Marischal College; but never raised his view higher than his present situation'. The local minister reported, 'he is a most industrious and successful teacher; labouring in his vocation from Sunday to Sunday, and from morning to night'. For this, he was paid the princely sum of £11. 3. 10d a year and the minister fulminated, 'How inadequate is this man's salary, although amongst the highest enjoyed by country schoolmasters' (OSA, 1982, XIV, p.20). Similarly, Hugh Miller, who attended Cromarty Grammar School, described his schoolmaster as, 'a scholar and an honest man…he had attended the classes in Aberdeen during the same sessions as the late Dr. Mearns, and in mathematics and the languages had disputed the prize with the Doctor; but he had failed to get on equally well in the world'. Like many other Scottish teachers, Miller's teacher also taught evening classes for young adults (Miller, 1874 edition, p.45).

Born on an Angus pendicle (smallholding) in 1800, John Ireland attended the parish school in Monifieth, and described his teacher as, 'a finished classical scholar', who taught French, Latin and Greek. Ireland left school at the age of 14 to begin work as an apprentice draper in Dundee (Ireland, 1878, p.24). An anonymous miner, born in 1828 in Eastwood, Renfrewshire, who went down the mines at the age of nine after his father's death, described his mixed experience of evening classes. He worked for two years as a drawer in the pits, 'in the meantime, I was attending evening classes, but with little progress'. However, he then signed up for evening classes in arithmetic taught by an outstanding teacher called David Home and enthused, 'I had a complete veneration for the skills of that man' (*The Commonwealth*, 25 October 1856). Another gifted schoolteacher influenced Ramsay MacDonald, born to a single mother in Lossiemouth in 1866. He attended the Free Church School, which he disliked and then the parish school, where he came under the influence of an exceptional teacher, James Macdonald. Ramsay MacDonald became a pupil teacher himself at the parish school. He moved to Bristol and then to London, where he discovered socialist ideas. He boasted to a friend in Lossiemouth in 1887 that at meetings of, 'the better kind of Socialist…Scotchmen reign supreme' (Marquand, 1977, pp.4–5, 21).

Not all experiences of school or evening classes were as positive as these. The minister of Kirkpatrick-Juxta, Dumfriesshire, complaining in 1791 of the low salaries paid to schoolmasters, reported, 'had not the present teacher been disabled for working as a common mason, he would have spurned such a livelihood as this'. The teacher's salary here amounted to some £11 a year, compared to a labourer's annual earnings of £8.16. 8d (*OSA*, IV, pp.345–6). The theme of people entering and staying in school-teaching because they were unable, through physical disability or lack of ambition, to do anything else, is a common one. For example, the self-taught botanist and geologist, Robert Dick, attended the parish school in Menstrie, Clackmannanshire, where the teacher, a man called Morrison, 'took to teaching because he had not limbs enough to fit him for anything else. He had only one arm' (Smiles, 1878, p.12). William Cameron, the crippled son of a Gaelic-speaking father, who worked as a mashman at a distillery, was born in Plean, Stirlingshire. He went to school at the age of four, with a teacher who was, 'an old decrepit man, who had tried to be a nailer, but at that employment he could not earn his bread. He then attempted to teach a few children but for this undertaking he was quite unfit'. Cameron attended this school for four years and, 'was not four months advanced in learning, although I was as far advanced as my teacher'. He went to another school for five years and learned some writing and arithmetic. He was apprenticed to a tailor at the age of 12 but went back to the parish school of St Ninians to learn Latin and at night learned arithmetic with a man called Robert McCallum. His parents were Burgher Seceders and, having watched an itinerant preacher on Glasgow Green making money from the collection, Cameron began preaching Erskine's sermons from memory and taking a good collection. He became an itinerant teacher himself and was employed by three farmers to teach their children, being boarded in one of their houses at ten shillings a week. After another spell at tailoring in Glasgow, he taught school in a rough coal mining area. Cameron reported, 'they had stoned a number of teachers out of the place before I went' but he persisted and in six months had built up a class of 30 reading the New Testament without the need for corporal punishment (Cameron, 1888, pp.5–15).

Corporal punishment at school is a recurring theme. Born in 1824 in Kirkmahoe parish, Dumfriesshire, John Paton went to the local parish school, where the teacher was able but with a ferocious temper. After receiving a flogging from this teacher, John refused to go back to school. His younger brother James persisted under a different master and went straight from the parish school to Glasgow University at the age of 14. At the age of 12, John began to work in the stocking trade with his father, working from 6.00 am till 10.00 pm. His meal breaks were spent studying Latin and Greek. He saved enough money to attend Dumfries Academy for six weeks and carried on studying in his spare time after leaving. He moved to Glasgow and got work with the West Campbell Street Reformed Church, distributing tracts to the non-attenders at Sunday school. Paton then trained as a teacher at the Free Church Normal Seminary in Glasgow and got a job at Maryhill Free Church School on the edge of Glasgow (Paton, 1889, pp.3–29).

Like William Cameron, John Paton found teaching a tough experience, 'The minister warned me that the School was a wreck and had been broken up, chiefly by coarse and bad characters from mills and coal pits, who attended the evening classes'. There were few pupils in the first week, about 18 in the day school and 20 in the night school, and he had great difficulty with them disrupting his class. But he stood his ground and the school began to succeed. He spent ten years working for the Glasgow City Mission and during this time, 'instituted a Bible Class, a Singing Class, a Communicants Class, and a Total Abstinence society'. Paton taught a Bible study class for Glasgow City Mission at 7.00 a.m. on a Sunday morning:

> attended by from seventy to a hundred of the very poorest young women and grown up lads of the whole district. They had nothing to put on except their ordinary work day clothes – all without bonnets, some without shoes. Beautiful was it to mark how the poorest began to improve in personal appearance immediately after they came to our class; how they gradually got shoes and one bit of clothing after another, to enable them to attend our other meetings and then go to church. (Paton, 1889, pp.55–65)

Other teachers received a mixed press. Thomas Carlyle (1795–1881), whose father was a prosperous stonemason from Ecclefechan, Dumfriesshire, and a member of the Burgh Seceder Church, left a characteristically waspish account of his schoolteachers in his semi-autobiographical work, *Sartor Resartus*. Carlyle went to the local parish school and then to Annan Academy and Edinburgh

University (Campbell, 1974, pp.1–4). He described his first schoolmaster as a 'downbeat, brokenhearted, underfoot martyr, as others of that guild are (who) did little for me, except discover he could do little'. At the Gymnasium, the teachers were, 'hidebound Pedants, without knowledge of man's nature, or of aught, save their lexicons and quarterly account books' (Carlyle, 1831, pp.81–4).

William Milne went to a subscription school in Lunanhead, Angus, where his first teacher was the 'Barefit minister'. When Milne returned to Forfar after a spell as an agricultural labourer in Kincardineshire, he attended an evening school to brush up on his arithmetic. However, this was not a success, as the teacher was an alcoholic who often failed to appear in the evenings (Milne, 1901, pp.35, 244). Alcohol problems amongst teachers were another recurring theme. The Glasgow radical, John Mackinnon, went to a variety of schools but remembered attending one in Clyde Street, Glasgow kept by a Mr Mackie, 'he was a pensioner, having been in the Army; he was a tolerably good teacher, but had a fault very detrimental to a Schoolmaster, he was not a teetotaller. Sometimes when he had been partaking too freely, there was no school for a day or two' (Mitchell Library, Mackinnon Mss.).

Because of low salaries, teachers were often forced to work long hours, teaching evening and Sabbath classes for extra fees, in addition to the usual school hours. Some teachers were obviously motivated by their love of learning, rather than financial reward. For example, Robert Cormack, the parish schoolmaster of Banchory-Devinick, Aberdeenshire, combined ordinary school hours with evening classes and Sunday school teaching. In 1798, it was reported that on Sundays, 'this indefatigable teacher attends them gratis from six o'clock in the morning till late in the evening' (OSA, XIV, p.20). A later example was the parish schoolmaster of Beith in Ayrshire, who in 1837 was said to be teaching 12 hours a day Monday to Friday, from 9.00 a.m. to 1.00 p.m. on Saturday and an active Sabbath evening school, attended by 300 people. His weekday evening schools were attended by 25 people over the age of 15, who were learning to read (Boyd, 1961, p.97).

Often, those from poorer families or from rural areas as opposed to small towns, experienced discrimination by teachers. In the late 1830s, Christian Watt attended a school between Fraserburgh and the fishing village of Broadsea where she lived. The school cost a penny a day and was attended by the children of 'would be gentry' from Fraserburgh, who were favoured by the teacher and looked down on the fishermen's children from Broadsea (Watt, 1988, p.14). Alex Smith described travelling from a Kincardineshire farm to attend Laurencekirk Secondary School in 1924. He and two other children from country primary schools were denied the chance to study Latin, which prepared children for university, unlike the Laurencekirk children. The master told them, 'You two from the country will have plenty to take on without that' (Smith, 1990, p.51).

Samuel Smiles and *Self Help*

After such narratives, it comes as little surprise to find that Samuel Smiles, the author of *Self Help*, was a Scot. He was born in Haddington, East Lothian on 23 December 1812 into a strict Presbyterian family belonging to the Cameronian sect. His father was a prosperous general merchant in Haddington and was able to send his son to local schools, then to the High School in Edinburgh and finally to Edinburgh University to study medicine. Haddington was the birthplace of the Protestant reformer, John Knox and in Smiles' youth it was well supplied with private and public schools and with no less than six libraries. It was also the birthplace of Samuel Brown, who founded the East Lothian Itinerating Library Scheme. However, the place was not to everybody's taste. Jane Welsh, who was born there and left for London and marriage to Thomas Carlyle, described it as, 'the dimmest, deadest spot in the Creator's universe...the very air is impregnated with stupidity' (Smiles, 1905, p.6).

Smiles became involved with adult education very early in life. When he was 14 and waiting to go to university, he helped with the chemistry experiments at the Haddington School of Arts. After the death of his father in the cholera epidemic of 1832, Smiles left Edinburgh and settled in Haddington as a country doctor. Scotland was over supplied with doctors and he found it hard to make a living. To supplement his income, he gave chemistry lectures at the Haddington School of Arts, which, 'were well attended by the leading mechanics of the town'. Three of the students, who worked as carpenters for an agricultural implement firm, used the classes to 'get on' in the world. Two went on to Edinburgh University, of whom one became a Presbyterian minister in Blackburn, Lancashire, the other headmaster of a large school in Hull. The third, Andrew Lamb, also moved to England and became General Manager of the Peninsular and Orient Steamship Company in Southampton (Smiles, 1905, p.31). In nineteenth-century Scotland, 'getting on' or self-improvement often meant 'getting out' of the country, either to England, as in these cases and that of Smiles himself, or further afield, as with Andrew Carnegie, whose family moved to Pittsburgh, USA, or John Muir, whose family emigrated to Wisconsin. Arthur Anderson, a Smilesian figure who had climbed from a humble fishing background in Shetland to become Chairman of the P&O Company, boasted in 1862, 'go to what part of the world you will, you are sure to meet two things – a Scotchman and a Newcastle grindstone' (Nicholson, 1932, p.106). J.M. Barrie, the playwright, the author of such successful whimsy as *Peter Pan,* who was born in the small Angus burgh of Kirriemuir, commented wryly, 'there are few sights in life more impressive than a Scotsman on the make' (McPherson, 1983, pp.229–30).

Smiles was impressed by Samuel Brown's East Lothian Itinerating Library Scheme, which grew from four to 47 libraries over a 20 year period, so that, 'there was scarcely an inhabitant who was not within a mile and a half of one of the institutions' (Smiles, 1905, p.30). When he moved south to edit the *Leeds Times* in 1838, he took with him this tradition of utilitarian self-improvement, developed in the small town atmosphere of Haddington, with its Presbyterian legacy of thrift, temperance and self-education. Leeds at this time was a booming industrial city, a stronghold of 'physical force' Chartism, a base for Feargus O'Connor and the *Northern Star*. The *Leeds Times* was founded as a way of countering Chartism and the *Northern Star*. It preached a more limited form of suffrage and Smiles became Secretary of the Household Suffrage Association. He condemned O'Connor as 'loud and mouthy' and disliked what he saw of the Chartist demonstration in London in September 1838, characterising the London Chartists as, 'loafers and idlers, not working men' (Smiles, 1905, p.37).

However, during his time in Leeds, Smiles was impressed by the ability of working men, 'to co operate together for mutual benefit and defence'. He noted that no less than 8,000 working men in Leeds belonged to the Manchester Oddfellows and something like £15,000 was subscribed annually by working men in the city for mutual assurance against sickness and accident. Whilst he approved of this type of working-class cooperation, he disliked strikes and calculated that strikes in the North of England in 1840 had cost the workers some £3 million in lost wages, 'virtually thrown away by the working people' (Smiles, 1905, pp.103–4).

Smiles combined newspaper editing with writing and teaching, in particular, teaching at Mechanics' Institutes. In March 1845, he was approached by a group of young working men who had established a mutual improvement society which met at an old cholera hospital in Leeds. They asked him to 'talk to them a bit' and the lecture series he gave to them under the title 'The Education of the Working Class' became the basis for his book *Self Help*. This book, described as, 'One of the great classics of working-class adult education', (Kelly, 1992, p.120) was designed to show that education was not simply a means of individual self-advancement but benefited the whole community. Smiles believed that, 'the education of the working classes is to be regarded in its highest aspect not as a means of raising up a few clever and talented men into a higher rank of life but of elevating and improving the whole class – of raising the entire condition of the working man' (Smiles, 1905, p.132). However, this was tempered by a thoroughly Calvinistic distinction between the 'elect' and the others; 'no laws, however stringent, can make the idle industrious, the thriftless provident or the drunken sober' (Smiles, 1859, p.1). This fits in well with utilitarian concepts of the deserving and undeserving poor, which underlay the 1834 Poor Law Amendment Act.

There was a strongly individualistic philosophy behind *Self Help*. In his lectures to the working men of Leeds, Smiles had pointed out that, 'their happiness and well being in after life must necessarily depend on themselves – upon their own diligent self culture, self discipline and self control'. However, he was sensitive to accusations that *Self Help* was merely promoting selfishness and protested, 'the duty of helping one's self in the highest sense involves helping of one's neighbours' (Smiles, 1859, pp.xii-xv). This is a variant of the concept of enlightened self-interest developed by Adam Smith. It was a theme picked up by many Victorian entrepreneurs, would be entrepreneurs and artisans. Arthur Anderson, the Shetland born Chairman of the P&O Company, remarked in his speech in 1862 at the opening of the first secondary school in Shetland, 'Self help and social usefulness are the true paths to social eminence' (Nicolson, 1932, p.107). Further down the social scale, Walter Freer, the son of a Glasgow handloom weaver, whose mother died when he was six and whose alcoholic stepmother forced him to leave home at an early age, remarked, 'for self help is the big thing in life. Let hardship engulf a lad, and, if he is of the right stuff, he will rise supreme to it – more, he'll make hardship a convenient stone to success' (Freer, 1929, p.19). The Dundee draper, John Ireland, was another enthusiast for self help and advised his readers to study, 'Smiles *Self Help*, Dodd's *Student Manual*, Platt on Business' (Ireland, 1878, p.89).

In later work, Smiles developed a critique of the unfettered *laissez-faire* theories that had created havoc in Victorian cities:

> Nobody adulterates our food. Nobody fills us with bad drink. Nobody supplies us with foul water. Nobody spreads fever in blind alleys and unswept lanes. Nobody leaves towns undrained. Nobody fills gaols penitentiaries and convict stations…Nobody has a theory, too, a dreadful theory. It is embodied in two words – *Laissez faire*…When people are poisoned by plaster of Paris mixed with flour, 'let alone' is the remedy…When people live in foul dwellings, let them alone. Let wretchedness do its work. (Smiles, 1875, p.337)

The central theme of *Self Help* was that success is based on the capacity and willingness of the individual for hard work rather than any God-given ability or inherited social position, the belief that 'common sense and perseverance' would triumph over adversity. The book took the form of short potted biographies of men (there was one female example) who had overcome humble origins, lack of education and other obstacles through hard work, perseverance, thrift and temperance. The objective was to provide an example and a role model for working men, particularly the skilled artisan who made up an important part of the 'new' industrial society. Self-education played an important role in this artisan culture and Smiles quoted with approval the historian, Edward Gibbon, 'every person has two educations, one which he receives from others and one more important which he gives himself' and Sir Walter Scott, 'the best part of every man's education is that which he gives himself' (Smiles, 1859, p.192).

In true Enlightenment fashion, Smiles believed that the role of education, 'should be to make the great mass of the people virtuous, intelligent, well informed and well conducted and to open up to them new sources of pleasure and happiness. Knowledge is of itself, one of the highest enjoyments'. However, education should be tempered with utility. Smiles looked down on the prizewinners he had known at school who, 'began as prodigies and ended as failures…In the battle of life, cramming is comparatively useless' (Smiles, 1905, pp.12, 132).

Self Help became a Victorian success story in its own right. The book sold 250,000 copies and was translated into all the main European languages. It influenced some surprising people. In spite of its strongly individualistic tone, *Self Help* was admired by Robert Blatchford, who thought it should be required reading in schools, and by Arthur Cook, the Communist Welsh miners' leader, who started out on the path of self-education by reading it. It was pirated in the USA, where it sold well, part of a boom in 'success literature' on both sides of the Atlantic. The American author, Horatio Alger, for example, was said to have reached fifty million readers with his stories of success (Briggs, 1990, p.127). However, even Smiles acknowledged that, 'Prodigality is much more natural to men than thrift and economy is not a natural instinct but the growth of experience and example' (Briggs, 2000, p.392). Self help, like the adult education institutions it permeated, appealed to the earnest minority who were willing to sacrifice time and money to the cause of self-education and self-improvement (Cooke, 2002, pp.135–43).

Self-help and self-education were an integral part of the cult of respectability that played such an important role in Victorian artisan culture. Literacy, combined with other characteristics such as hard work, temperance and thrift, was one of the pillars upholding the ideal of the respectable artisan (Harrison, 1971, p.3; Johnson, 1979, pp.75–102; Knox, 1999, p.42). Not only middle-class philanthropists but also many working-class organisations supported this ideal, based on self-respect and independence. It was an ideal that did not lend itself easily to revolutionary activism, as it placed a premium on individual effort and conformity. It could also lead to the exclusion of other important groups, such as immigrants, unskilled workers and women. In Scotland, it fitted in well with Calvinistic ideas of the elect and the others. The autobiographies studied suggest that the ideal could create considerable tensions, when faced with the harsh realities and insecurities of working-class life, and the counter attractions of popular culture represented by pubs and alcohol, popular sports and gambling, fairs and markets. As E.P. Thompson has argued, 'the educated universe was so saturated with class responses that it demanded an active rejection and despisal of the language, customs and traditions of received popular culture' (Thompson, 1986a, p.14). Many of those writing give the impression of learning as a somewhat isolated activity that could alienate them from their family, friends and workmates, in spite of a tradition of literacy and self-improvement in some communities

(Thompson, 1968a, p.14). Indeed, some found the tensions too much. Charles Campbell, a Glasgow cotton spinner, wrote his memoirs while awaiting trial in 1826 for the murder of his common-law wife in Glasgow. He was found guilty but insane. Hugh Miller, who began his working life as a stonemason and became the editor of the Free Church publication, *The Witness*, ended it by killing himself. Robert Tannahill, the Paisley weaver/poet, also ended his life by suicide, when his poetry collection was rejected by two publishers. Another weaver/poet from Paisley, Alexander Wilson, had to flee to the USA in 1794 because of his support for the Friends of Liberty (Leonard, 1990, pp.8, 38).

These pressures were particularly intense on women. Christian Watt wrote her memoirs in Cornhill Infirmary, Aberdeen, where she was confined for over 40 years with mental illness. Janet Little described how a critic reacted with derision to the idea of a milkmaid poet. Janet Hamilton, mother of ten, had to read surreptitiously and hide her books in a hole in the wall, if she thought someone was coming into the house. Ellen Johnston, the 'Factory Girl' poet, considered suicide as a young girl, and later was ostracised and physically attacked by her fellow female mill workers in Dundee.

However, this picture of lonely strivers groping their way towards self-improvement in isolation can be exaggerated. In many working-class communities in Scotland, this isolation was relieved by strong elements of mutual support – readers' clubs, discussion groups, reading aloud in groups, mutual improvement societies and so on. These important activities have generally been under-recorded by historians but they do emerge as significant features in the lives of many of the autobiographers. Of course, those who wrote autobiographies were an unrepresentative minority. They were drawn disproportionately from certain groups such as poets and writers, religious activists and missionaries, popular journalists, and those involved in radical social and political movements, from early Owenites and cooperators, to the Chartists, radical Liberals and socialists. Whereas the literary life could be isolating and stressful, particularly for the less successful, other careers offered better ways of coping with the problems of upward social mobility. Missionaries such as David Livingstone, Mary Slessor and John Paton moved from humble backgrounds through a supportive religious network and eventually left Scotland to spread the message of Christianity to far flung places. Radical political and social movements could provide a similar support system for the upwardly mobile artisan. The autobiographies of early Owenites, cooperators, Chartists, radical Liberals, trade unionists and socialists give the impression of a fairly self-contained world with its own values and support mechanisms. Similarly, the expansion of the press and its search for new mass markets in the second half of the nineteenth century opened up new employment possibilities for self-educated men, who might have found it harder to achieve success in more established middle-class occupations. This will be considered in the next chapter.

Chapter 4
'The age of philanthropy and good will towards men': urbanisation, industrialisation and responses: 1850–1914

The unexampled efforts now making in every part of the kingdom for the intellectual and physical improvement of the lower classes of the community, distinguish the present, as the age of philanthropy and good will towards men. The middle classes vie with the rich in promoting the great and good work of education.

(J.W. Hudson, *The History of Adult Education,* 1851)

The growth of heavy industry in the west of Scotland

The period from 1850 to the outbreak of the First World War was marked by population growth and economic expansion in Scotland. The Scottish population grew from 2,888,000 in 1851 to 4,760,000 in 1911 (Kenefick, 1998, p.98). Population growth was heavily concentrated in west central scotland, where the expansion of heavy industry was fuelled by local coal and ironstone deposits, plus the pivotal trading position of Glasgow as 'The Second City of the Empire'. The worldwide growth of railways and the rapid expansion of the steam-powered British merchant marine, led to Glasgow and Clydeside becoming a world leader in building steam locomotives and shipbuilding. The expansion of heavy industry in the west of Scotland was closely linked with the invention of the 'hot blast' iron ore smelting process in 1828 by James Beaumont Neilson, the engineer of the Glasgow Gas Works (Bremner, 1869, pp.39–40). Characteristically, Neilson was an enthusiast for self-improvement and encouraged the workers at the Glasgow Gaslight Company to set up a library, where, 'they might meet every evening throughout the whole year, to read and converse, in place of going to the ale house'. The workmen then organised classes for themselves, led by Alexander Anderson, a joiner who had attended classes at the Andersonian Institution, Glasgow (Claxton, 1839, pp.208–10; Smiles, 1863, pp.149–61). Neilson gave the address at the opening of the Glasgow Gas Workmen's Institution and contrasted the happy state of those engaged in, 'the study of literature and the arts' with 'the votary of sensual enjoyments' whose youth was 'a scene of riot and dissipation' till they sank into 'an early and unlamented grave' or eked out 'a lingering and miserable existence, despised and shunned by the virtuous and happy' (*Glasgow Mechanics' Magazine,* 1825, p.157).

The 1850s and 1860s were a period of relative prosperity and social consensus. The period saw attempts by employers across Britain to woo their workforce, particularly skilled workers, by sponsoring libraries and adult education activities, and social and musical events, often linked with temperance. In 1851, James Hudson described how:

> The manufacturer finds it profitable to form schools and factory libraries, to rear amateur bands of musicians amongst his workmen, to encourage frugality by savings banks, benefit societies, sick clubs, clothes clubs, burial associations and by occasional tea meetings, at which, he and his family partake, to destroy that barrier between men, which pride and wealth sometimes ungraciously erect. (Hudson, 1851, p.vi)

Textile firms in both Dundee and Paisley sponsored similar events, aimed to reduce the social distance between employers and employed. In Paisley, for example, the Coats Thread Company organised day excursions to Edinburgh for its workers, who turned out en masse in 1857 to welcome James Coats and his American bride back from their honeymoon (Knox, 1999, p.109). On 24 May 1862, a public lecture was held in the Corn Exchange, Dundee for 1,000 female mill workers to listen to advice, 'which emphasised the importance of self respect and women's household duties' (Whatley, 2000b, p.85). The opening of Baxter Park in Dundee in 1863 was the occasion for an outburst of civic pride, recorded in a poem by Ellen Johnston, the 'Factory Girl'. Nearly 17,000 people subscribed to a statue of Sir David Baxter, the donor of the park, which was unveiled at the opening, 'a very considerable of the entire sum subscribed being in the pence of the industrious classes, including not a few of the female millworkers of the town' (*Dundee Yearbook, Supplement,* 1901, p.18). In the Midlothian coalfields, the mine owners donated libraries, schools, bowling greens and parks to mining communities and provided assistance for widows of men killed in colliery accidents (Knox, 1999, p.109–10).

In the Lanarkshire coalfields, the dominant iron-manufacturing firm was Baird and Company, who in 1868 employed 9,000 men and produced 300,000 tons of pig-iron a year, a quarter of all Scottish production, from 42 blast furnaces (Bremner, 1869, p.36). In 1849, it was reported that Bairds had built a church and, 'a magnificent establishment for all the branches of elementary education' for their workers and schools in other mining villages. Another firm (Wilsons) had established a lending library for its workers, part of a policy to cut down on excessive drinking (*Parliamentary Papers,* 1849, XXII, p.12). In 1845, Alexander Whitelaw, who became a partner in Baird and Company, noticed a deterioration in the quality of iron produced in the week after pay day, 'in consequence of the men not being entirely masters of their own actions' through drink (Campbell, 1979, p.224). In these circumstances, the temperance movement had considerable appeal to employers. By the 1860s, Temperance Societies and Bands of Hope had been established at Calder, Gartsherrie and Calderbank Ironworks (Campbell, op. cit.). One historian has characterised the temperance movement as having, 'the short term aim of increasing the usefulness of skilled workers…and the long term aim of spreading bourgeois values' (Pollard, 1963, p.268). However, for many workers, it was a grassroots movement, linked to economic survival and artisan self-respect.

In 1867, the owners of the Woodside and Hill collieries in Larkhall, Lanarkshire provided a soiree for their workers and their families. The partners and manager gave an address, professing, 'great interest in the workmen's welfare, and their earnest desire that there should always be goodwill on both sides'. In the same year, a Literary Association was formed at Quarter, under the chairmanship of Colin Dunlop, for the 'moral and literary improvement' of the workers. It was hoped to, 'foster a spirit of social intercourse amongst all classes in which master and servant, superior and inferior, can mingle for a time and enjoy the same intellectual treat, thus smoothing the distinctions of rank, alleviating the toils and cares of life, and realising in some measure that long wished for and happy time "when man to man the world o'er, shall brothers be for a' that"'. The historian of the Lanarkshire miners commented, 'Such ideas of respectability, self-help and class harmony were ambiguous doctrines, and not necessarily incompatible with the exclusive outlook of mid-Victorian trade unionism' (Campbell, 1979, pp.230–1). By 1868, Bairds were still making, 'Liberal provision for the education of the children of the workpeople' and the success of a large cooperative store was said to have been assisted by 'the fostering care' of the Company (Bremner, 1869, p.40). The store, operated by a joint committee of management and men, replaced an oppressive truck system operated by Bairds through a company store (Campbell, 1979, p.221).

Technical education – the challenge of Germany

The success of Prussia in the Franco-Prussian War of 1870 sent alarm bells ringing throughout Britain. As early as 1839, the Glasgow *Chartist Circular* had compared Scottish elementary education unfavourably with a number of other European countries, including Prussia (*Chartist Circular,* 28 September 1839, p.19). By 1870, there was unease about Prussia's military success, linked to the increasing technical requirements of modern warfare. As the century progressed, and Prussia was transformed into Germany under the direction of Bismarck, there was growing alarm at the rapid advance of German industry and the way in which technical education in Britain lagged behind its European counterparts. In 1881, a UK commission on technical education was set up under the chairmanship of Sir Bernhard Samuelson, in response to fears that industry in France and Germany was forging ahead of Britain because of better education systems (Paterson, 2003, pp.89–90). At the opening of the Baxter Technical Institute, Dundee in 1888, a Mr Swire Smith gave an address on 'Technical Education'. His address highlighted growing competition from Germany in Britain's traditional export markets, particularly the USA, where German exports had increased by 335 per cent in the period 1860–1887, compared to a modest 19 per cent increase in British exports in the same period. Smith used the example of aniline dyes, a British invention, where Germany was pulling ahead of Britain, due to inadequate, 'levels of knowledge of chemical science on the part of the English chemical manufacturer as compared with the Germans and the Swiss' (*Dundee Yearbook*, 1888, p.98).

In Scotland, technical and scientific education had been promoted on a voluntary basis by Mechanics' Institutes, as outlined in Chapter 2. The idea of state sponsorship for scientific and technical education was a new concept in Britain in the 1850s and 1860s. The Central School of Design opened in London in 1837 and Scotland soon followed suit, with Schools of Design in Glasgow (1844) and Paisley (1848). The emphasis here was on textile design. The Great Exhibition of 1851 gave a fillip to design and in 1852 a Department of Practical Art was created under the auspices of the Board of Trade. A year later, it became the Department of Science and Art. There was grudging admiration for the quality of technical education in Germany – its technical high schools and municipal trade schools. However, the Education Department of Scotland remained suspicious of purely technical and scientific education. Simon Laurie, Secretary of the Church of Scotland Education Committee claimed, 'the Shorter Catechism has done more to make Scotland efficient in the world's work than mathematics or chemistry can ever do' (Anderson, 1995, pp.161–2, 265–6).

Existing evening classes were given a boost by the Education (Scotland) Act of 1872, which allowed school boards to provide evening schools for those over 13 years of age. The classes qualified for grants under the Scotch Code of 1874. These continuation classes at first continued to provide largely remedial education in reading, writing and arithmetic but gradually diversified into teaching commercial and technical subjects, as well as domestic subjects for girls. By 1899–1900, student numbers had reached 82,000, of whom 15,000 were over the age of 21. Continuation classes attracted financial support from local and central government – government grants totalled £47,000, with local rates accounting for £33,000 and student fees £8,000 (Butt, 2000, p.183). By 1911, continuation class enrolments had grown to 144,815 (Paterson, 2003, p.91). Some education authorities took their responsibilities seriously. Edinburgh, for example, could boast that a quarter of its 14-18-year-olds were in evening classes in 1910 and a further quarter were still in school (Anderson, 1995, p.280). Glasgow tried to make continuation classes compulsory but was thwarted by the reluctance of employers to support training. The Technical Schools (Scotland) Act of 1887, a response to the Samuelson Inquiry, had little impact, as no parliamentary grants were available for any school provided by local authorities. Similarly, technical colleges in Scotland had to rely on voluntary initiatives for their funding and buildings. In Dundee, for example, Sir David Baxter, a textile magnate, left £20,000 in his will in 1872, 'for the erection and endowment of a Mechanics' Institution in Dundee'. This bequest was used to found the Baxter Technical Institute, the forerunner of Dundee College of Technology, which eventually became the University of Abertay, Dundee (Cooke, (ed.), 1980, pp.70–1).

One of the beacons of technical and scientific education in Scotland was the Andersonian Institution, Glasgow, the ancestor of Strathclyde University. Its origins have been described earlier but it continued to expand in the second half of the nineteenth century. In the 1830s, it had targeted the middle classes by offering a course on the 'History of the Principles of Painting' which attracted, 'one of most fashionable audiences perhaps ever congregated in any classroom in our city' (Marwick, 1930, p.195). Its professorial staff often came from less than conventional backgrounds. Dr John Taylor, Professor of Physics from 1846–62, a pioneer of photography and a popular lecturer, had been a surgeon on an East Indiaman and was an advocate of universal suffrage, annual parliaments and the secret ballot (Fraser, 2000, p.50). The Professor of Mathematics was Alex Laing, an ex-handloom weaver, who had been a schoolmaster, then an academic. At Glasgow University, the first Professor of Civil Engineering, Lewis Gordon, delivered a course of popular lectures on his subject in 1848–9, whilst John Pringle Nicol, Professor of Astronomy, gave similar lectures to large audiences (Marwick, 1931, pp.88–90). Tom Bell (born 1882) attended evening classes on Geology and French in the Andersonian College, Glasgow, paying two shillings for a six-month course. He also joined classes in Astronomy run by the West of Scotland Astronomical Society and English Literature classes taught by Professor Eyre Todd (Bell, 1941, p.66).

The Dundee-born George Barnes, who became Secretary of the Amalgamated Society of Engineers, discovered on a tour of the German engineering industry in 1898 that, 'In the application of science to industry they were ahead of Great Britain' (Barnes, 1924, p.54). Another Scot, James Stuart (1843–1913), a pioneering figure in English university extension, who held the first Chair of Mechanism and Applied Mechanics at Cambridge, was well aware of the high priority given to technical education in Germany compared to its relatively low profile in Scotland. In an address given in Dundee in 1901, he referred to the greater expenditure on education by Britain's economic rivals such as Germany, Austria and the USA. He contrasted Darmstadt, Germany, a town of 57,000, where the Technical High School had been rebuilt in 1895 at a cost of £130,000, with Dundee, with a population of 160,000 in 1901, where University College, Dundee and the Technical College had both struggled for funds (Stuart, 1901; Cooke, 1998).

University extension and literary ladies

James Stuart was a key figure in the English University Extension Movement, which sought to extend university education socially to women and skilled workers and geographically to the growing industrial towns and cities of the north of England and Midlands. He was born in 1843 in Balgonie, Fife, where his father was a partner in a flax spinning mill. The family were Congregationalist in religion and there was a tradition of political radicalism and social activism in the family. Stuart's mother knew Mary Godwin, the daughter of Mary Wollstonecraft and her husband, William Godwin. When the Hungarian patriot, Kossuth, came to speak at Cupar in Fife, Stuart's father made the speech of welcome. He was a paternalistic employer who established schools and Sunday schools, a lending library and a temperance association for his workers. Like Samuel Smiles, James Stuart became involved in popular enlightenment/adult education early in life, when he acted as librarian in his father's works library, when still at school (Stuart, 1911; Cooke, 1998).

From Madras College in Cupar, Fife, James Stuart went on to study at St Andrews University and then Trinity College, Cambridge, where he graduated as third Wrangler in the Mathematical Tripos in 1866 and became a fellow of Trinity in the same year. Also in the same year, Stuart confided to his mother his plans for creating, 'a sort of peripatetic university the professors of which would circulate among the big towns and thus give a wider opportunity for such teaching' (Stuart, 1911, p.155). His allies in this movement were the campaign for women's access to higher education, spearheaded by the North of England Council for the Higher Education of Women, and the Labour movement, including the Rochdale Pioneers and the Crewe Mechanics' Institute. His other powerful allies were the industrial towns and cities of the English Midlands and the north of England, who were lobbying for a higher education presence in their towns. The university extension movement began at Cambridge in October 1873 with lecture courses held in Derby, Nottingham and Leicester for working men (Political Economy in the evenings), 'ladies' (English Literature in the mornings) and, 'young men engaged in business' (Force and Motion in the evenings). The example of Cambridge was quickly followed by London (1876) and Oxford (1878) (Goldman, 1995; Cooke, 1998, pp.824–5).

James Stuart was seeking to bring the more 'democratic' traditions of the Scottish universities into the elitist atmosphere of Cambridge. He stood squarely in the tradition of the Scottish Enlightenment in that he saw education as a bulwark against revolutionary change and class conflict, not as a contributing factor to it. In a speech to the Leeds Ladies Educational Association in 1871, Stuart observed, 'It seems to me on the contrary that nothing could more tend to work against that class distinction than any efforts we may make towards a system in which our rich and poor, our men and women, should be taught by the same individuals' (Cambridge University, BEMS 1/11). Similarly, his address at the opening of University College, Dundee (UCD) on 5 October 1883 claimed, 'Ignorance and uncultivated barbarism of mind are the most efficient instruments of social disintegration and revolution' (Stuart, 1883, p.26). However, the opportunities for university extension were limited in Scotland, where three of the four cities already had an ancient university, with the exception of Dundee. Moreover, student fees in Scotland were much lower than in England and there was a tradition of popular access to university education. The Argyll Commission reported in 1868 that, in Scotland, six times as many students per head of population received a university education as in England and that something like one-fifth of all Scottish university students had working-class origins (Anderson, 1983, p.157). The limited impact of university extension in Scotland was attributed by the 1919 Report of the Ministry of Reconstruction to the 'democratic character' of the Scottish Universities and, 'the fact that the intramural classes are more readily accessible to all classes of the population than is the case in England' (Ministry of Reconstruction, 1980 edition, p.289).

Significantly, the founder of UCD, Mary Ann Baxter of Balgavies, a member of a prominent Dundee textile manufacturing family, and a Congregationalist like James Stuart, donated £115,000 to establish, 'a college for promoting the education of persons of *both* sexes and the study of science, literature and fine arts' (Walsh, 1968, pp.375–8; Schafe, 1982, p.11). At the opening of UCD, it was claimed of Mary Ann Baxter, 'her main object was that the College should impart instruction and enlightenment to the working classes' and Provost Moncur of Dundee also saw the College as, 'a fountain of learning not for the privileged few but for the million'. The opening ceremonies ended with an evening lecture to working men by Professor Ewing on 'Electricity as a Motive Power' (*Dundee Yearbook*, 1883, pp.93–4).

From its inception, UCD targeted women students and in 1883–4 announced that, 'in the event of the 8 to 9 am Classes proving inconvenient to Ladies, there may be similar classes formed in the afternoon'. A physics course was, 'arranged specially for the convenience of Ladies' in which, 'the various branches of Physics will be discussed in a simple manner.' This proved unnecessary, as the women admitted performed very well academically and the special physics class was discontinued in 1885–6. However, although women could attend classes on an equal footing with men, they were not permitted to matriculate until the Universities (Scotland) Act of 1892 (Spackman and Paul, 2000, pp.196–7). Some outstanding female students came through UCD. Mary Lily Walker (1863–1913), for example, came from a middle-class background in Dundee, the daughter of a solicitor. She was an exceptional student and every year between 1884–8 won first prizes in subjects ranging from Latin, literature and history, to botany, zoology and physiology. She became the warden of the Grey Lodge Settlement in Dundee, the secretary of the Dundee Social Union and was one of the first two women elected to the Dundee Parish Council (Baillie, 2000, pp.122–50).

The older Scottish universities had been involved in attempts to widen access for women since 1867 when the Edinburgh Ladies' Educational Association (ELEA) was formed, which was followed by similar associations in Glasgow, Aberdeen and St Andrews. The ELEA claimed a membership of 160 and attendances of 265 women at lectures. By 1872, Edinburgh University was awarding a Certificate in Arts to those who attended classes and passed in three subjects. Subjects included English Literature, Latin, Greek, Logic, Moral Philosophy, Political Economy, Theory of Education, Fine Arts, Mathematics, Biblical Criticism, Physics, Botany, Physiology and Zoology. At Glasgow, 'lectures for ladies' were arranged in 1868 and systemised by 1877 by the foundation of the Glasgow Association for the Higher Education of Women (Shearer, 1969, pp.146–8; Moore, 2000, pp.319–33). In the same year, a Ladies' Educational Association was formed in Aberdeen and St Andrews launched its LA (later LLA) scheme, which allowed women to sit exams in various centres across the country. The Edinburgh Association established the 'St George's Hall Oral and Correspondence Classes' in 1876–7, whose students, 'varied in age from girls of fifteen to mature women,' average numbers being 120 oral and 550 correspondence students. The longest lasting of these schemes was the 'Literary Ladies' scheme at St Andrews, where some 900 women were admitted between 1898 and 1904 and over 1,000 between 1907 and 1911. The scheme finally closed in 1931 (Smart, 1968; Bell and Tight, 1993; Moore, 2000, pp.319–33).

Popular journalism

The same period that saw middle-class women knocking on the doors of Scottish universities to gain entry, also saw the emergence of a mass newspaper-reading public. Following the repeal of the Stamp Act in 1855, many cheap newspapers sprang up, aimed at the lower middle classes and the 'respectable' working-class market. Some of the publishers of these newspapers had previously published chapbooks for the country trade, such as the Randle and Macnie Press in Stirling, one of the leading chapbook producers, who launched the *Stirling Observer,* or the Johnstone family of Falkirk, from a similar background, who published the *Falkirk Herald.* Many of the editors of these new cheap publications came from an artisan background themselves and had often followed a Smilesian path of self-improvement. They were often continuing an earlier tradition from the period of the unstamped press. For example, Alexander Campbell (1796–1870), a Glasgow joiner, Owenite socialist missionary and early cooperator, was a regular contributor to the unstamped press in the 1830s, particularly the *Herald to the Trades Advocate,* an early trade union newspaper, described by a fellow radical as, 'two penny unstamped, conducted by the late Mr Alexander Campbell' (Fyffe, (ed.), 1980, p.3). Campbell later wrote for the main working-class newspaper in Scotland, the *Glasgow Sentinel,* published weekly from 1850 to 1877 (Donaldson, 1986, p.4; Macdougall, 1985, p.94). Another largely self-taught radical editor was James Paterson, the Ayrshire printer who founded the *Kilmarnock Chronicle* in 1831 to spearhead the campaign for the Reform Act of 1832. Paterson continued in a career in journalism as Dublin correspondent of the *Glasgow Liberator* and eventually as a contributor to *Kay's Edinburgh Portraits* (Paterson, 1871, pp.99–101, 148–9).

The 'new' editors included William Latto of the *People's Journal,* a former handloom weaver and Chartist, William Scott of the *Montrose Review,* another ex-handloom weaver, and W.H. Murray of the *Falkirk Herald,* a former shoemaker. Other editors from similar backgrounds included George Penny, an ex-handloom weaver and local historian, who became publisher of the *Perthshire Advertiser and Strathmore Journal,* James Bridges, ex-railwayman, editor of the *Perthshire Advertiser,* William Alexander, of the *Aberdeen Free Press,* a mutual improver from a crofter/blacksmith background, and William McCombie, the founding editor of the *Aberdeen Free Press,* who combined newspaper work with farming (Donaldson, 1986, pp.4–5; Alexander, 1992 edition, pp.7–8; Penny, 1836, p.viii). To these could be added the Edinburgh printer, David Pae, (1828–84), the son of a Perthshire miller, who after a spell editing the *Dunfermline Press,* became the founding editor of the Dundee-based *People's Friend* (Pae Mss.; Pae, 1858, pp.vii-xiv). Another self-made editor was James Annand, born in 1843 on a croft near Peterhead, who began life as a blacksmith and ended it as editor of the *Newcastle Chronicle* and, briefly, as Liberal MP for East Aberdeenshire (Hodgson, 1908, pp.8–171).

An example of the 'new' type of cheap newspaper was the *People's Journal,* launched on 2 January 1858 and aimed at the working-class market. The brainchild of the remarkable John Leng of the *Dundee Advertiser,* it combined advanced liberal opinions with a popular literary element and a news service. Its prospectus complained of cheap newspapers, 'utterly unworthy of the intelligence and character of the respectable portion of the working classes'. The *People's Journal* would concern itself with, 'freely publishing letters and communications from working men, reporting their meetings, epitomising the newly published biographies of men like Livingstone and Stephenson, who have raised themselves from poverty to lofty reputations…and co-operating generally in every movement having for its end the intellectual and social advancement of the people'. Its tone was one of somewhat relentless self-improvement, temperance and the domestic virtues. On 14 March 1868, it claimed that:

> instead of the Saturday evening alehouse there is the Saturday evening fireside – instead of the excited or half sottish 'jaw' there is the 'news' of the week, with a fresh supply of wholesome literature...a love for reading is thus engendered among communities of good average intelligence, where before the introduction of the *Journal* in dozens of families no trace of any volume could be found but the Bible, the Church Record and the Children's school-books. (Donaldson, 1986, pp.11, 21)

The *People's Journal* had a close relationship with its readers. Robert Barclay, the son of an Aberdeenshire weaver and crofter, and a strict teetotaller and mutual improver, described how he was thrilled when the *Journal* published a poem he had submitted (Barclay, 1985, pp.11–6). James Annand got his start in journalism by writing articles first for the *Peterhead Sentinel* and then for the *People's Journal* (Hodgson, 1908, p.17).

The founding editor of the *People's Journal*, William Latto, was a classic autodidact. Born at Ceres in Fife in 1823, he received a rudimentary education before starting work as a herd boy around the age of ten, then transferring to handloom weaving at 14. He was a Chartist, a supporter of Feargus O'Connor and the 'physical force' branch of the movement. He was active in the foundation of the Free Church at Ceres in 1843 and became a campaigner for free trade. He studied English grammar from a textbook attached to his loom and the minister of the Free Church taught him and lent him books. By 1846, Latto had become the master of a small subscription school and a freelance writer. A bursary enabled him to attend the Free Church training college at Moray House, Edinburgh and he taught at Johnshaven, near Inverbervie, Kincardineshire for 11 years before entering full time journalism (Donaldson, 1986, pp.28–9).

The *People's Journal* was so successful that it spawned the *People's Friend* in 1869 to take the overspill of articles and readers' contributions. Its founding editor was David Pae, who had been contributing articles to the *Journal* since 1863. He was born in Buchanty, Perthshire in 1828, the son of a miller who drowned in the River Almond when David was a child. His mother took her son back to her family home in Coldingham, Berwickshire, where he was educated at the parish school. He was apprenticed at an early age to Thomas Grant, an Edinburgh printer and publisher. David Pae was a devotee of the theatre and a keen student of the Bible. As a young man at the time of the Crimean War, he published a millennial tract, *The Coming Struggle,* which sold over 100,000 copies and caused something of a sensation. It was a wide-ranging tract, which attacked both the growing power of Czarist Russia and the Papacy and predicted the Jews return-ing to Israel. In 1855, he began to write theatre reviews for the Edinburgh-based *North Briton* but found his metier with the publication of a serial novel, *Jessie, the Bookfolder; or the Heroism of Love,* which appeared simultaneously in the *North Briton* and the Glasgow-based *Penny Post.* During a relatively short life, David Pae wrote no less than 50 novels, which were serialised in newspapers in Scotland and the north of England. Their titles and improving tone – *Lucy the Factory Girl, or the Secrets of the Tontine Close; The Heiress of Wellwood, or Swindlers and their Victims; The Cloud on the Home, or a Wife's Devotion;* and *Mayhew the Millspinner, or the Stolen Will* are reminiscent of George Miller's *Cheap Magazine* of the 1810s. In 1859, Pae became editor of the *Dunfermline Press* and in 1863 was engaged by John Leng to write for the *People's Journal* (Pae Mss.; Donaldson, 1986, pp.77–100).

Even in the 1850s and 1860s, these newspapers faced an uphill struggle in terms of the reading ability of their audience. An article in the *Aberdeen Free Press* in 1853 commented on, 'the greater part of our labourers and ploughmen', that, 'to confine them an hour at a book is just like condemnin' the criminal to an hour o' the treadmill'. In 1860, an anonymous correspondent wrote to the *Free Press* to complain that, 'after fifty years experience, or nearly so, of working men, I unhesitatingly affirm, that an infinitesimal number only owe the Schoolmaster anything…many of those who have been benefited by educa-tion…cannot attribute it to their school-training but rather to their indomitable energy, in overcoming the want of it'. Reading the newspapers aloud was one way of overcoming these deficiencies. William Lindsay, the publisher of the Aberdeen edition of the *People's Journal,* was born in 1821, the son of a shoe-maker from Newhills, near Aberdeen. His father's business prospered and from the age of 12, Lindsay earned his living as a reader, reading the newspapers to groups of his father's workers while they worked. Lindsay became a prominent moral force Chartist, a temperance reformer, campaigner for the Anti-Taxes on Knowledge Association, a founding member of the Northern Co-operative Company and an early socialist. The *Free Press* reported in 1854 that children often read to older people, 'Noo, the laddie reads clearly and distinctly, an should a hard word occur, the dictionary is readit, so that naething is lost – the haill circle, be it muckle or little, gatherin information, and maist o' a', the min' o' the youthfu' reader is led to expand' (Donaldson, 1986, pp.16, 19–21).

Patrick Geddes – citizenship, culture and the environment
Patrick Geddes (1854–1932) was a polymathic figure characterised by one his-torian as 'a resilient outsider' and 'a throw back to the universal intellect of the Enlightenment' (Harvie, 1994, p.101). He was born at Ballater in Aberdeenshire, the youngest son of a former sergeant major in the Black

Watch. The family moved to Perth where Geddes attended Perth Academy. Geddes despised examinations and never completed a conventional academic education. After a brief period at Edinburgh University and the Royal School of Mines in London, he moved on to the University of Paris where he developed a lifelong attachment to French culture and French thought. He was overwhelmed by the cultural institutions of Paris – the theatre, the National Library, the Conservatoire, artists' studios etc. Many years later he wrote, 'Our true University is thus in the City; nay more, it is the City, great Paris herself' (Meller, 1993, p.34).

Geddes began to develop theories of urbanisation based on French models whilst living in Scotland, one of the most densely urbanised countries in Europe, with cities like Dundee and Glasgow which displayed some of the most extreme problems of bad housing and poverty. His concept of 'citizenship' sought to define the relationship of the individual to a mass urbanised society, by emphasising humanising factors such as the development of the local community, the conservation and interpretation of historic buildings, the development of parks and open spaces and cultural development. He believed that the city was not simply an economic unit but an organic entity with its own identity and evolutionary development, based on family structures, social and cultural traditions, hence his concept of 'Work, Place and Folk,' an adaptation of the ideas of the French social theorist, Frederic Le Play. The citizen was defined in relation to their urban setting and 'citizenship' was seen as fulfilling the functions of the clan or the tribe in earlier societies. Education for citizenship therefore had to function not simply at a political or economic level but also at a cultural and spiritual level (Cooke, 2001, pp.193–208).

In 1889, at the age of 35, Geddes was offered the Chair of Botany at University College, Dundee. The Chair was endowed by a friend of Geddes, James Martin White, who specified that the Professor should only teach and live in Dundee for three months a year during the summer term. This gave Geddes ample time to pursue his other multifarious activities and he remained Professor of Botany at Dundee for the next 30 years, eventually leaving to take up the full-time Chair of Civics and Sociology at the University of Bombay in 1919 (Macdonald, 2000a, p.148). He was active in many educational and social movements, including the University Settlements in Edinburgh and Dundee, University Extension in Scotland in the 1880s and 1890s and the Edinburgh Summer Meetings from 1890 to 1895. These were modelled on the Oxford Summer Meetings, which had developed for extension students from 1888 onwards, and where Geddes had taught in 1890 (Goldman, 1995, p.94). In his Edinburgh Summer Meetings from 1893 onwards, he began to develop ideas of pan-Celtic Nationalism, influenced by his contacts with the Irish nationalist movement. To support this, he began an Edinburgh-based publishing venture with William Sharp, producing the 'Evergreen,' a forum for Irish and Scottish writing (Cooke, 2001).

Figure 4 Patrick Geddes with a Botany field trip, University College, Dundee, c.1890
(Source: University of Dundee, Archives)

Geddes's ideas on citizenship and citizenship education are revealed in his Report for the Carnegie Dunfermline Trust on *City Development: A Study of Parks, Gardens and Cultural Institutes* published in 1904. This report came out of a bequest of $2.5 million by the American millionaire and philanthropist, Andrew Carnegie, to his birthplace of Dunfermline in Scotland. Dunfermline was an industrial town in Fife founded on textiles but with a historic centre and a mediaeval abbey. Pittencrieff Park in Dunfermline was purchased and Geddes was commissioned to write a development plan. The plan quoted Ruskin on the mediaeval love of cities and was a plea for utilitarian municipal schemes to be replaced by wider cultural ones. Geddes argued that, 'something more than open spaces, music in the parks, municipal trams and steam boats and a generous employment of the rates is needed to develop cities as they ought and might be'. The plan involved the development of Pittencrieff Park and the neighbouring mediaeval Abbey with the conservation of ancient buildings and the development of new social institutes, libraries, museums, art galleries, a nature palace, a labour museum, an open-air museum, a crafts village, an art institute, a music hall and a Civic Union. The Civic Union would be a model of participatory citizenship in that it would advise the Trust on the development of cultural facilities in Dunfermline. Another proposal was for a City Improvement Association, loosely based on models such as the Edinburgh Cockburn Association and the Freiburg Improvement Association in Germany, both early examples of voluntary urban conservation bodies (Geddes, 1904, pp.2, 224).

This was education in the broadest sense with a strong emphasis placed on physical as well as cultural activities – the plans included a men's gymnasium, tennis courts and a bowling green as well as an open-air theatre. The museum complex proposed for Dunfermline would form the basis of a Summer school programme based on the American Chautauqua model. Geddes argued for cross-disciplinary studies and links with Scottish Universities in any proposed Summer school development. The proposals had a strong temperance emphasis in that the Social Institutes were planned as, 'successful substitutes for the public house'. They would have a large room for entertainment and music would play an important part in their role, plus indoor and outdoor games. They would be linked with, 'temperance reform, civic progress and education in social life' (Geddes, 1904, pp.37, 176).

Geddes saw women as playing a key role in these institutes, 'The whole policy of Social Institutes must be strongly influenced by women'. Later in the report he argued, 'our next statement of the ideal of democracy must thus be no mere restatement of the rights of man, as with the French Revolution, nor of the rights of woman...it involves an increasing satisfaction of the ideals of woman and these on both a temporal and a spiritual phase' (Geddes, 1904, pp.39, 198). However, Geddes was no feminist – he saw woman as the biological nurturer and disliked radical feminism and the suffrage campaign. The role of woman was, 'to fulfil her true biological duty as wife, romantic companion and ideal mother. Her role was to inspire her man to know intuitively what needs to be done: to nurture cultural and spiritual values, which were the potent elements for generosity, the highest quality of social evolution' (Meller, 1993, p.7).

In 1907, Geddes ran a tutorial class in Battersea under the auspices of London University, a year earlier than R.H. Tawney's more celebrated tutorial classes for the Workers' Educational Association in Rochdale and Longton. The subject matter of this and subsequent classes reflected Geddes's wide range of interests – 'The History and Principles of Biology', 'The Evolution of Life, Mind, Morals and Sociology', 'Nature Study and Geography in Education', 'Contemporary Social Evolution', 'The Evolution of Occupations' and 'The Evolution of Cities' (Ministry of Reconstruction, 1980 edition; Meller, 1993, pp.146–7; Goldman, 1995, p.117).

However, many of Geddes's activities were a reaction against what he believed to be the overly academic approach of much of British adult education in this period. He laid heavy emphasis on cultural, spiritual and moral education, on informal methods and the generalist tradition as opposed to specialisation. This can be seen by his use of museums as teaching tools, by his involvement in numerous overseas exhibitions and by his use of drama in education. In 1912, he organised a 'Masque of Mediaeval and Modern Learning' to celebrate the 25th anniversary of the foundation of University Hall, Edinburgh. This was the sort of large-scale informal educational and cultural project dear to Geddes's heart. It involved 650 'active participants' enacting a pageant of learning over the ages for a middle-class audience. For Geddes, this meeting of Town and Gown was in the best traditions of Scottish education and contrasted with, 'that other separation of Town from Gown which has long been a main drawback of Oxford' (Geddes, 1913, p.31).

The Masque contained a powerful plea for a general education to, 'keep pace with the vast growth of knowledge and again take the generalisation of "all things to be our province"; and interest ourselves in histories, literatures, languages, sciences, incomparably beyond the present depressed condition of the student' (Geddes, 1913, p.65). This was in keeping with the generalist traditions of Scottish education, which was coming under increasing pressure from the second half of the nineteenth century onwards (Macdonald, 1999).

Geddes distinguished between the 'urban' and the 'rural' response to cities, favouring the latter (Meller, 1993, p.144). Geddes himself grew up in Perth, a traditional Scottish burgh, although rather larger and more diverse than the small towns of Haddington or Dunbar, the base for earlier Scottish adult educators such as George Miller, Samuel Brown or Samuel Smiles. It is questionable how far he was comfortable with sprawling industrial cities such as Glasgow or Manchester, or even the industrial town of Dundee where he held a Chair for 30 years. His town planning schemes were usually concerned with towns or cities with a historic core such as Edinburgh, Dunfermline or Dublin or further afield, Jerusalem or the Muslim city of Lucknow in India. Geddes was a thoroughgoing internationalist. An address he gave in 1890 contrasted the vigour of the French and German university systems and the resources spent on them with the more inward looking and less well resourced system in Britain. He argued for more foreign work and travel by students and for the Scots College in Paris to be revived (Geddes, 1890, pp.5–8).

Geddes's most influential writing appeared in the period before and during the First World War – a time of great social ferment when trade union membership was growing and socialist ideas were beginning to enter the mainstream of British politics. It was an era that saw the Easter Rising of 1916 in Ireland and the Russian Revolution of October 1917. The period also saw the emergence of the Workers' Educational Association and the Labour College movement; the first based on partnership with existing educational institutions, including the universities, the second suspicious of any links with the institutions of a capitalist society.

Education and the labour movement
The growth of the labour and cooperative movement in the nineteenth and early twentieth centuries saw significant developments in working-class adult

education. Glasgow was an uneasy melting pot for refugees from both the Irish Famine and the Highland Clearances, who were exposed to poverty, disease, gross overcrowding in housing and the harsh realities of urban living and industrialisation. Here, there seems to have been a continuous tradition of radicalism stretching from Owenism, to Chartism, to secularist and socialist societies. Dr G.B. Clark, for example, described how his father was Secretary of the local Chartist Society in Glasgow, 'and many of the men whom I met in my youth were extreme politicians – Radicals, Chartists, and Socialists'. Clark vaguely remembered the 'Noddy Kirk' in Great Hamilton Street, 'the headquarters of Robert Owen's early socialist movement. But my recollections are much clearer of the last two Socialist missionaries in Glasgow – Lloyd Jones and John Buchanan'. Buchanan carried on a printing and publishing business in Glasgow, including *The Weekly Times, The Penny Post* and *The Sentinel,* which afterwards was taken over by Alexander Macdonald of the Miners' Union (*Forward,* 11 June 1910).

After Owen's organisation ceased, the Eclectic Society was formed in Glasgow, many of its members being former followers of Owen. The Society was founded on the basis of secularism and took as its texts Owen's *New Moral World* and Tom Paine's *The Age of Reason* and *The Rights of Man.* The Society operated in a thoroughly didactic way as Clark explained:

> There were two meetings in the Eclectic Hall on Sundays, one in the forenoon when a social or political subject was considered and an evening one, when a scientific, philosophical or religious question was discussed. The speakers were often local men, but sometimes lecturers came from London, among whom were several leaders of the Secularist movement, such as George Jacob Holyoake, the two Editors of the *National Reformer,* 'Iconoclast', (Charles Bradlaugh) and Dr George Sexton. Holyoake had at one time been a Socialist missionary in Glasgow and was the principal leader of the Secularist organisation which replaced the socialist one. (*Forward,* 11 June 1910)

Towards the end of the 1860s, George Sexton, 'an able scientific man and a Socialist' was appointed as lecturer for a year, but the experiment was not a success. Like Robert Owen, Sexton became a Spiritualist and later a lecturer for the Christian Evidence Society. Dr G.B. Clark eventually became Assistant Physician at the Royal Sick Children's Hospital in Edinburgh. He was a supporter of temperance, female suffrage and Irish Home Rule, and became President of the Highland Land League and MP for Caithness (*Forward,* 11 June 1910).

The Eclectic Society and similar organisations were minority activities, but the Cooperative movement in Scotland boasted a mass membership. From the second half of the nineteenth century, many Scottish Cooperative Societies began to establish educational programmes for their members. As early as 1863, the St Rollox Society in Glasgow decided, 'That two and a half per cent be taken from the profits, to be applied for educational purposes, such as taking a commodious house in the district, and supplying books, newspapers, periodicals, etc., so that the members might pass an hour or so in the evening profitably'. In another example, the Kilmarnock Equitable Society set aside a modest 16 shillings for education on its foundation in 1860. Forty years later, this had grown to £406, and by 1910 the society had a library of, 'several thousand volumes of informing works, while the reading rooms are plenished with the current daily, weekly and monthly literature. Lectures are also arranged for the members by the educational committee, while classes on various subjects are carried on during the winter months'. In the same year, it was reported that at St Cuthbert's Association in Edinburgh, 'Classes for bookkeeping and kindred subjects are carried on during the winter months; musical evenings, by their own choir and orchestra, are held monthly, where a co-operative address is introduced, which seems to be much appreciated by the large audiences; a women's guild, with branches in different parts of the city, has lectures on subjects that must be helpful in everyday life'. Similarly in Glasgow, in 1910, it was claimed of the Glasgow Eastern Society that, 'Its lending library, its reading room, its classes, and its guilds all speak of intelligent administration' (Maxwell, 1910, pp.118–202).

The Cooperative movement placed considerable emphasis on female education, although in strictly delineated and domesticated terms. In 1889, for example, the Education Committee of the Kinning Park Society, Glasgow began domestic economy classes for women, which led to the foundation of the Scottish Cooperative Women's Guild in 1892, with 14 branches and 1,491 members (Lucas, 1920, p.62; Paterson, 2003, p.96). The Guild championed the domestic virtues, 'the information gained by the women at these guilds will greatly improve the domestic arrangements, and make homes happier and brighter. Sick nursing, ambulance work, and some knowledge of the general laws of health are simply invaluable in the workman's household and have too long been neglected. Add to this, instruction in dressmaking, millinery, fancy-work etc. and it will be readily conceded that the guild is of inestimable value to the ordinary household' (Maxwell, 1910, p.358).

Towards the end of the nineteenth century, a number of early socialist groups in Scotland established discussion classes and worker study groups focusing particularly on the teaching of economics, industrial history and the writings of Karl Marx. Tom Bell, for example, joined an Economics Class run by the Social Democratic Federation on the south side of Glasgow in 1902. The class leader was a self-taught engineer called George Yates, who became a draftsman and designer of Glasgow Central Station and the railway bridge. Yates read and spoke French and German and was strongly internationalist in outlook. Bell recalled:

We had two and a half hours tuition; reading out aloud; questions and answers to last week's lessons; short discussion and examination of homework; after which tea was made and for another hour we talked and discussed freely on all manner of political and educational subjects. (Bell, 1941, pp.38–9)

From 1905, Bell took over the running of these classes, which he continued to teach for the next 15 years. He described the teaching and learning methods, designed to produce tutors for future classes:

These had to be studied, memorised and discussed thoroughly for perhaps the first four weeks. The student would study Wage Capital and Labour at home. At the class we would read it over paragraph by paragraph, round the class. This practice aimed at helping the students to speak fluently and grammatically. At the following class meeting, questions would be put and answered, and the points raised thoroughly understood by everyone, the results of each lesson being summarised by the leader. This method was applied in the same way to industrial history. Later on, simple lessons on historical materialism and formal logic were added. So that, after six months of this, every worker who went through the entire series came out a potential tutor for other classes. (Bell, 1941, p.57)

Edwin Muir, the distinguished poet, born on a croft in Orkney in 1887, eventually became the Warden of Newbattle Abbey, Scotland's only residential college for adult education (Muir, 1940, p.30). He moved to Glasgow in his youth, and recalled going to meetings of the Clarion Scout Rambling Club before the First World War, 'every Sunday evening we attended a speakers class run by an old and experienced socialist. Working class mothers, dock labourers, suffragettes, and all sorts of people attended the class. Each of us, after a few weeks' instruction, had to get up on a platform and address the others for ten to twenty minutes, after which we had to answer their questions' (Muir, 1954, p.12).

This type of radical adult education was typical of the west of Scotland and the Fife coalfields in this period. It was one of the reasons why many British socialists saw Scotland as the template for radical change. For example, H.M. Hyndman, the London stockbroker and founder of the Democratic Federation, which became the Social Democratic Federation, claimed in 1911:

Scotland was the country in which the independent labour movement began...it seemed probable that Scotland, by far the best educated part of the United Kingdom, would come to the front and take the lead in the political arena on behalf of the disinherited class. (Young, 1992, p.48)

The most prominent socialist adult educator of this period in Scotland was John Maclean, who was born in 1879 in Pollockshaws, then an industrial village on the edge of Glasgow. He was the son of parents belonging to the Secession Church, whose families had been evicted during the Highland Clearances. His father died when Maclean was 11 and his mother survived by working as a weaver, then running a small shop. Maclean attended Pollockshaws Academy and Queen's Park Secondary School and worked as a pupil teacher at Polmadie School from 1896–8. Maclean was a committed lifelong learner himself. He studied at the Free Church Training College from 1899 to 1900 and on graduating as a teacher, enrolled as a part-time student at Glasgow University, graduating as MA in 1904. He then attended continuation classes at Glasgow Technical College from 1904 to 1907 in chemistry, mathematics and physics. In 1900 he had joined the Progressive Union in Pollockshaws. This was a debating and discussion society with a strongly secular and radical bent. A convinced tee-totaller, Maclean gave a lecture to the Union on 'Poverty, Drink and Crime' in January 1901 and soon became its secretary (Milton, 1973, pp.15–20).

Maclean began to teach Marxist economics for the Social Democratic Federation from 1906 onwards. From 1908 until his imprisonment for anti-war activities in 1916 he taught economics in evening continuation classes. A teachers' strike was organised in 1913 by the Scottish Socialist Teachers' Society (STTS). It was held in Neilston, Renfrewshire, 'over the payments for Evening Continuation Classes. A strike committee was formed and pickets were posted at the schools to stop blacklegs' (Young, 1992, p.140). The Secretary of the SSTS, which was behind the strike, lived next door to Maclean in Pollockshaws. In February 1913, Maclean addressed the Clarion Scouts in Glasgow on the subject of Marxian economics:

> I want you to go home and read the works of Karl Marx. If you read one or two good books they will do more good to your head and to your heart than a library of rubbish. What we need in this country is an educated working class. The millennium, if it is to come, must come from an educated working class. (Bell, 1944, p.24)

This radical and anti-capitalist approach commanded more support in Scotland than the Workers' Education Association, (WEA) which believed in a partnership between working-class organisations and universities. The WEA had been founded in 1903 by Albert Mansbridge, a Battersea clerical worker, and by 1907 had qualified for a government grant aid for its classes in England and Wales. Following a visit by Mansbridge to Scotland, a WEA branch was formed in Springburn, Glasgow by a group of teachers as early as 1905. However, the WEA struggled to get a footing in Scotland, which had a different legal framework for adult education, a different and more accessible university system, and a more vigorous independent working-class education movement than England. There was fierce internecine warfare between the WEA and other socialist education organisations in Scotland, who accused the WEA of collaboration with the ideological allies of capitalism (Cooke, 2000, pp.267–77; Duncan, 2003, p.178). These rivalries were to intensify with the outbreak of the First World War, as John Maclean and other socialist leaders were accused of, and eventually imprisoned for, anti-war activities because of the pacifist and internationalist approach they advocated.

More influential in the longer term was the rise of municipal planning, pioneered by Glasgow, but followed by other urban centres such as Edinburgh and Dundee. As early as 1855, the Glasgow Corporation Water Act advanced a scheme to bring pure water into the city from Loch Katrine in the Trossachs. This ambitious project, opened by Queen Victoria in 1859 at a cost of £1.5 million, was a pioneering effort planned not by socialists, but by Liberals and Tories. In the second half of the nineteenth century, Glasgow Corporation moved into gas supply, tramlines, public baths and laundries, a telephone service, police, fire services, parks, libraries and art galleries (Smout, 1986, pp.44–5). Culture and education were seen as part of an all embracing whole, provided by the council in much the same way as water or gas supplies. The People's Palace, for example, was opened on Glasgow Green in the East End of the city on 22 January 1898. Modelled on the People's Palace in the East End of London, it consisted, 'practically under one roof, of a museum, picture gallery, winter garden and music hall' (Glasgow Museum, 1998, p.12). Foremost amongst the musical groups to make their reputation in the new public space was the renowned Glasgow Orpheus Choir, a mixed choir which had developed out of a choir at Toynbee House, Glasgow, founded for working men by, ' a small group of West End social reformers' along the lines of Toynbee Hall in London (Roberton & Roberton, 1963, p.15).

Chapter 5

'Moving towards an abyss': the two World Wars and the inter-war period: 1914–1945

For no one can doubt that we are at a turning point in our national history. A new era has come upon us. We cannot stand still. We cannot return to the old ways, the old abuses, the old stupidities. As with our international relations, so with the relations of classes and individuals inside our own nation; if they do not henceforth get better they must needs get worse, and that means moving towards an abyss. It is in our power to make the new era one of such progress as to repay us even for the immeasurable cost, the price in lives lost, in manhood crippled and in homes desolated.

(Ministry of Reconstruction, *Report on Adult Education*, 1919)

The impact of the First World War

The First World War had a traumatic impact on Scotland. Of the 557,000 Scots who enlisted in all services, 26.4 per cent lost their lives. This compared with an average death rate of 11.8 per cent for the rest of the British army between 1914 and 1918. As well as this enormous loss of life, the First World War also had a major impact on the west of Scotland economy, as the area was transformed into, 'a vast national arsenal for the mass production of ships, shells, guns and other munitions' (Devine, 1999, p.309). In this atmosphere, when there was great pressure to move to mass production methods using less skilled or female labour, there was resistance from skilled male workers leading to major disputes amongst engineering workers in firms like Weirs, Albion Motors, Beardmores and Barr and Stroud. In 1915, Lloyd George appointed William Weir, who had a reputation as one of the most anti-union employers, as controller of munitions for Scotland. The engineering unions had agreed to ban all strikes for the duration of the war, on condition that the government would restore pre-war working practices at the end of the war. The suspicion that the government would renege on the agreement led to a series of unofficial strikes led by a group of shop stewards linked to the Clyde Workers' Committee, including members of the Socialist Workers' Party such as Willie Gallacher, Arthur McManus and John Muir.

Independent working-class education

It was against this background that the legend of 'Red Clydeside' developed. In October 1915, Glasgow women led a successful rent strike, involving 25,000 tenants, contrasting the behaviour of Glasgow's rack-renting landlords with the sacrifices of their husbands and sons in the trenches. At the same time, John Maclean and others were involved in an internationalist anti-war campaign in Scotland, arguing that workers should not sacrifice their lives for a capitalist war. The immediate post-war years were marked by industrial depression and attempts at wage-cutting by many firms, which was met by widespread strike action in Clydeside and the Fife coalfields. The Forty Hours' Strike was marked by a riot in George Square, Glasgow on 31 January 1919, when there was a confrontation between police and thousands of strikers who had assembled there. From late 1920, however, mass unemployment overtook virtually every sector of the Scottish economy – coal, steel, shipbuilding, heavy engineering and textiles (Foster, 1998, pp.225–6). In Dundee, in 1923, the largely female Jute and Flax Workers' Union waged a bitter strike for 27 weeks at Camperdown Works, Lochee with two periods of lock-out throughout Dundee (Walker, 1979, p.486).

In this atmosphere, it was difficult for working-class organisations to stay neutral and independent working-class education, which regarded collaboration with existing educational institutions with suspicion, found much more grass-roots support in Scotland than the Workers' Educational Association (WEA), which argued for partnership with universities and education authorities. For example, in 1918/19 the WEA had run only six classes in Scotland – one in Aberdeen and the rest in Edinburgh. By contrast, the Scottish Labour College (SLC) in the same period had run 17 classes in economic and political subjects with 1,500 enrolments, mostly in the west of Scotland. The Glasgow Plebs League, another independent working-class organisation, had run 19 classes in the same period with enrolments of about 1,000 (*Ministry of Reconstruction,* 1980 edition, pp.290–1). Scotland, particularly the west, was the stronghold of independent working-class education in the UK. By comparison, in its other stronghold of South Wales, there were 1,200 students in classes in 1917 (McIlroy, 1996, p.266).

The Plebs League and the Central Labour College were the creation of dissident students at Ruskin College, Oxford in 1908. They formed the Plebs League to campaign for a Marxist-orientated programme of education and set up the Central Labour College in London in 1911, supported by the South Wales Miners' Federation and the National Union of Railway Workers. A crucial element in the argument for a Labour College was that of independence from State control, as opposed to the concept of partnership with the universities favoured by the Workers' Educational Association. In 1915, a proposal for a Labour College for Scotland appeared in *Forward*:

the universities and other institutions of higher education have for their object the training of men and women to run capitalist society in the interests of the wealthy. We think the time has come for an independent college, financed and controlled by the working class in which workers might be trained for the battle against the masters. (Duncan, 1992, p.109).

John Maclean believed in, 'such education as will make revolutionists' and argued for a working-class press and a Scottish Labour College (SLC) to teach adult workers, independent of any schools or universities, which he saw as being influenced by the ideology of the ruling classes. At the launch of the SLC at the Cooperative Hall, Glasgow on 12 February 1916, Maclean was imprisoned in Edinburgh Castle. A speech 'A Plea for a Labour College in Scotland', written jointly by Maclean and James Macdougall, was delivered by Macdougall and argued:

I am firmly convinced that the workers must establish and maintain their own colleges to equip themselves of their own specific task as a class...More and better working class papers and magazines are needed, if the people are going to get facts instead of fiction, working class instead of capitalist leading articles...the principle study ought to be Economics. At a Labour College economics must be taught fundamentally from the labour standpoint. Otherwise we ought to send our students to the capitalist universities. Our students must make the writings of Marx and Marxian scholars the basis of their studies; otherwise the College becomes an expensive luxury. (NLS, Acc. 5120, Box 6, p.1)

The SLC had an inauspicious start as many of its key supporters amongst the labour activists – John Maclean, James Macdougall, James Maxton and John Muir – were in prison for 'anti-war' strike activities. Others who were active in the Clyde Workers' Committee were deported from the Glasgow area. John Maclean was released from prison in June 1917 and in the following winter ran a Marxist economics class for 500 people in the Central Halls in Glasgow and another for 100 people in Govan. In the winter of 1917 there were 17 classes organised by the SLC, 14 in the west of Scotland, three in Fife. The Glasgow Plebs League organised another 11 classes in Glasgow and at Dumbarton and Clydebank (NLS, Acc. 5120, Box 6, p.1).

The planned Day College was slow to materialise because of lack of funds but by 1919/20 the SLC was running 30 classes with 854 students in Glasgow and 51 classes in other parts of Scotland with some 2,000 students. In September 1920, a Day College for nine students began at rented premises in St Vincent Street, Glasgow. Classes ran from 9.00 a.m. to 4.00 p.m. from 1 September to 26 December for a fee of £5. The reading list included *Das Kapital* but also books on English grammar and elementary algebra. The morning sessions were mainly economics, industrial and political history but included maths, Esperanto and public speaking. The afternoon programme was farmed out to the Scottish Business Training College in Bath Street and included shorthand and bookkeeping, which Maclean insisted would be useful skills for labour activists. Evening classes ran from 7.30 to 9.30 p.m. and included two taught by Maclean – English composition and public speaking on Mondays and economics and mathematics on Tuesdays. The cost was five shillings a term for one subject, extra subjects being 2/6d each. There was also a Sunday class taught by Maclean (economics) and J.P. Gready (industrial history). The SLC set up an appeal for student bursaries on 1 September 1919. Bursaries were fixed at £35 for a four-month course (NLS Acc. 5120, Box 6, p.1; Duncan 1992, pp.115–21).

Figure 5 John Maclean with students outside the Scottish Labour College, Glasgow, 1920-21 (Source: National Library of Scotland)

The SLC also attempted to carry the gospel to other parts of Scotland. An article in *Forward* dated 5 June 1920 reported on 'What Dundee is Doing'. The previous week a course of ten lectures had been held on 'Economics and Social Revolution', the tutor being John Maclean, who had recruited at factory gates in Dundee. They had failed to get the University Lecture Hall for the class and had to fall back on the Independent Labour Party (ILP) Hall. The class had enrolled 200 and could have taken more. Earlier correspondence in *Forward* revealed some of the background to the Dundee situation. On Saturday, 8 May 1920, the Rev. Richard Lee of Dundee denounced the WEA as favouring capitalism and the war, citing a book with articles by Arthur Greenwood, Seton Watson, Zimmern and others as a, 'striking and emphatic defence of the war'. In the same issue, James Thomson, Secretary of Dundee and District WEA, defended his organisation. Although the WEA had held classes on University College, Dundee premises, St Andrews University had not tried to influence the curriculum or choice of tutors. The local authority had paid the tutors but, 'a minority of the LEA, strangely enough, suspected the WEA of being a Socialist propaganda association'. Their industrial history class made extensive use of mutual instruction and the students covered a wide spectrum of political opinion:

> A student, who had made a special study of the Trades Guilds, discussed the subject from the platform; a member of the ILP contributed an original analysis of prices and wages; the lecture on the Chartist movement was delivered by 'an extreme Marxian', a strong opponent of the war, an SLP-er who prepared the lecture and decided its scope and content. (NLS Acc. 5120, Box 6, No 1)

Disputes over accommodation with official bodies such as School Boards and universities were a continuing theme of SLC correspondence, often contrasted with more favourable treatment for the WEA. For example, an article in *The Worker,* dated 3 November 1917, by John Maclean claimed:

> Now the WEA is being galvanised into activity in Scotland. Lord Haldane helped at the opening of the branches in Edinburgh and Dundee. More significant still, Dr. Boyd of Glasgow University made a savage attack on Marxian education a fortnight ago when opening the Kilmarnock branch of the WEA...His speech, and he is President of the Educational Institute of Scotland, reveals quite clearly the exact motive underlying this new outburst of WEA ism. (Young, 1992, pp.146–7)

On another occasion, a request for a room for an SLC class in Renton was rejected by the School Board and J.P.M. Millar reported, 'The Chairman of the Board, a Commercial Gentleman of the Cloth however suggested that they take a class under the WEA. Tutor was to be provided, paid for by the Board, etc., etc. Truly the Non Biased People have many friends in strange places' (NLS, Acc. 5120, Box 6, No 4). In Edinburgh, Kemp Smith, the Professor of Philosophy, taught a philosophy class for the Edinburgh WEA in 1920, and was noted for his, 'resourcefulness and boldness in his efforts to stem the encroaching tide of Marxism as it came eastwards' (Davie, 1986, p.51).

The case for the WEA was made by W.H. Marwick, a WEA Staff Tutor, in a letter in *Forward*, dated 27 February 1921. He argued the case for impartial education for working people as, 'the right of all and not merely a leisure class, to enter into the cultural heritage of mankind and to develop their powers – intellectual and aesthetic – to their fullest capacities'. Marwick also believed in the need for a high standard of knowledge and intelligence by workers, 'if economic and political democracy are to be realised in a social commonwealth'. He stressed the need for democratic control by the students, for cooperation between students and tutor and for impartiality, 'which some confound with compromise' (NLS Acc. 5120, Box 6, No 1).

Other disputes focused on personalities and continuing problems over lack of funds. The first full-time Secretary of the Scottish Labour College was William Leonard, a member of the Cabinet Makers' Union, who became Secretary in 1916 and 'went back to my tools' in 1919, citing 'internal differences'. Leonard became Convenor of Shop Stewards in four shipyards and in 1931 was elected as MP for St Rollox in Glasgow. In April 1923, a third Secretary resigned. Francis Rafther wrote to hand in books, papers and office keys and added as a parting broadside, 'I bitterly regret that I consented to act as Secy. after Lyle gave up the job. I have neglected my home, wife and baby all for the College. I am also pounds out of pocket but never again. It was hurtful of Com. Millar doubting my integrity but I can assure him that my reputation stands as high as his in the movement'. 'Comrade Millar' was J.P.M. Millar, who was emerging as a leading light in the movement. Born in Edinburgh in 1893, Millar came from a middle-class background and worked in an insurance company before being converted to socialism and joining the No Conscription Fellowship, serving time in prison for anti-war activities. He eventually became the Secretary of the National Council of Labour Colleges (Millar, 1979, pp.45–9). Millar continued to pursue Rafther, seeking details of disputed accounts, but fell foul of Rafther's redoubtable wife, Christina. She wrote to Millar from Strattord Street, Maryhill, Glasgow, 'if I had my wish this would never have transpired because he would never have associated himself with socialism of any kind. I am entirely against the whole movement…I have already told you socialism is only a game with fools doing the no pay jobs and the bigheads getting the salarys…Allow me to close my letter with congratulations on the unity which seems to cement all your dealings with one another' (NLS. Acc. 5120, Box 6, No 2).

Bitter sectarian disputes were a continuing feature of the movement, reminiscent of those in the Presbyterian churches in the eighteenth and nineteenth centuries. For example, an article in *The Vanguard* described a meeting of the Provisional Committee of the SLC, when the Chairman, John M'clure, moved for the dismissal of John Maclean in Maclean's absence. This provoked a backlash in which M'clure was accused of leaving the Socialist Labour Party and joining the Independent Labour Party in 1919. In a phrase reminiscent of the Stalinist show trials, M'clure was accused of being, 'boosted by the official wire pulling gang, some of whom have openly or secretly backed up the WEA'. The article went on to claim, 'The Government backs up the WEA as a means of staying the progress of Marxist education' (NLS Acc. 5120, Box 6, p.1).

The WEA was a favourite target, and some years later, when there was a proposal to reorganise the SLC, the Glasgow District wrote on 14 August 1928 to protest, 'let every friend of the Labour College movement realise as never before that the Glasgow College stands for real and genuine Independent Working Class education such as inspired the work of our late comrade John Maclean when he founded the SLC and not for its development into a glorified form of the WEA standing for a similar neutrality in the struggle for the emancipation of the working class' (NLS Acc. 5120, Box 6, (6)).

Not all disagreements were so intense. An ongoing dispute between the Greenock branch of the Scottish Labour College and the Brassmoulders' Union centred on the claim that Brassmoulders' Union members were being turned away from SLC classes in Greenock, although the Union contributed to SLC funds. An exasperated E. Wilson wrote from John Street, Gourock on 21 February 1924 that the complaint was a hardy annual without any foundation. He reported that the Secretary of the Brassmoulders was a member of the SLC District Committee and received details of all classes, adding, 'I suggest you are mistaken in the name, which is not Brassmoulders but Brassfaced Union' (NLS, Acc. 5120, Box 6, (4)).

By the 1930s, the Scottish Labour College had been absorbed by the National Council of Labour Colleges (NCLC) and had ceased to be Marxist and revolutionary in its purpose, in spite of left wing rhetoric. The NCLC provided an adult education service to the broad Labour movement, a good deal of it through correspondence education, together with the publication of the *Plebs* newspaper, which sold 6,000 copies monthly and a large output of pamphlets (Millar, 1979; McIlroy, 1996).

The Ministry of Reconstruction Report on Adult Education 1919

After the War, the Liberal government set up a Committee on Adult Education under the auspices of the Ministry of Reconstruction. Its terms of reference were, 'to consider the provision for, and possibilities of, Adult Education (other than technical and vocational) in Great Britain and to make recommendations'. The Board of Education was suspicious about the work of the Committee and insisted that the words 'other than technical and vocational' should be added to restrict the remit of the enquiry. These ministerial turf wars extended to Scotland where the Scottish Education Department, 'manifested an even greater complacency about the need for post war developments in adult education' (Taylor, 1980, p.30).

The Committee had a number of members with Scottish connections and it published a section on Scotland. The Scottish members included Robert Climie, a Kilmarnock town councillor, trade union organiser and treasurer of the Scottish Trade Union Congress. Climie became the Labour MP for Kilmarnock in 1923. Another Scot was James Morton, a textile employer with mills in England and Scotland. He was active in preparing the Scottish sections in the report. Two other members had links with Glasgow University. Professor Henry Jones had been born in Wales but held the chair of Moral Philosophy at Glasgow for the last 30 years of his life. An Idealist philosopher, Jones was a liberal and a friend of Lloyd George (Fraser, 2000, p.109). R.H. Tawney was a Balliol man who was teaching at the London School of Economics during the period of the Committee. However, his first teaching post was at Glasgow University as an Assistant Lecturer in Economic History and he had travelled from Glasgow at weekends to teach his WEA tutorial classes in Longton and Rochdale (Taylor, 1980, pp.31–4; Cooke, 2000b, p.268).

The cultural and educational differences between Scotland and England became clear in the historical section of the report where it was reported that the university extension movement, although founded by a Scot, James Stuart, 'never took root in Scotland' (Ministry of Reconstruction, 1980 edition, p.27). The same phrase was used of the Adult School Movement, which by 1914 had only five schools in Scotland with a total membership of just over 500. Similarly, the Workers' Educational Association did not make an appearance in Scotland until 1913, 'since when war conditions have hampered development'. The differences between the two countries in the immediate post-war period were summed up by a Scottish educationalist, 'it would be wise to assume therefore that non-vocational adult education of an organised nature is at present non-existent in Scotland' (Ministry of Reconstruction, 1980 edition, p.295). This in spite of the fact that some 2,500 students in Scotland were enrolled in adult classes with various independent working-class bodies in 1919, by far the largest number in any part of Britain.

The emphasis of the report was on an elite, 'the natural aristocracy that is among any body of men', who were the target groups for university tutorial classes. The mass of the population should receive 'two educational essentials', which were:

a) the development of an open habit of mind, clear sighted and truth lov-
ing, proof against sophisms, schivalists, claptrap phrases and cant; b) the
possession of certain elementary information and essential facts about
such main questions as the Empire, the relations between Capital and
Labour, the relations between science and production and other such subjects. (Ministry of Reconstruction, 1980 edition, p.5)

Most Scots who gave evidence to the Committee took up a position of superiority. An 'official source' claimed that:

traditionally every parish school in Scotland aims at providing instruction
of a non-vocational kind to its older pupils. Secondary education, the
facilities for which are abundant, is almost purely non-vocational. The
result is that a very much larger proportion of the lower middle class population of Scotland find opportunities of access to the universities, and
take advantage of them than in any other country I know of. To put it
briefly the class of people whose needs regards non-vocational education
are catered for in England by the Workers' Education Association and
such like organisations, in the circumstances of Scotland have little difficulty in finding the way to the universities, where they pursue non-
vocational studies in a much larger proportion than they do at, say the
newer Universities of England. (Ministry of Reconstruction, 1980 edition, p.294).

However, other Scots giving evidence disagreed and the Committee itself came
to the conclusion that the more open and democratic tradition of Scottish education was changing, 'with the increasing growth of industrialisation, conditions
in Scotland are more and more approximating to those south of the border'.
Most Scots left school at 14 and were subject to the same economic, political
and social pressures as those south of the border, so that there was, 'a similar
need for adult education, and a similar desire springing up for its satisfaction'
(Ministry of Reconstruction, 1980 edition, p.295).

The solutions proposed by the Committee centred on education for citizenship with particular emphasis on the role of grass roots and democratic
voluntary organisations such as trade unions, adult schools and cooperative
societies, who were to be given as much self-determination as possible in devis-
ing their own educational programmes. In his covering letter to Lloyd George,
the Committee Chairman, A.L. Smith, made a moving (and very early) plea for
a system of universal and lifelong learning:

adult education must not be regarded as a luxury for a few exceptional
persons here and there, nor is the thing which concerns only a short span

of early manhood.... adult education is a permanent national necessity, an
inseparable aspect of citizenship, and therefore should be both universal
and lifelong. (Ministry of Reconstruction, 1980 edition, p.5)

The report recommended that extra-mural university education departments
should be established in Scotland along the same lines as those south of the border, which would however require a change in the method of paying government
grants. It further recommended that the Scottish Education Department should
establish a standing joint committee of representatives of the universities, the
Local Education Authorities and voluntary organisations to consult on the provision of adult education.

The Scottish School Boards were responsible for continuing education
classes and evening schools, which were mainly concerned with vocational and
technical education and aimed at young people rather than adults. The
Committee commented that the low rates of pay for evening class tutors did
not encourage the retention of, 'adequately equipped and suitable teachers for
adult work'. Many School Boards viewed evening classes on subjects other than
the purely vocational as potentially subversive or socialistic and this suspicion
was mutual. A Scottish trade union official reported, 'there can be no doubt of
the suspicious hostility with which a large and intelligent section of the working class view classes run by School Boards' (Ministry of Reconstruction, 1980
edition, pp.207, 293).

The legal framework in Scotland was different from that in England and
Wales, where voluntary bodies could obtain recognition by the Board of
Education and receive grants directly from the Board. This had, 'secured the
independence of their classes, given students a voice in the selection of a
teacher, and enabled the arrangements to conform to the wishes and needs of
the students themselves'. By contrast in Scotland, classes organised by a voluntary organisation could only be eligible for grant if they were brought under the
auspices of a School Board. This system continued under the Education Act of
1918, although the local education authority, with the sanction of the Scottish
Education Department, could, 'contribute to the maintenance of any educational institution or agency, where such contribution appears to the Department
desirable for the educational benefit of persons resident within the education
area of the authority'. The same system applied to university tutorial classes in
Scotland and in the opinion of the Committee had hampered their development because of 'the absurdly inadequate' fees paid to tutors and other
difficulties that were placed in the way of the partnership between voluntary
organisations and universities. In Aberdeen, tutorial classes were run by a joint
Committee of the University, the School Board and the WEA, whereas in
Edinburgh they were run by an advisory committee of the WEA on which the
university had membership. The Report recommended that education authori-

ties in Scotland should include members interested in adult education on their new advisory councils and that the Scottish Education Department should consider making grants direct to voluntary organisations (Ministry of Reconstruction, 1980 edition, pp.108, 198, 293–4).

The report argued that the state should subsidise the widest range possible of educational activities for adults regardless of religious or political affiliation provided that they were, 'concerned with serious study'. It believed that, 'the practical evil today is not too much study by students for their sectarian bias, but too little study of any kind'. However, it was not well disposed towards the Labour College movement and described the Labour College in London as, 'frankly partisan in its outlook'. A recent innovation praised by the Commitee was an evening school run by the School Board in Dundee for young women mill workers in which basic instruction was given in English, arithmetic, history and geography, the rest of the time being devoted to dancing, gymnastics, music, sewing and knitting and, 'discussions on subjects of interest to young women' (Ministry of Reconstruction, 1980 edition, pp.118–9, 293).

Education authorities, the universities and the WEA

After the First World War, the Education (Scotland) Act of 1918 replaced School Boards with directly elected county and city education authorities. It also transferred Roman Catholic and Episcopalian schools to the new authorities, with safeguards for their religious character. As a result of this and the 1919 report, an administrative structure began to emerge for the provision of adult education by local authorities, the universities and voluntary bodies such as the Workers' Educational Association. In this partnership the local authorities were dominant as they had control of the purse strings, unlike England and Wales where university extra-mural departments and the WEA could apply to become 'Responsible Bodies' and qualify for direct government funding. The Scottish response to the 1919 report came slowly. Glasgow University established an extra-mural committee in 1924, followed by Edinburgh in 1929, but it was not until 1934 that adult education regulations were introduced empowering local authorities (not central government) to cooperate with universities and voluntary bodies (Fieldhouse, 1996, p.207). In Scotland, financial control remained firmly with the local education authorities.

Of the voluntary organisations, which made a significant contribution to informal adult education, the Scottish Women's Rural Institute and the Scottish Co-operative Women's Guild both targeted women. The first Scottish branch of the WI was founded at Longniddry in 1917, but by 1938/9, there were 1,000 institutes with 50,000 members. As well as 'Jam and Jerusalem', the Institutes provided lectures on topics such as health, child welfare, diet, housing and water supplies. The Scottish Co-operative Women's Guild, founded in 1892, had a similar impact in urban centres. It grew from 14 branches and 1,491 members in 1892 to 421 branches and 32,854 members in 1938. Its curriculum was similar to the SWRI, except for an emphasis on the principles of cooperation (Paterson, 2003, p.96).

In the field of workers' education, the balance of provision in Scotland was different from England. The Workers' Educational Association initially struggled to survive in Scotland. By 1926/7, there were sixteen Scottish branches of the WEA with 818 members, and Scotland accounted for only 6 per cent of the 30,000 WEA enrolments in Britain (Bryant, 1984, p.11). Between 1920 and 1931, the Scottish WEA employed a full-time tutor-organiser, W.H. Marwick, but financial difficulties led to his post being discontinued and he had to move into the extra-mural department at Edinburgh University. By contrast, the Scottish Labour Colleges, with a more radical educational, social and political agenda, continued to grow until 1926/7, when enrolments peaked at 6,598. The impact of the General Strike in 1926 and the economic depression that followed, led to a steady decline in activity, to reach a low of 2,202 students in 1932/3 (Paterson, 2003, pp.93, 98).

The period also saw the increasing separation of vocational and technical education from liberal adult education, with the lion's share of funding going to the former. From 1901, Scottish Central Institutions had been responsible for higher technical education under the control of the Scottish Education Department, whilst evening continuation classes provided preparatory and basic craft and commercial courses. In 1919, the Royal Technical College, Glasgow was included in the list of institutions funded by the new University Grants Committee, because much of its teaching was recognised as being of university level by a 1913 Ordinance of the University of Glasgow. The Scottish Woollen College at Galashiels was created a central institution in 1922 and the Scottish Academy of Music in 1939 (Butt, 2000, p.186).

In 1930, education authorities replaced committees in the 35 counties, with the power to develop post-school vocational education. In Glasgow, five evening class continuation centres were converted into full-time day and evening colleges, beginning with Stow College in 1934. However, in the depressed economic conditions of the 1930s, there was little support from Scottish employers for day release schemes. By 1938/9, grant-aided continuation class enrolments in Scotland totalled 190,000, with 21,000 being in central institutions, representing very little advance on the situation before the First World War (Butt, 2000, p.186). The lack of basic technical education was to cause serious skill shortages during the Second World War, and longer-term, for the Scottish economy as a whole.

In 1939, a survey of non-vocational adult education in Scotland found that local authorities ran 189 courses, compared to 47 run by university extra mural departments, 30 by university settlements and five by the WEA. Total enrolments were 9,300, with a total of about 4,500 students, of whom half were women. The classes were concentrated in the four large cities and about 38 per cent of students were in the age group 25–35. Most students were in paid work (88 per cent of the men and 68 per cent of the women). Of those in paid employment, 44 per cent of men and 25 per cent of the women were in skilled working-class jobs. The most popular subjects were foreign languages and literature (1,894 enrolments), citizenship, international affairs and economics (1,748) and psychology (1,270) (Cochrane and Stewart, 1944).

Residential adult education

In December 1931, Lord Lothian decided to offer Newbattle Abbey to the Scottish universities, 'to be used in perpetuity as an educational centre for Summer Schools and...for the kind of University Extension work which ...(was) being done so successfully at Harlech College in Wales'. Coleg Harlech had been inspired by the example of the Danish Folk High Schools and Lothian visited Denmark and Sweden in the summer of 1936, with his Warden Designate, the Rev. Alexander Fraser. Lothian, a Liberal whose family wealth derived from coal mining royalties, planned an explicitly Christian and anti-socialist mission for Newbattle. On 4 October 1939, he wrote to Fraser:

> I am sure in my own mind that Newbattle Abbey College cannot succeed without that force of Christianity at the top and adequately infused in the staff. The central conclusion I formed after our tour of Denmark and Sweden was that the real success of the folkschools depends on what old Grunding (N.F. Grundtvig) had put into them and when they were run by mere intellectuals or Marxists they really did more harm than good to their inmates...It is the same in Scotland. Unless NAC is founded on that spirit – symbolised by the Chapel – it will...breed a destructive, harshly intellectual temper in its members, corrosive and corrupting. (Ducklin and Wallace, 2000, p.293)

Newbattle Abbey College opened in January 1937 with somewhat half-hearted support from officialdom, including the four ancient Scottish universities, the local authorities and the Scottish Education Department (SED). The universities agreed to become trustees of the College, on condition that it involved no cost to them. The Carnegie Trust gave £15,000 for the reconstruction of the building and another £14,000 was raised privately for capital equipment and running expenses. The local authorities agreed to offer bursaries and the SED offered a capitation grant of £28 for each student completing the proposed one-year course (Ducklin and Wallace, 2000, p.294).

The problem was that residential adult education was expensive compared to other models of adult education in Scotland. Newbattle Abbey College cost £7,000 a year to run for 26 students in 1936/7 and had no endowments. Unlike Denmark, there was no tradition of residential adult education in Scotland, where most adult education was provided both locally and cheaply, often self-financed by the students themselves. Indeed, the SED capitation grant of £28 was more generous than that paid to Scottish Central Institutions. Compared to England, university education in Scotland was usually city-based and non-residential, and could often be accessed relatively cheaply on a part-time and evening basis. Scottish officialdom was also uneasy with the non-utilitarian aims of Newbattle. An SED memo of 18 January 1939 noted, 'So far as Adult Education is almost entirely concerned with broad cultural education, it is difficult to reconcile the aims of Newbattle with those of a Central Institution'. Furthermore, the College's target audience of working-class Scottish students was suspicious of its Christian and anti-socialist credentials. Lothian wrote to Fraser on 4 October 1939 sympathising with him in his hard job of coping with, 'the executive committee or the hard materialist underlying point of view of many of the students from the industrial areas'. When war broke out in September 1939, the College was turned over to the army and that year's intake of 55 students was put on hold (Ducklin and Wallace, 2000, p.294).

Industrial decline, emigration and the Second World War

The inter-war years were a difficult transition period for the Scottish economy and Scottish society. The decline of Scotland's traditional industries and the resulting unemployment was marked by an old solution – emigration. After a steady growth in population since the beginnings of the census in 1801, Scotland's population recorded an absolute decrease between 1921 and 1931, when the population fell from 4,882,500 to 4,843,000. In the same period, 523,981 Scots left Scotland, of whom 446,212 went overseas, the rest moving to other parts of the UK. This was simply the peak of a long drawn-out process – between 1861 and 1931 a staggering 2,620,392 Scots left the country, mostly emigrating overseas (Kenefick, 1998, pp.98–105).

The ailing Scottish economy was eventually revived by the outbreak of the Second World War. Heavy industry and shipbuilding were kept busy producing armaments and building replacements for shipping sunk by enemy action. The Dundee jute industry was turned over to the manufacture of sandbags. The war also saw the emergence of centralised state planning under Winston Churchill's Coalition Government. Churchill appointed Tom Johnston, former Red Clydesider and Labour MP, as regional commissioner for civil defence and then in February 1941 as Secretary of State for Scotland. Johnston came from a background of benevolent paternalism in local government. He had served on Kirkintilloch Town Council between 1914 and 1918 where:

To a modern observer the range of successful municipal enterprises engaged in by Johnston and his cronies in that ancient but semi-industrial town outside Glasgow seems incredible. They boosted higher education by holding popular boxing and dancing classes for those who also agreed to study English or mathematics; they formed a big, long lived municipal bank to invest local money in building waterworks, gas and roads; they set up a municipal cinema, built municipal showers and houses, and bought bulk orders of English suits and baby food and sold them on at cost price; and they pasteurised milk and improved the food supply for poor children, halving the infant mortality rate in three years. (Devine, 1999, pp.551–2)

This type of municipal socialism owed something to the paternalism practised by some Victorian firms and rather more to the collectivist principles of the Scottish cooperative movement. It drew heavily on the traditions of municipal intervention practised by Liberal and Tory councils in Scottish cities from the 1850s onwards. It was this kind of paternalism by Labour councils in Scotland, together with soldiers' and civilians' experience of wartime and the activities of the Army Bureau of Current Affairs during the war (Fieldhouse, 1996, p.55) that contributed to the massive increase in the Labour vote in Scotland after the war. In the 1945 election, which returned a majority Labour government to Westminster for the first time, Labour won 37 seats in Scotland and received nearly 48 per cent of the Scottish vote (Devine, 1999, p.555).

Chapter 6

'A lamp to light the feet of their children': post war reconstruction and educational expansion: 1945–1975

I know how my grandfather's, even my father's, generation felt about education. They were very romantic about it. They thought of it as a kind of lamp to light the feet of their children, so that we need not stumble and hurt ourselves as they had done, or as armour buckled around us so that we could meet in fair fight all who stood in our way. They never doubted that our fight would be anything other than their fight and with them and of them and for them.

(Jennie Lee, This Great Journey, 1963)

Central planning and the post-war boom

Centralised state planning, begun under a Coalition government in wartime conditions, continued after the Second World War under a majority Labour government, which saw the creation of the National Health Service and the nationalisation of the railways, the coal industry, the iron and steel industry, and electricity. Scotland benefited from a strongly dirigiste approach by the Board of Trade, which was able to create 'development areas' for special assistance in terms of acquiring land, building advance factories and capital assistance. By 1950, Scotland had attracted 13 per cent of all new industrial building in Britain and several American multi-national companies such as Honeywell, IBM, Euclid and Goodyear had become big players in the Scottish economy. At the same time, traditional industries, such as shipbuilding and heavy engineering, were undergoing a renaissance. Between 1948 and 1951, Scottish shipbuilders launched no less than 15 per cent of the world's tonnage and 33 per cent of UK tonnage (Devine, 1999, pp.556–7).

Politically, the dominant Labour party was committed to increasing state planning and centralisation and had moved away from earlier commitments to Home Rule for Scotland. Although the Scottish Nationalist Party leader, Robert McIntyre, won the party's first ever Parliamentary seat, Motherwell, in a war time by-election in 1945, the seat was lost in the general election that followed and the SNP's electoral hopes faded. However, the Scottish Convention campaigned for Scottish self-government from 1947 onwards and in 1949, the Covenant movement collected two million signatures in favour of Home Rule (Devine, 1999, pp.565–6).

The Scottish Institute of Adult Education

Similar issues of identity lay behind the foundation of the Scottish Institute of Adult Education in 1949, although its origins were almost accidental. A Scottish Branch of the British Institute of Adult Education had been established in 1928 under the chairmanship of Sir James Irvine, Principal of St Andrews University. In 1946, the Ministry of Education in England set up the National Foundation for Adult Education to support local authorities in their adult education activities and to encourage cooperation between them and voluntary organisations. In 1949, the National Foundation and the British Institute merged under the Secretaryship of Edward Hutchison to form the National Institute of Adult Education. This left the Scottish Branch of BIAE out on a limb and it was decided to form a separate organisation for Scotland, if the question of funding could be solved. The new organisation drew its membership from the local authorities, the universities and the Workers' Educational Association, although most of its funding was provided by the local authorities. Sir Hector Hetherington, the Principal of Glasgow University, took a leading role and academics rubbed shoulders with WEA activists, local authority officials and councillors, and members of voluntary organisations such as trade unions, churches and the SWRI (Inglis, Cooke and Inglis, 1989, pp.1–2).

The Institute held annual conferences and from 1951 published the journal *Scottish Adult Education* three times a year. Its Honorary Secretary and Treasurer was W.D. Ritchie, recently retired Director of Education for Selkirkshire, and its early debates focused largely on arrangements for collaboration between universities, local authorities and voluntary organisations and such matters as university standards in adult education. In 1957, Tom Lansborough, Director of Education for Clackmannanshire, succeeded Ritchie as Honorary Secretary, a post he was to hold for the next 14 years until his replacement by a full-time paid Secretary. The annual income of the Institute in 1966 was a paltry £700. The Institute's ambition was always larger than its tiny budget. It relied on a great deal of goodwill and unpaid effort from its members. In 1971, on the retiral of Tom Landsborough, the SED was persuaded to come up with the money to appoint a full-time Secretary. After a short-lived tenure by Brenda Main, John Taylor was appointed Executive Officer in 1974. He came from an administrative background in Edinburgh University and had a commitment to a 'new' and emerging area of adult education – adult literacy work (Inglis, Cooke and Inglis, 1989, pp.3–37).

Adult education and youth and community work

The period was marked by a steady growth in numbers of adult students enrolled – for example student enrolments in non-vocational further education more than doubled in a 20 year period from 104,000 in 1952/3 to almost 218,000 in 1972/3 (Bryant, 1984, p.18). There was also increasing professionalism of adult education with a growing number of full-time staff appointed in education authorities, the universities and the WEA. This marked a change from a more loosely structured movement dependent on a good deal of voluntary effort to a more professional ethos. In spite of this, there was a feeling that all was not well with adult education in Scotland. In Fife, for example, the Labour-controlled Education Committee, 'concerned at the continually falling enrolments in Adult Education Classes' set up a Working Party on Adult Education in 1963. This recommended that, 'the traditional academic range of adult education be widened to include the variety of subjects which are offered by Further Education evening centres, by arts and crafts clubs, and by voluntary organisations'. This recommendation led to the appointment of adult education staff to each Technical College in Fife and a specialist member of staff to the Directorate (Fife County Council, 1964).

At national level, representatives of the Scottish Institute of Adult Education met with the Scottish Education Department from 1960 onwards to discuss, 'the establishment of these conditions which would ensure the progressive development of adult education in Scotland'. Adult education was defined as, 'Formal and informal cultural activities, aesthetic as well as intellectual, requiring participation, both for the development of the individual and for active citizenship under changing conditions'. Financial support, or the lack of it, was seen to be a key issue and it was recognised that, 'most of the problems presented for solution appeared to call for answers in financial terms'. In 1968, an SIAE Working Party Report on the Finance of Adult Education in Scotland revealed that SED administrative grants for the provision of adult education outside the education authorities in 1966 amounted to a mere £42,235, with the lion's share (£20,600 or 49 per cent) going to Newbattle Abbey College, the rest going to the Extra-Mural Committees of Glasgow, Edinburgh and St Andrews Universities (£12,000 or 28 per cent) and the remainder to the Workers' Educational Association. Teaching costs were subsidised by education authorities, although the degree of subsidy varied widely across the country. The Report highlighted three areas of concern for adult education – the growth of leisure, the rapid obsolescence of knowledge and increasing numbers of women returning to the workplace. It noted, 'adult students more and more tend to be already highly educated'. This would become a central theme of the Alexander Report on adult education. As solutions, the report proposed the creation of a career structure for teachers and administrators in adult education and training courses for the army of part-time teachers in the field. It also called for better accommodation for adult education, such as adult centres, adult wings in schools, short-term residential colleges and the expansion of long-term residential colleges (SIAE, 1968, pp.3–6, 17).

At the same time, the local authority youth service was diversifying, expanding and becoming professionalised as 'youth and community work' through full-time training courses based in the Colleges of Education, first at Moray House, Edinburgh and Jordanhill, Glasgow, then in Aberdeen and Dundee. The rapid expansion of the youth and community service followed the recommendations of the 1964 Kilbrandon Report, *Children and Young Persons in Scotland* (the Scottish counterpart of the 1960 Albemarle Report). By 1968, the Report of the Standing Consultative Council on Youth and Community Service recommended that the government, 'promote, within the sphere of informal further education, further development of the youth and community services and to foster co-operation among the statutory and voluntary organisations concerned' (Martin, 1996b, pp.131–2). This was an attempt to instil a clearer educational purpose into the youth and community service and at the same time, to correct the perceived failings of the adult education service to address the needs of those who had received little formal education. This formed the unwritten agenda of the Scottish Education Department and was an important influence on the Inquiry into Adult Education, chaired by Professor Kenneth Alexander, which reported in 1975.

The expansion of higher, technical and further education

The 1960s were a period of educational expansion. There was steady growth in provision by universities, central institutions and further education colleges. The three sectors also moved closer together in the development of degree-level work. In the 1960s and 1970s, the two leading Advanced Technical Colleges in Glasgow and Edinburgh were transformed into Strathclyde and Heriot Watt Universities, and degree-level work was encouraged in central institutions and further education colleges. In 1967, Queen's College, Dundee became independent of St Andrews as the University of Dundee, and Stirling was founded as Scotland's only 'new' university. By 1970, there were 11 central institutions in Scotland funded by the SED (the Scottish universities were funded by the (UK) University Grants Committee). The central institutions included five colleges of technology, three art colleges, two colleges concerned with domestic science, and the Royal Scottish Academy of Music and Drama, based in Glasgow. Their teaching staff in 1970 was about 900, but this was set to grow dramatically in the next two decades. Teacher training colleges, also SED funded, had seen expansion from their bases in the four Scottish cities in the 1960s, with the creation of colleges at Callendar Park, Falkirk and Craigie, Ayr in 1964, and Hamilton in 1966 (Anderson, 2000, p.171; Butt, 2000, pp.186–91).

Further education (FE) colleges also expanded considerably in this period after the publication of a White Paper *The Future of Technical Education* in 1956. The White Paper was followed by increased capital spending on college facilities – some £12 million over five years followed by a further £3.5M in 1959. In 1961, another White Paper, *Technical Education in Scotland*, recommended further expansion over the next two decades and a strategy for a training structure to support the growing Scottish economy. From 1957 to 1972, no less than 30 new FE Colleges were built in Scotland, starting with Reid Kerr College in Paisley and ending with Glasgow College of Technology. Further education in Scotland grew rapidly from a very underdeveloped base. In 1956, there had been fewer than 700 full-time FE staff; by 1970 this had risen to about 4,000, based in about 80 colleges and centres. Some were very small, about half having fewer than 20 full-time teachers per institution, but 12 had over 120 full-time staff each (Butt, 2000, pp.187–8) Because of the part-time nature of many further education courses, many colleges recruited substantial numbers of adult students and this pattern was to intensify over the next two decades. An interesting innovation was the Special Recruitment Scheme to encourage older students to enter teaching. This scheme, an early example of adult access, offered financial support for adults to study on a full-time basis in an FE College for 'O' Grades and Highers, for entry to university or teacher training college. Other colleges laid more emphasis on the development of degree-level full-time courses and this was to lay the foundations for the eventual transformation of an institution like Glasgow College of Technology into Glasgow Caledonian University.

The Open University in Scotland

A major innovation came with the foundation of the Open University (OU). This UK based organisation, set up in 1969, began teaching its first intake of 25,000 students in 1971, of which some ten per cent came from Scotland. The OU was important not only in its own right but also as a catalyst in producing high-quality distance learning materials, imaginative use of the electronic and print media and collaborative arrangements with other educational organisations. It had strong Scottish connections. It was floated by the Leader of the Labour Opposition, Harold Wilson, as a 'University of the Air' in a speech in Glasgow in September 1963. After the election of a Labour government in 1964, Wilson entrusted the idea to Jennie Lee, Minister for the Arts, the daughter of a Fife miner and widow of Aneurin Bevan. She insisted on two principles: firstly, it was to be a proper university, independent and autonomous, with degree awarding powers and academic standards comparable to other universities; second, it was to be open to all without any prior entry qualifications (Sargant, 1996, p.291). Its first Vice-Chancellor was another Scot – Walter Perry, a medical graduate of St Andrews University. Similarly, the OU's degree structure, with its general first year, bore more similarities to the generalist tradition of Scottish universities, than to more specialised English degrees. The biographer of Jennie Lee noted perceptively, 'The OU's distinctive texture came not from Chicago (to which (Harold) Wilson looked), nor from the National Extension College (to which (Michael) Young looked) but from Scotland' (Hollis, 1997, p.305).

The OU offered courses over a wide range of subjects, it gave students a good deal of choice and degrees were based on the accumulation of credits. Initially, four foundation courses were offered in Mathematics, Understanding Science, Literature and Culture and Understanding Society (Sargant, 1996, p.292). The OU provided an important model for other educational institutions who wished to develop more flexible models of education, catering for part-time, mainly adult students. There was a steady growth of part-time professional and degree courses in Scottish universities, central institutions and further education colleges, often with a distance element. A key element in the success of the OU was its close links with the BBC, and the educational mission of the BBC was to have significant spin-offs in another successful venture, the adult literacy campaign of the 1970s.

One paradoxical result of this expansion of educational opportunity was a growing divide between the educational 'haves' and the 'have nots', which was to become a central theme of the Committee of Inquiry into Adult Education in Scotland. The dilemma was well summed up by Jennie Lee, describing her upbringing in the West Fife coalfields and the idealistic attitude her family had towards education. However, the consequences of increasing educational opportunity were generally to create a competitive meritocracy with very different attitudes. Jennie Lee commented wryly, 'it is very hard for the old idealistic socialist when he sees graduates from the working class home turn into small town snobs' (Lee, 1963, p.92).

Chapter 7
From adult education to lifelong learning: 1975–2005

Those to whom adult education should be of most value are least involved.
(*Adult Education: The Challenge of Change*, 1975)

For many years Scotland has been admired and envied for its achievements in educa-
tion. Our distinctive qualifications structure and traditions of excellence have made us
highly regarded internationally. Traditionally we have led the way in terms of positive
change and innovative progress. But somewhere along the line education has ceased to
capture the imagination of a large part of the Scottish population...We want to make
a reality of educational opportunity for all.
(Donald Dewar in *Opportunity Scotland*, 1998)

De-industrialisation and globalisation

The discovery in May 1970 of the giant Forties oilfield in the North Sea some
110 miles off Aberdeen transformed the economic, and ultimately the political,
landscape of Scotland (Devine, 1999, p.585). Aberdeen became a boom town,
supplying and servicing the oil rigs, and the Scottish National Party revived its
electoral fortunes with the slogan, 'It's Scotland's Oil'. One reason the SNP
were able to do so well in the 1974 elections was the contrast between the
wealth created in the North-East by North Sea Oil, largely controlled by multi-
national corporations, and the rising levels of unemployment and de-
industrialisation in the rest of the country, particularly in the Labour heartlands
of the west of Scotland. From the 1970s, Scotland's traditional industries such
as coal mining, shipbuilding, iron and steel and textiles went into steep, and in
some cases terminal, decline in the face of global competition (Payne, 1998,
pp.73–95).

This had profound long-term social and economic consequences.
Traditional heavy industries, largely dominated by male semi-skilled and
unskilled full-time workers, were replaced by newer multi-national controlled
industries like electronics, with a much higher proportion of female (often part-
time) workers. Like other parts of Western Europe, the Scottish economy
experienced the growth of knowledge-based industries such as information

technology and bio-medical research, often linked to university campuses. Other developments have been the growth of financial services, particularly in the Edinburgh area, and the mushrooming of call centres across Scotland.

Economic and social change has been accompanied by political and cultural change in Scotland, with a growing sense of Scottish, as opposed to British, identity. The Labour Party remains the dominant political presence, but the increasing strength of political nationalism has meant that Labour has had to come to terms with home rule or devolution. The confusion over the Scottish devolution referendum in 1979 brought down the Labour government in Westminster, and ushered in the era of the arch centraliser, Margaret Thatcher. Devolution had to wait another 20 years until the election of a Labour government in 1997 brought about the establishment of a Scottish Parliament two years later, nearly 300 years after its abolition in 1707.

There has been a 'cultural renaissance' in Scotland in the same period, particularly in the fields of literature, painting, popular music and traditional music and song. A number of nationalist historians have seen this as a response to Scotland's status as a 'stateless nation' (Harvie, 1998, pp.293–5). Prominent recent Scottish writers include the novelists Alasdair Gray, whose work is strongly influenced by issues of national identity, Irvine Welsh of *Trainspotting* fame, Alison Kennedy, and the playwright Liz Lochhead. In the field of painting, Peter Howson, Ken Currie and John Bellany are key figures in a whole generation of largely Glasgow-trained artists (Macdonald, 2000b, p.210). Glasgow is also the centre of a thriving popular music scene, the home of bands such as Franz Ferdinand, Snow Patrol and Belle and Sebastian, all Mercury Award nominees in 2004, whose music sells worldwide.

There has been a revival of interest in traditional Scottish music, dance and song, both in Scots and Gaelic. This increasingly strong sense of national identity is mirrored in other small countries across Europe and can be seen as a response to globalisation, to multi-national corporations, to increasingly remote governments and to fears of a 'Macdonaldisation' of culture across different countries and continents. In Scotland, a strong national identity has survived, helped by a separate Scottish framework of law, education and religion within the British state, the result of the Act of Union in 1707.

The Committee of Inquiry on Adult Education, 1975 (The Alexander Report)

In May 1970, the Secretary of State for Scotland appointed a Committee of Inquiry under the Chairmanship of Professor Kenneth Alexander. This was the Scottish equivalent of the Russell Inquiry into Adult Education in England and Wales, which published its report in 1973. The publication of the *Alexander Report* in 1975 coincided with local government reorganisation in Scotland in

1974. The Wheatley Commission had resulted in the replacement of numerous small authorities, by nine double-tier regions and three single tier island authorities.

The Alexander Committee was heavily influenced by the UK *Gulbenkian Report* on community work (1968), which had recommended a 'community development approach', as practised in Educational Priority Areas and Community Development Projects. Scotland had already seen a significant expansion of the Youth and Community Service as a result of the *Kilbrandon Report* of 1964 (Martin, 1996b, pp.131–2). The terms of reference for the Alexander Committee were:

> To consider the aims appropriate to voluntary leisure time courses for adults which are educational but not specifically vocational; to examine the extent to which these are being achieved at present; and with due regard to the need to use available resources most effectively, to make recommendations. *(SED*, 1975, p.vi)

The Chairman of the Inquiry, Kenneth Alexander, was Professor of Economics at Strathclyde University in Glasgow and later became Head of the Highlands and Islands Development Board and then Principal of Stirling University. He had strong links with the Labour Party in Scotland, and had taught in adult education classes organised by the Workers' Educational Association. The Vice-Chairman, Dr D. Dickson, was a former Senior Chief Inspector in the Scottish Education Department (SED) and was part of a strong SED presence on the Committee. In addition to the Vice-Chairman, the SED supplied three assessors and the Secretary, D.R. McFarlane.

The Committee had a membership of 21, of whom four retired or resigned, one of whom was replaced. Membership was drawn from the universities (six), Directors of Education (two), Chairmen, Education Committees (two, one female) and teachers in further and secondary education (two). Other members included a County Treasurer, a Further Education College Principal, a Workers' Educational Association District Secretary, a Training Officer from British Steel, Motherwell, a Trade Union Congress Regional Education Officer, a social worker (female), the Warden of the Palace of Art, Bellahouston, Glasgow, and John Round, Principal Lecturer in Youth and Community Services, Jordanhill College of Education, Glasgow, who was an influential figure on the Committee. There were only two female members – Mrs. T.P.D. Murray, the Conservative Chairman of Angus Education Committee, a former Chairman (sic) of the Scottish Women's Rural Institutes and a prominent Girl Guider, and Miss J. Vaughan, a social worker in Midlothian (SED, 1975, pp.viii-ix).

Probably because of Kenneth Alexander's background in economics, the Committee took care to place Scottish adult education in its social, cultural and economic context. Part One of the report began by defining terms, followed by a short historical section, a brief review of the current position and a comment on the inadequacy of contemporary statistics. Part Two began with an analysis of the 'Determinants of Change', which were grouped under three headings – technological, social and educational. The report commented:

> Education, although an agent of social change, is very much affected by other elements in society, the most powerful of which are perhaps technology, economic development and social structure…It is too limiting a view, however, to see education as simply responding to social needs as if it were merely a servant of society. The educational system is itself a main agent of change inasmuch as it affects the character of social and technological change, the pace at which new knowledge and attitudes are diffused throughout society and the quality of life in the broadest sense. (SED, 1975, p.19)

This contrasts with the views of the American sociologist, C. Wright Mills, who argued in the late 1960s:

> Families, churches and schools adapt to modern life; governments, armies and corporations shape it; and as they do, they turn these lesser institutions into means for their ends…. Schools select and train men (sic) for their jobs in corporations and their specialized tasks in the armed forces. (Mills, 1967, p.4)

The *Alexander Report* argued that work had become, 'so highly specialised and so subject to frequent innovation' because of technological change that adult education was needed for workers to, 'mobilise knowledge with speed' (*SED*, 1975, p.21). On social change, the report noted the increasing numbers of older people in the Scottish population, leading to an educational gap between young and old. In an echo of the 1919 Report, the Committee argued that, 'a democratic society, if it is to function effectively, must have an educated and well informed electorate'. It went further, in a rather obvious case of special pleading by claiming, 'A strong, broadly based and *highly professional* system of education for adults is one of the best guarantees of a healthy democracy' (SED, 1975, p.22, my italics). The *highly professional* claim owed a good deal to effective lobbying by Departments of Youth and Community Services in Scottish Colleges of Education. The history of the German Folk High Schools under the Weimar Republic in the 1930s, and their subsequent fate at the hands of the National Socialists, suggests that a highly professional system of adult education is no guarantee of democracy, or indeed of institutional or even personal survival (Friedenthal-Haase, 2000, pp.167–81).

Other points made by the report as regards social change included the growth of leisure, which opened out, 'exciting possibilities for expanding both the quantity and quality of adult education' (SED, 1975, p.23). The report also commented on rapid changes in employment patterns leading to high and sometimes highly-localised levels of unemployment. As regards educational change, the report saw education as, 'a continuing experience spread over the whole of life', a view taken by the 1919 Report, some 60 years earlier (Cooke, 2000b, pp.267–79). In many ways, however, the *Alexander Report* was remarkably farsighted, arguing that education should no longer be, 'concerned solely or primarily with the training of the intellect' and that there should be, 'a transfer of emphasis from teaching to learning'. It forecast the massive expansion of higher education in Scotland, and welcomed the growing trend for initial education to concentrate on key skills (SED, 1975, p.24).

The report saw education 'as a lifelong process and learning as a, 'basic characteristic of life...by no means always associated with an educational institution' (SED, 1975, p.25). It identified four main aims for adult education – the reaffirmation of individuality, the effective use of the resources of society, fostering the pluralist society, and education for change. The reaffirmation of individuality was seen as a counter to, 'the growing technological basis of our society, the dehumanising aspect of many kinds of work and the impact of the mass media, all of which tend to erode individuality and paradoxically to increase a sense of isolation and alienation' (SED, 1975, p.26). The report singled out groups that were particularly likely to be affected by this sense of isolation and alienation. They included the family (often isolated in parenting), the elderly, whose numbers in the population were increasing, the disadvantaged, often caught in a generational cycle of deprivation, the handicapped and those who needed remedial education.

The disadvantaged included those with literacy problems, prisoners, the handicapped, those living in areas of multiple deprivation and in isolated rural areas. Behind all this lay concern for what the report called, 'the non-participants...the great majority of adults in Scotland who do not attend and never have attended, any classes or courses'. Those taking part in adult education in Scotland had a relatively high socio-economic status and were more likely to have higher educational qualifications than the population as a whole. The Committee found that those with least initial education were least likely to be taking part in adult education (SED, 1975, p.15).

The effective use of resources meant health and consumer education, areas such as diet and exercise and the use of credit. Fostering the pluralist society included trade union education, the educational needs of immigrants and foreign workers, and the educational role of voluntary organisations. Education for change examined community development, what the French call 'animation', and recommended, 'Adult education should participate increasingly in community development and much more experimentation is needed' (SED, 1975, p.31). Education for change included social and political education, environmental education, bridging the educational gap between young and old, understanding science and technology, and professional updating, a brief reference to what was to become a major growth area in universities and elsewhere.

To achieve these aims, and in the light of the Local Government (Scotland) Act, 1973, the Report recommended, 'adult education should be regarded as an aspect of community education and should, with the youth and community service, be incorporated into a community education service' (SED, 1975, p.35). This meant that a numerically weak and underdeveloped adult education service was incorporated into a much better staffed and resourced youth and community service, with, 'very different ideological roots and cultural policies'. It also had the unintended effect of isolating the weak adult education sector from, 'the wider field of adult and continuing education' (Martin, 1996b, pp.131–2). Ironically, the years after the publication of the *Alexander Report* saw a dramatic reduction in enrolments in adult education classes, due to the changing priorities of the new community education service and to cuts in local authority budgets leading to steep fee increases. Enrolments, which had risen steadily from 185,000 in 1968 to 240,000 in 1975/76, fell by 32 per cent in a year to a low of 164,000 in 1976/77. They made a small recovery to 171,463 in 1978/79 (Horobin, 1980, pp.5–6, 1983, pp.5–10). In 1986, Scottish Education Department administrative funding was withdrawn from university extra-mural and continuing education departments (Kirkwood, 1990, pp.308–9) and in 1987 from Newbattle Abbey College, Scotland's only adult residential college, ostensibly to fund the new Scottish Wider Access programme (Ducklin and Wallace, 2000, pp.291–301). Four years later, in 1991, the Scottish Institute of Adult Education closed its doors due to precarious public funding (Standish, 1999, p.644).

The coming of mass higher education

There has been a massive expansion in higher education in Scotland in the last ten years, similar to that taking place in the rest of Europe. From 1990/91 to 2000/01, the number of students, both part-time and full-time, in all types of Scottish higher education virtually doubled from 137,928 to 262,913. By 2001, the participation rate in full-time higher education by age 21 had risen to 50.4 per cent, compared with 17.8 per cent in 1980/81. As in other European countries, women's participation rates in Scottish higher education overtook men's in this period. In 2001, the female participation rate by age 21 was 56.1 per cent, compared to 44.9 per cent for men (Paterson, Bechofer and McCrone, 2004, pp.108, 185) The period saw the end of the binary divide and the conversion of Scottish Central Institutions into universities. A significant part of the expansion of student numbers has been an emphasis on recruiting adult students as undergraduates, and universities have mainstreamed their continuing education operations. The period has been marked by growing competition between universities, both for student numbers and for research funding, and marketing has come to have a much higher profile in higher education (Anderson, 2000, pp.171).

Access courses began to develop in Northern Ireland and England in the 1970s. The earliest ones in Scotland were in the university sector – in Glasgow (1979) and Dundee (1980). These original access courses were for adults but later most universities developed more intensive courses for disadvantaged school leavers – Glasgow again being the pioneer. In 1987 Strathclyde Regional Council established a consortium linking further education colleges and higher education institutions in developing and providing access courses. This became the basis for a national Scottish Wider Access Programme (SWAP), established in 1988, which operated on the basis of regional consortia and targeted both

Figure 6 Adult access student, Dundee University, 1989

under-represented groups, and areas such as science and technology, where there was a perceived shortfall in student numbers (Osborne and Gallacher, 1995, pp.224–51). At the same time Scottish Universities through their Continuing Education Departments (usually former extra-mural departments) continued to develop in-house access courses, which are now offered in most universities, a higher proportion than in England and one which has no equivalent in other European countries, reflecting the long tradition of regional links between Scottish universities and their communities (Cooke, 1995b).

There has been a steady growth in more open and flexible learning systems delivered by print-based or electronic systems. The role model has been the Open University but its methods have been adopted by the community education service, who use OU short courses, and by FE Colleges, who have developed open learning and drop-in centres. Within higher education, many universities have developed distance-learning courses, mainly for professional training, but including cultural studies, such as the University of Aberdeen's Certificate in Scottish Studies or the University of Dundee's Award in Modern Scottish History, developed jointly with the Open University. The most ambitious recent example is the University of the Highlands and Islands, a consortium of FE Colleges from Perth to Inverness and Wick, which uses a mixture of face-to-face teaching and open learning to deliver its courses.

Further education colleges, the Community Education Service and schools

A high proportion of students in Scottish further education colleges consist of adults. In 1989/90, for example, 55 per cent of all students in Scotland registered on vocational further education courses were over 20 (SOED, 1992, p.18). By 2000/01, some 7 per cent of the Scottish population aged 30–39 were enrolled either full-time or part-time in further education, compared with 6 per cent of the same age group who were enrolled in full-time or part-time higher education. Some 9 per cent of the population aged from 40–49 were enrolled in part-time or full-time courses in further or higher education in the same year. Participation in both higher and further education fell off steeply after the age of 50 (Paterson, Bechcofer and McCrone, 2004, p.184). Work in further education colleges includes collaborative work with the Community Education Service to extend access to further and higher education, provision for students with special needs, prison education, work with ethnic minorities and short courses for industry. A good deal of this 'new' work is outreach work and community based. Much of it reflects not only changing attitudes, but also a change in the demographic base and the decline in traditional industries, leading to the virtual disappearance of craft apprenticeships, which were the staple of much college provision in the past. The incorporation of further education colleges in 1993, the outcome of a White Paper entitled *Access and Opportunity* (1991), led to their removal from local authority control and being placed under the Scottish Office. This has been accompanied by growing competition and more aggressive marketing, often aimed at adults. There has also been a blurring of the divide between higher and further education, with many higher education courses offered in further education colleges (Leech, 1999, pp.50–6).

Community education in Scotland includes both youth work and aspects of community development and adult education. It has been defined in the following way, 'Community Education is informal, community-based and brings the educational process to people and places the formal education system does not easily reach, thereby increasing access to all forms of education and training' (SOED, 1992, p.15). Many of those taking part are not registered in the way that students are in further or higher education. Because of this informality and the fact that a good deal of community education is provided by voluntary organisations rather than by local authorities, statistics on community education participation are hard to come by. However, in 1996/97 it was estimated that some 255,000 adults were involved in community education activities. Of these, 94,000 received 'substantial educational' support from the community education services, the great majority being classified as learning 'in groups', and 15,000 learning in a 'one-to-one' situation (Scottish Educational Statistics Annual Review, 1998).

How effective has community education been in developing the Alexander agenda of informal outreach work with those not already involved in adult learning programmes? A detailed study of policy, organisation and provision in community education and leisure and recreation in three Scottish regions was commissioned by the Scottish Education Department and carried out from October 1981 to October 1983. The regions involved were Central, Fife and Tayside, and some work was also carried out in the largest Scottish region, Strathclyde, comprising some 50 per cent of the total population. The report was rather circumspect in its conclusions but found little evidence of developmental work with adults being carried out by community education services, concluding, 'there is little sign in mainstream Youth and Community and Community Education of deliberate and systemic programming for the creation of developmental work.' It also criticised the way in which the 'non-directive' approach of community education tended to be biased against more cognitive and structured educational work, which was often seen as 'elitist'. The Report commented, 'While non directive methods have their place, workers frequently do not have sufficiently developed areas of knowledge and skills to create appropriate curricula and learning methods for particular groups of participants or non-participants' (Alexander, Leach and Steward, 1984, pp.445–6). Looking back in 1996 on the achievements of the community education service created by his Committee of Inquiry some 20 years earlier, Sir

Kenneth Alexander felt, 'that the delivery of the service is judged to have fallen short of what supporters feel should have been achieved' (McConnell, (ed.), 1997, p.v).

The non-directive approach within community education reflected the influence of community development thinking, and of writers such as Carl Rogers, whose ideas were prominent in Scottish community education training courses at this time. These formed an uneasy combination in training courses with utilitarian ideas of professional competence. There was a strong anti-theoretical, even anti-intellectual, tradition within community education, based on mistrust of the professional teacher, combined with a growing managerial culture. The generic community education worker was seen as having competence in community work, adult education and youth work. The danger was that this could lead to over inflated expectations (Kirkwood, 1990; Alexander and Martin, 1995, pp.82–96; Shaw and Crowther, 1995, pp.204–18). An influential alternative for some was offered by the ideas of the Brazilian educator, Paulo Freire. In Lothian region, for example, the Adult Learning Project was started in Gorgie/Dalry in Edinburgh in 1977 by a group of local women, supported by a community worker and a community education worker. Lothian Region Community Education Service applied for an urban aid grant, and three full-time workers and a secretary were appointed in 1979. This project used the ideas of Freire in an urban, Western context, using themes such as 'Living in Gorgie/Dalry', 'Health and Well-being' and 'Parents and Authority' (Kirkwood and Kirkwood, 1989). Whilst this Edinburgh ALP project was both successful and long-running, (Galloway, 1999) in the wider context, Freire's emphasis on the empowerment of the colonised and the dispossessed did not sit easily within the bureaucratic framework of Scottish local authorities.

The 1960s saw the rise of a number of 'new' social movements, particularly feminism. Women had provided a disproportionate number of students in non-vocational adult education for many years. Surveys carried out in the early 1970s on behalf of the Alexander Committee, for example, showed they made up some 64 per cent of enrolments in Scotland (SED, 1975, p.124). However, most full-time staff working in adult education were male, and the distinctive position of women learners was slow to be recognised. In Scotland, feminist ideas began to enter the curriculum in the late 1970s, initially in informal adult classes organised by community education departments, the WEA and university extra-mural departments (Thompson, 1995; Barr, 1999). This was earlier than in mainstream degree programmes or other formal courses, and demonstrated the way in which, at its best, informal adult education was able to function as a 'critical space' in which new ideas could be developed and critical and creative thinking carried on. A similar process was at work in English adult education in the late 1950s, where people like Richard Hoggart and Raymond Williams began to develop, in university adult education classes, out of response to learners' interests, the subject that eventually became known as 'Cultural Studies' (Steele, 1995, pp.48–9; Fieldhouse, 1996, p.212; Steele, 1997).

From the late 1970s, women-only courses, influenced by feminist thinking, began to develop in community settings, such as Maryhill in Glasgow, Ardler in Dundee or Raploch in Stirling. In the more formal sphere, organisations such as Edinburgh University began to develop women-only courses to encourage women back to study, such as the 'New Horizons' course, which began in 1976. At the same time, articles on women's issues began to be published in the *Scottish Journal of Adult Education* and conferences were organised, such as the one held in March 1979 on 'Women, Education and Training', sponsored by the Equal Opportunities Commission and the Scottish Institute of Adult Education (SIAE). In the early 1980s, the Manpower Services Commission began to fund FE Colleges and universities to run 'Wider Opportunities for Women' courses, initially with funding for childcare provision, aimed to encourage women back to the workplace after having children (Smith, (ed.), 1979; Wilson, (ed.), 1981). In 1983, SIAE appointed Elisabeth Gerver as its first female Director, part of a more general trend towards the feminisation of the workplace. For example, Glasgow University appointed Lalage Bown as the first female Professor of Adult Education in the UK, and the first two female District Secretaries of the WEA in the UK were both in Scotland (Inglis, Cooke and Inglis, 1989, p.58; Barr, 1999, p.74).

One of the success stories of community education post-Alexander was the adult basic education service. Its origins, however, lay outside both Scotland and the community education service, in the BBC, which launched its 'On the Move' series in 1975. The television programme, centring around two removal men, was linked to a free telephone referral service and one-to-one teaching by volunteers. The adult literacy movement, which developed out of this BBC initiative, used innovative methods such as the use of television for publicity and teaching purposes, volunteer tutors and a combination of one-to-one and group teaching. In the four years between 1975 and 1979, 11,883 adult literacy students were 'dealt with' by regional authorities and voluntary organisations in Scotland – 2,826 from Glasgow, 1,347 from Lothian and 1,293 from Lanarkshire. A survey of 700 students in three divisions of Strathclyde Region showed that they fell into three main categories – the 'under achiever', the 'slow learner' and those who could read but had difficulty writing and spelling. Other adult literacy provision included work with adults with special needs, ethnic minorities, prisoners and the long-term unemployed (SED, 1980; Duncan, 1999).

Research on participation rates in adult education in Scotland in the late 1980s showed that 42 per cent of adults had taken part in some form of educational activity in Scotland since leaving school. The survey found that social class was a major determinant of participation in adult education. Some 74 per cent of socio-economic groups A and B had returned to education at some time, while 77 per cent of groups D and E had never returned to post-compulsory education (Munn and Macdonald, 1988, pp.9-11). This was in line with findings elsewhere in the UK and in the USA, that adult participation in education was clearly related to an individual's position in the social system. Research in the USA, for example, characterised adult literacy programmes as a 'creaming system', attracting only those individuals in tune with middle-class norms and values (Hayes and Darkenwald, 1988). In the early 1990s, a survey was carried out of 50 adult returners in a variety of educational settings in Scotland – higher education, further education, community education and schools. It revealed that adult returners had strongly utilitarian reasons for returning to education, similar to many of the autobiographers discussed earlier. When asked their reasons for participating in education, 24 said 'to get a better job' and 17 'to gain qualifications'. Other reasons included 'self-satisfaction', 'interest' and 'for progression'. Many people had a mixture or a hierarchy of goals (Blair, McPake and Munn, 1993). A study of adults in schools in the early 1990s claimed, 'Scotland is unique in Europe in the extent to which it promotes adult student participation in secondary schools' (Blair, McPake and Munn, 1994, p.6). Strathclyde Regional Council had a particular commitment to this policy, although financial stringency and the abolition of the regional authorities in 1996 have led to a decline in numbers taking part. Adult enrolments in daytime school classes reached a peak of 14,000 in 1990 but have fallen since then. Some 80 per cent of secondary schools in Scotland make provision for adults although many schools only have very small numbers enrolled. There is a long tradition in Scotland of the adult use of schools, dating back at least to the parochial school tradition of the eighteenth century. The encouragement of adults to re-enter school is not unrelated to demographic patterns and falling school rolls in inner-city areas.

Although many older people take part in a variety of learning activities, some programmes are geared specifically towards their particular needs and interests. They include the Discovery Scheme, a voluntary organisation based in Dundee, which is an adaptation of the Duke of Edinburgh Award Scheme for the fifty-plus group, with elements of outdoor education, community service and structured learning in its programme. In the west of Scotland, the University of Strathclyde's Senior Studies Institute organises a wide range of learning activities for the over fifties and runs an associated research programme, often with a European dimension (Coare and Thomson, 1996, pp.81–4). Another educational organisation for older people with a Scottish dimension is the University of the Third Age, a self-help organisation, which offers classes and skills teaching by members for members.

Opportunity Scotland 1998

The concept of lifelong learning was picked up by New Labour, after its election victory in 1997, as part of its strategy of 'education, education, education,' in response to globalisation. The 'Third Way' (borrowed from the Clinton administration in the USA) saw an education strategy as one way of coping with the pressures of global competition, through better schools, wider access to higher and further education and lifelong learning. Lifelong learning was seen not only as producing a better-trained workforce, but also as a way to, 'tackle social exclusion' and encourage better citizens (*Scottish Office*, 1998). These were all continuing (and unsolved) themes from the *Alexander Report*, with the imminent arrival of a Scottish Parliament in Edinburgh adding an extra twist to the tail (Cooke, 1999).

In his introduction to *Opportunity Scotland*, the then Secretary of State for Scotland, Donald Dewar, acknowledged that, 'We live in a highly competitive world characterised by fast changing technologies,' and saw lifelong learning as making, 'a major contribution in building a modern Scotland and a strong society where people understand the importance and benefits of developing their abilities and talents'. In a specific reference to globalisation, *Opportunity Scotland* registered concern that, 'jobs are changing with continually developing technology and pressure to keep up with foreign competitors' (*Scottish Office*, 1998, pp.2–4). This was hardly a new concern. James Stuart, the Scots-born pioneer of university extension at Cambridge, had drawn attention to the superiority of German technical education over Scotland as early as the 1880s (Cooke, 1998b).

The themes of *Opportunity Scotland* were raising awareness, improving access, extending participation and therefore tackling social exclusion, encouraging progression and ensuring quality. The core of the Green Paper was a ten point action plan, which included a Scottish University for Industry, a National Grid for Learning, additional students in further and higher education, new Individual Learning Accounts, the expansion of the University of the Highlands and Islands, the expansion of the New Deal and the New Futures schemes, Modern Apprenticeships, all 16–17 year olds in work to have the right to study for level 2 or equivalent, Higher Still to be established, plus a Scottish Credit and Qualifications Framework through SCOTCAT, and finally, a strategic framework for the further education sector to promote collaboration and cut down, 'needless competition' (*Scottish Office*, 1998, p.5). Many of these themes were part of existing government initiatives, which had been cobbled together in an attempt to make a coherent policy on lifelong learning. They were very 'Treasury friendly', as they generally involved public money that had already been committed, and involved very little additional public spending.

The unspoken subtext to *Opportunity Scotland,* was the failure of the Scottish education system, including schools, further and higher education institutions, and community education, to deliver significant benefits to that section of the

Scottish population that *Opportunity Scotland* referred to as the 'socially excluded', and that the *Alexander Report* had characterised as 'the non-participants' or the 'disadvantaged', over 20 years earlier. The government saw lifelong learning as an elegant solution to at least two major problems – social justice and international competitiveness. Donald Dewar's introduction spelled out, 'we ignore the economic importance of lifelong learning – for individuals, business and for national prosperity – at our peril…sustained investment in learning opportunities and training is the key to personal and business success' (*Scottish Office*, 1998, p.2). The government saw the new Scottish Parliament as being in a position, 'to influence and advance a learning society' in Scotland. Lifelong learning was part of a wider agenda to tackle social exclusion, help people back to work, and extend new learning opportunities.

The Scottish Parliament report on lifelong learning

This challenge was taken up by the new Scottish Parliament. In 2001, its Enterprise and Lifelong Learning Committee carried out an Inquiry on Lifelong Learning and published *Interim* and *Final Reports* on the Web. The Committee, which was composed of Members of the Scottish Parliament, began its inquiry on 9 July 2001 with its terms of reference:

> To inquire into the need for a long term, comprehensive strategy for continuing post-compulsory education and training in Scotland which meets the needs and aspirations of individuals and society as a whole in respect of quality, relevance, efficiency, effectiveness, accessibility, accountability, funding levels and structures and delivery mechanisms. (Scottish Parliament, 2002a)

Witnesses to the inquiry cautioned against placing, 'too much emphasis on the economic aspect of lifelong learning…seeking a broader definition encompassing the cultural, civic, individual and social inclusion aspects of lifelong learning'. The Committee agreed and decided not to adopt an upper age limit for the inquiry, focusing instead on, 'the continuous development of knowledge and skills aimed at enhancing the individual's quality of life and society's well being' (Scottish Parliament, 2002b).

The globalisation debate dominated the agenda of the inquiry, with some political spin given to social inclusion for those bypassed by global competition. Amongst the seven key questions the Committee asked at the beginning of its inquiry, five were directly related to the workplace and international competitiveness. They included, 'will the current strategic direction of lifelong learning policy meet Scotland's economic objectives' and, 'How effective and relevant are current funding mechanisms, levels, performance targets and patterns of distribution in meeting Scotland's economic and social needs?' The remaining three questions were concerned, firstly with how effective current routes and pathways through learning were in responding, 'to the changing needs of Scotland's labour markets', secondly with promoting learning opportunities in the workplace and integrating the worlds of work, education and training, and finally with, 'What can we learn from international experience of the development of lifelong learning strategies and from international benchmarks and comparisons to improve Scotland's international competitiveness?' (Scottish Parliament, 2002a, 2002b)

The reports were set in the context of rapid social and economic change. Scotland's economy had changed radically and by 2002 over 63 per cent of Gross Domestic Product originated in the service sector, 20 per cent from financial and business services alone. An ageing population meant that 80 per cent of the projected working population in 2020 were currently in employment:

> In other words, if Scotland is to have a trained, self-motivated and competitive workforce in twenty-five years time, provision will have to focus more on those currently in work than it has done in the past. (Scottish Parliament, 2002b)

Other concerns mirrored those of the *Alexander Report* and *Opportunity Scotland*. Concern for social justice largely centered on, 'learning as an important route out of poverty for individuals, their families and communities, as well as help narrow the gap between rich and poor in society'. Another concern was with citizenship, where, 'a *reasonable* lifelong learning education' (my italics) was seen as necessary to help people, 'participate actively in modern society' (Scottish Parliament, 2002a, p.4). On economic development, the Committee proposed as a key objective, 'the creation of a prosperous, high wage, high productivity, internationally competitive economy, based around high performance work practices', which sounds very like the rationale for the educational reforms carried out in Denmark from the early 1990s onwards (Cooke, 1995c).

It has to be said that the quality of argument in this *Interim Report* falls far short of the *Alexander Report* or even *Opportunity Scotland*. For example, its aim for a lifelong learning strategy was, 'to create a culture where everyone has the desire and the opportunity to continuously develop their knowledge and skills, thus enhancing their quality of life and the well being of society' (Scottish Parliament, 2002a, p.6), which is the equivalent of being in favour of motherhood and apple pie. The broader, humanistic approach that characterised the Alexander Report has been replaced by a more impoverished and jargon-ridden language. The age of Orwellian Newspeak is almost upon us.

Like the *Alexander Report,* back in 1975, the Scottish Parliament reports were concerned with, 'those who are least likely to participate in learning' and with targeting under-represented groups. They were also concerned with education for active citizenship, in the light of soaring rates of non-participation in elections. The solution to the problem of non-participation and unequal take up of educational opportunities amongst different social groups was a system of educational entitlement. Significantly though, the reports proposed that the system should be 'budget neutral', and that there was a strong case for redistribution of resources. Other proposals included streamlining financial support in further education, a Learning Smartcard, Business Learning Accounts, credit-based funding for providers and the merging of the separate funding bodies for further and higher education in Scotland.

In a strong echo of the *Alexander Report*, the Committee noted with concern that Scottish Enterprise had reported, '800,000 Scots of working age had very low literacy and numeracy skills' and that, '24 per cent of Scots in employment have no qualifications'. Like Alexander, it was concerned about this, 'tail of low achievement' and concluded, 'public policy must address the other 50 per cent'. The reports then spelled out a list of social groups who were being poorly served by the existing education system, which was virtually identical to that listed by the *Alexander Report* 27 years earlier – people from deprived backgrounds or areas, ethnic minorities, older people, those in remote or island communities, people with disabilities and those with care responsibilities (Scottish Parliament, 2002a, 2002b). Unlike *Opportunity Scotland*, the reports did acknowledge the ageing of the Scottish population, and identified a major gap in participation in education by older men, over the age of 55. They were also concerned about support for disabled learners, and the difficulties in attracting young working-class men into learning opportunities.

The Scottish Executive published its response in February 2003. It defined lifelong learning in the widest terms, 'Lifelong learning encompasses the whole range of learning: formal and informal learning, workplace learning and the skills, knowledge, attitudes and behaviour that people acquire in day-to-day experience.' It took a broad view of the potential benefits of lifelong learning, which should bring not only economic benefits but, 'the achievement of other social goals such as civic participation, sustainable development, improved health and wellbeing, reduced crime and greater social cohesion' (Scottish Executive, 2003, p.7). This view of the impact of education, particularly its ability to reduce crime, is reminiscent of the attitudes of the Scottish Enlightenment, the ministers who contributed to the *Statistical Accounts* and early adult educators such as George Miller, the Dunbar bookseller, or Robert Owen of New Lanark.

When the question was asked 'How well does the current lifelong learning system perform?' the document highlighted the 50 per cent participation rate in higher education, but pointed out that the proportion of 15–18 year olds not in employment, education or training in Scotland in 2001 was 11.8 per cent, well above the OECD average of 8.6 per cent. Significantly, only 71 per cent of this age group were in education in Scotland, compared to an average of 80 per cent for the OECD as a whole. More worrying still, some 23 per cent of adults in Scotland (800,000 people) were estimated to have low levels of literacy and numeracy skills. Of this 800,000, 650,000 were of working age and 520,000 were in employment. Here, the document set targets of improving literacy and numeracy skills of an additional 70,000 adults by 2006, in addition to the 80,000 already being helped. A good deal of faith was placed in e-learning and it was planned to expand the number of Public Internet Access Points (PIAPs) from the current number of 390, of which 196 were in areas of social exclusion. The document also identified some 3,000 'graduate practitioners' working in the field of community learning and development in Scotland in both public and voluntary agencies. It believed they had a key role to play in the overall strategy but was vague about what this role would be (Scottish Executive, 2003, pp.31–4, 42, 45–8).

Postscript

A DfEE Gallop Survey on Adult Learning in the UK in 1996 estimated that some 38 per cent of the Scottish population were current/recent learners. This was lower than the figures for England (42 per cent) but higher than those for Wales (37 per cent) or Northern Ireland (28 per cent). The survey also found that those with higher socio-economic status and more initial education and training were much more likely to return to learning than other people. Similarly, unemployed or retired people had much lower levels of participation than those in work or seeking work (Sargant, 1997; Field and Schuller, 2000). The *Lifelong Learning Strategy for Scotland* reached similar conclusions (Scottish Executive, 2003).

A declining and ageing population presents major problems for Scottish society and the Scottish economy. Most Western European societies face similar problems, but Scotland has the lowest population growth of any European country. Whereas both England and Wales have experienced a slow increase in population, the Scottish population has fallen every decade since 1971. Indeed in 2001, the Scottish population of 5,064,000 is smaller than it was in 1951. Adults in the fifty plus age group now constitute some 31 per cent of the Scottish population and it is estimated that this proportion will increase over the next 40 years. In common with other Western European countries, Scotland is also becoming a more individualistic and isolated society, certainly in terms of housing and living arrangements. Small households consisting of one or two people are now the norm, amounting to 63 per cent of all Scottish households in 2001; indeed, single person households now make up 33 per cent of all households. The family household with children is a minority. This is linked to a number of trends, common throughout Western Europe – longer life expectancy, low birthrates and higher divorce rates (Paterson, Bechhofer and McCrone, 2004, pp.10–31).

The fact that government-sponsored enquiries and reports into adult education/lifelong learning in Scotland over the last 30 years keep returning to similar themes of underachievement and lack of social justice may reflect increasing frustration by policy makers at what they see as the intractability of some of Scotland's social and economic problems. On the positive side, there are rising levels of prosperity amongst the population as a whole, there has been a cultural renaissance in many areas of the arts, and there is at last a new Parliament in Edinburgh. In education, student numbers entering higher education in Scotland are at record levels and student retention rates in higher education are amongst the best in Europe. Scottish universities still retain their international reputation for teaching and research, although with increasing difficulty because of low levels of core funding.

However, new business start up rates in Scotland remain depressingly low compared with England or many other European countries and levels of poverty, sub-standard housing, and bad health are unacceptably high by Western European standards. There is increasingly a feeling that the Scottish school system, once considered to be the jewel in the crown, does not deliver for a significant minority of the Scottish population and that education after school is failing to redress the balance. The market-driven system appeals to those who have had a longer initial education and are in work with a comfortable income. Significant groups such as working-class men, the long-term unemployed, ethnic minorities, and retired people are under-represented in adult learning activities. There is continuing interest in adult education for a more informed and participatory democracy and in addressing issues such as Scottish identity, nationhood and culture. This lies behind attempts to promote the idea of Scotland as a Learning Society and even Edinburgh as a City of Lifelong Learning, which has been associated with the biennial adult education conferences organised by the University of Edinburgh (Kirkwood, 1990 and Martin, 1996a, pp.99–113).

With so many adults entering the educational mainstream, it is becoming questionable whether there is a distinctive role for adult education institutions any longer (Thomson, 2001). The mainstreaming of university adult education provision has led to increasing emphasis on accreditation, quality assurance and conformity with existing models of degree provision. Other parts of the system, such as FE Colleges or community education, are facing similar pressures to produce a 'one size fits all' model, based on a nationwide system of competence-based credits with bureaucratically defined 'levels'. There is a paradox here in that the more adults enter the mainstream, the less 'critical space' there is for distinctive forms of adult education, including most importantly, the space to innovate and for learners to influence the curriculum themselves.

In this book, I have tried to focus on adult learners themselves, as much as on the providers of adult education and its changing institutions. This marks a conscious attempt to examine the history of adult learning from the learners' point of view, i.e. 'bottom up' rather than 'top down'. This approach highlights the distinctively Scottish/Calvinist culture of self-improvement and self-education, which has been influential world-wide because of the Scottish diaspora (Herman, 2003). The scale of emigration from Scotland meant that Scottish ideas of popular education, self-improvement and self-education were carried to many other countries, including England, Canada, the USA, Australia, New Zealand and so on. My argument is that this Smilesian culture of self-improvement, whilst having an obvious appeal to middle-class industrialists and entrepreneurs, also had great resonance with many skilled artisans, however hard it might be to live up to in real life. This challenges the assumptions underlying many previous histories of British adult education, which have emphasised the socio-political role of adult education, and its contribution towards helping the labour and trade union movement both challenge and come to terms with the economic and political system. By drawing on the accounts of learners themselves, I would argue that the book demonstrates that many adult learners were concerned at least as much with individual advancement and 'getting on' in life, as with the advancement of their social class as a whole. Indeed, the Labour movement itself was often used as a ladder of social mobility by many of its more ambitious and successful activists.

An alternative standpoint was that represented by John Maclean and other radical socialists in the early twentieth century. This challenged the idea of 'neutral' education provided by the State, arguing that, 'the working class standpoint in economics is bound to be different from that of capitalists' (Milton, (ed.), 1978). Nonetheless, it was equally rooted in Calvinistic ideals of temperance and respectability. As his daughter has pointed out, the Glasgow Highland community in which John Maclean was brought up, 'exalted those self-regarding virtues which tended to make and save money – hard work, thrift and sobriety' (Milton, 1973, p.16).

Adult and continuing education in Scotland today exhibits the same tensions as it always has between serving the needs of the economy, the interests of the individual, or fostering the democratic society. One major change is that adults have moved on to the mainstream educational agenda, although how far Labour's commitment to educational entitlement and the concept of Lifelong Learning is rhetoric rather than reality remains to be seen. However, significant shifts have taken place in the last few years and the majority of Scots now continue in either higher or further education after leaving school. Given that all the research evidence is that the longer initial education people have, the more they are likely to participate in adult education in later life, this has implications for future adult education provision in Scotland. Lifelong learning, however, is unlikely to be the educational panacea that some have claimed. A recent writer has characterised it as, 'primarily a mode of social control that acts as a new disciplinary technology to make people more compliant and adaptable for work in the era of flexible capitalism' (Crowther, 2004, p.125). Another has drawn attention to the concept of, 'the knowledge poor' and claimed, 'lifelong learning has raised the stakes, and helped embed inequality' (Field, 2000, p.113). One undoubted problem is the increasing gap between the educational 'haves' and the 'have nots', although education is simply one facet of a larger economic, social and cultural divide in Scotland, linked to poverty, unemployment, low expectations, low quality housing, bad diet, drug and alcohol abuse and poor health. It cannot be helpful that an increasing amount of adult education/lifelong learning is priced at a level suitable only for those in employment, or for employers themselves to pay. The replacement of student grants by loans in terms of financial support may also act as a disincentive against older learners re-entering full-time education.

Scotland remains a divided and contradictory society in many ways. It is a country where supporters of the national rugby and football teams sing 'Flower of Scotland', but where supporters of the two major football teams fly respectively the Union Jack and the Irish Tricolour. Glasgow is not only the city of Adam Smith, the home of great architects and designers such as Alexander 'Greek' Thomson and Charles Rennie Mackintosh but of sectarianism and Rab C. Nesbitt. Edinburgh is the city of the New Town and the Scottish Enlightenment, but also of Irvine Welsh's *Trainspotting* and the spiritual, if not the geographical, home of that powerful fable of the divided self – Robert Louis Stevenson's *Dr Jekyll and Mr Hyde*. To be effective, any vision of a Learning Society will have to appeal to people's hearts as well as to their heads, to the irrational and creative as well as to the rational and functionary. The education system in Scotland has not generally been good at doing this and the increasing emphasis on vocationalism and qualifications is in danger of erecting as many barriers to learning as it dismantles. The ultimate question remains – Dr Jekyll or Mr Hyde, which one is the lifelong learner?

References

Manuscript sources

Cambridge University Archives
Board of Extra-Mural Studies Papers (BEMS)

Mrs. Judith Cooke, Dundee
Pae Family Papers

Dornoch Heritage Society, Dornoch, Sutherland
Gilchrist of Ospidale Mss

Dundee City Archives
Memoirs of Alex Moncur, 1869

Mitchell Library, Glasgow
Autobiography of Sir Patrick Dollan – "From the miners' row to the Lord Provost's room"

Letters of John Mackinnon, Carnbroe Ironworks, to his son, James

National Library of Scotland, Edinburgh
Diary of Charles Hutcheson, 1820-1848

Notes by Janet Livingstone for Dr Blaikie

Scottish Labour College Papers

Printed sources

Books and articles

Alexander, D. Leach, TJ. and Steward, T.G. (1984) *A Study of Policy, Organisation and Provision in Community Education and Leisure and Recreation in Three Scottish Regions,* Nottingham: Department of Adult Education, University of Nottingham

Alexander, D. and Martin, I. (1995) 'Competence, curriculum and democracy', in Mayo, M. and Thompson, J., (eds.), *Adult Learning, Critical Intelligence and Social Change,* Leicester: National Institute of Adult Continuing Education (NIACE)

Alexander, W. (1992 edition) *Rural Life in Victorian Aberdeenshire,* Edinburgh: Mercat Press

Altick, D. (1957) *The English Common Reader. A Social History of the Mass Reading Public 1800-1900,* Chicago: Chicago University Press

Anderson, R.D. (1983) *Education and Opportunity in Victorian Scotland: Schools and Universities.* Edinburgh: Edinburgh University Press (EUP)

Anderson, R.D. (1995) *Education and the Scottish People,* Oxford: Clarendon Press

Anderson, R.D. (2000), 'Scottish universities', in Holmes, H. (ed.), *Scottish Life and Society: Education,* East Linton: Tuckwell Press

Baillie, M., (2000) 'The grey lady: Mary Lily Walker of Dundee'', in Miskell, L., Whatley, C.A. and Harris, B. (eds.), *Victorian Dundee. Image and Realities,* East Linton: Tuckwell Press

Bain, A. (1904) *Autobiography,* London: Longmans, Green and Company

Barclay, R. (1985) *Reminiscences of an Unlettered Man,* Aberdeen: Aberdeen University Press

Barnes, G. (1924) *From Workshop to War Cabinet,* London: Herbert Jenkins

Barr, J. (1999) 'Women, adult education and really useful knowledge', in Crowther, J., Martin, I. and Shaw, M. (eds.) *Popular Education and Social Movements in Scotland Today,* Leicester: NIACE

Bathgate, J. (1895) *Aunt Janet's Legacy: Recollections of Humble Life in Yarrow in the Beginning of the Century,* Selkirk: George Lewis

Bell, R. and Tight, M. (1993) 'The maddest folly: Scotland, the certification of Women and the St Andrews LLA', in Bell, R. and Tight, M., *Open Universities: A British Tradition?* Buckingham: Society for Research in Higher Education and Open University Press

Bell, T. (1941) *Pioneering Days,* London: Lawrence and Wishart

Bell, T. (1944) *John Maclean, Fighter for Freedom,* Glasgow

Bethune, A. and J. (1884), *Tales of the Scottish Peasantry,* London and Glasgow: Hamilton Adams and Thomas Morrison

Blair, A., McPake and Munn, P. (1993) *Facing Goliath: Adults' Experiences of Participation, Guidance and Progression in Education,* Edinburgh: Scottish Council for Research in Education (SCRE)

Blair, A., McPake, J. and Munn, P. (1994) *Adults in Schools,* Edinburgh: SCRE

Boyd, W. (1961) *Education in Ayrshire through Seven Centuries,* London: University of London Press

Bremner, D. (1869) *The Industries of Scotland. Their Rise, Progress and Present Condition,* (1969 reprint) Newton Abbott: David and Charles

Briggs, A. (1990) *Victorian People. A Reassessment of Persons and Themes 1851-67,* London: Penguin

Briggs, A. (2000) *The Age of Improvement 1783-1867,* 2nd edn London: Longmans

Brougham, H. (1825) *Practical Observations on the Education of the People,* London

Brougham, H., (1871) *The Life and Times of Henry, Lord Brougham, Written by Himself,* 3 Volumes, Edinburgh and London: Blackwood and Sons

Brown, C., (1981), 'The Sunday school movement in Scotland', *Records of the Scottish Church History Society,* 21

Brown, C. (1997) *Religion and Society in Scotland since 1707,* Edinburgh: EUP

Brown, C. (1998a) 'Religion' in Cooke, A.J., Donnachie, I., MacSween, A. and Whatley, C.A. (eds.) *Scottish History: 1707 to the Present, Vol. I, The Transformation of Scotland, 1707-1850,* East Linton: Tuckwell Press

Brown, C., (1998b), 'Religion', in Cooke, A.J., Donnachie, I., MacSween, A. and Whatley, C.A. (eds.) *Scottish History: 1707 to the Present, Vol. 2, The Modernisation of Scotland, 1850 to the Present,* East Linton: Tuckwell Press

Brown, S. (1856) *Some Account of Itinerating Libraries and their Founder,* Edinburgh

Brown, W. (1830?), *Memoir Relative to Itinerating Libraries*, Edinburgh: Waugh and Innes

Bryant, I. (1984) *Radicals and Respectables: the Adult Education Experience in Scotland*, Edinburgh: Scottish Institute of Adult and Continuing Education, (SIACE)

Bryce, T.G.K. and Humes, W.M. (eds.) (1999) *Scottish Education*, Edinburgh: Edinburgh University Press

Buchan, J. (1980) *The Expendable Mary Slessor*, Edinburgh: St Andrews Press

Burns, R. (no date) *The Works and Correspondence of Robert Burns*, Glasgow: William Mackenzie

Burnett, J., Vincent, D. & Mayall, D. (eds.) (1984-9) *The Autobiography of the Working Class: An Annotated, Critical Bibliography*, 3 Volumes, New York: New York University Press

Burt, E. (1998 edition) *Letters from a Gentleman in the North of Scotland to his Friend in London*, Edinburgh: Birlinn

Burton, J.H. (ed.) (1908-1970) *Register of the Privy Council of Scotland*, 16 Volumes, Edinburgh

Butt, J. (1996) *John Anderson's Legacy: The University of Strathclyde and its Antecedents 1796-1996*, East Linton: Tuckwell Press

Calder, A. (1996) 'Livingstone, self-help and Scotland', in Mackenzie, J.M. and Skipwith, J. (eds.), *David Livingstone and the Victorian Encounter with Africa*, London: National Portrait Gallery

Cameron, W. (1888) *Hawkie, the Autobiography of a Gangrel*, Glasgow: David Robertson

Campbell, A.B. (1979) *The Lanarkshire Miners: A Social History of their Trade Unions 1778-1874*, Edinburgh: John Donald

Campbell, C. (1828) *Memoirs of Charles Campbell at Present Prisoner in the Jail of Glasgow. Including his Adventures as a Seaman and as an Overseer in the West Indies*, Glasgow: James Duncan

Campbell, I. (1974) *Thomas Carlyle*, London: Hamish Hamilton

Campbell, R.H. (1982) 'The enlightenment and the economy', in Campbell, R.H. and Skinner, A.S. (eds.), *The Origins and Nature of the Scottish Enlightenment*, Edinburgh: John Donald

Carlyle, T. (1831) *Sartor Resartus: The Life and Opinions of Herr Teufelsdnochel* (1896 edition) London: Chapman and Hall

Carlyle, T. (1843) *Past and Present*, (1897 edition), London: Chapman and Hall

Carlyle, T. (1887) *Reminiscences*, London: Macmillan

Carlyle, T. (1894 edition) 'Chartism', in *Critical and Miscellaneous Essays*, Vol. VI, London: Chapman and Hall

Carnegie, A. (1920) *Autobiography*, London: Constable

Carruthers, G. (1998) 'Culture', in Cooke, A. J., Donnachie, I., MacSween, A. and Whatley, C. A. (eds.), *Modern Scottish History 1707 to the Present*, Vol. 1, East Linton: Tuckwell Press

Carter, I. (1976) 'The Mutual Improvement Movement in North East Scotland in the nineteenth century', *Aberdeen University Review*, XLVI, No. 4

Chambers, W. (1967 edition) *Memoirs of the Chambers Brothers*, London: Galahad Press

Clark, A. (1995) *The Struggle for the Breeches. Gender and the Making of the British Working Class*, Berkeley: University of California Press

Claxton, T. (1839) *Hints to Mechanics on Self Education and Mutual Instruction*, London: Taylor and Walton

Clunie, J. (1954) *Labour is my Faith. The Autobiography of a House Painter,* Dunfermline: Romanes

Coare, P. and Thomson, A. (eds.) (1996) *Through the Joy of Learning: Diary of 1,000 adult learners,* Leicester: NIACE

Cobbett, W., (1833) *A Tour in Scotland,* (1984 edition) Aberdeen: Aberdeen University Press,

Cochrane, C. and Stewart, D. M. (1944) *Survey of Adult Education in Scotland 1938-1939,* Edinburgh: British Institute of Adult Education (Scottish Branch)

Cockburn, H. (1856) *Memorials of his Time,* Edinburgh: Adam and Charles Black

Cockburn, H. (1874) *Journal of Henry Cockburn,* 2 Volumes, Edinburgh: Edmonton and Douglas

Combe, A. (1824) (reprinted 1972) 'The religious creed of the new system', in *Motherwell and Orbiston: Three Pamphlets,* New York: Arno Press

Combe, A. (1825) (reprinted 1972) 'The way to increase the value of land, capital and labour. With an account of the establishment at Orbiston in Lanarkshire', in *Motherwell and Orbiston: Three Pamphlets,* New York: Arno Press

Cooke, A.J. (ed.) (1980) *Baxters of Dundee,* Dundee: Department of Extra Mural Education, University of Dundee

Cooke, A.J. (1995a) 'Cotton and the Scottish Highland clearances – the development of Spinningdale 1791-1806', *Textile History,* 26(1): 89–94

Cooke, A.J. (1995b) 'From Grundtvig to Gradgrind - Danish and Scottish models of access compared', *Journal of Access Studies,* 10(1)

Cooke, A.J. (1995c) 'Denmark', in Davies, P. (ed.), *Adults in Higher Education, International Perspectives in Access and Participation,* London: Jessica Kingsley

Cooke, A.J. (1998a) 'Lifelong learning policy in Scotland", in Taylor, R. and Watson, D. (eds.), *Lifelong Learning Policy in the UK. UACE Occasional Paper No 23,* Cambridge: Universities' Council for Adult and Continuing Education (UACE)

Cooke, A.J. (1998b) 'James Stuart and the origins of English university extension', in Friedenthal-Haase, M. (ed.), *Personality and Biography: Proceedings of the Sixth International Conference on the History of Adult Education,* Frankfurt: Peter Lang

Cooke, A.J. and Donnachie, I. (1998) 'Industrialisation in Scotland 1707–1850', in Cooke, A.J., Donnachie, I., MacSween, A. and Whatley, C.A., (eds.), *Modern Scottish History 1707 to the Present,* Vol. I, East Linton: Tuckwell Press

Cooke, A.J., (1999) 'Opportunity Scotland – Lifelong learning and the Scottish universities', *Scottish Journal of Adult and Continuing Education (SJACE),* 5(2): 77–88

Cooke, A.J. (2000a) 'Adult and continuing education in Scotland', in Holmes, H. (ed.), *Scottish Life and Society: Education,* East Linton: Tuckwell Press

Cooke, A.J. (2000b) 'Scotland and the 1919 report', in Cooke, A.J. and MacSween, A. (eds.), *The Rise and Fall of Adult Education Institutions and Social Movements,* Frankfurt: Peter Lang

Cooke, A.J. (2001) 'Patrick Geddes and the concept of citizenship', in Bron, M. and Field, J. (eds.), *Adult Education and Democratic Citizenship III,* Wroclaw: Lower Silesian University College of Education

Cooke, A.J. (2002) 'Samuel Smiles and the ideology of Self Help' in Nemeth, B. and Poggeler, F. (eds.), *Ethics, Ideals and Ideologies in the History of Adult Education,* Frankfurt: Peter Lang

Cooke, A.J. (2004) 'From adult education to lifelong learning: changing policy frameworks for adult education in Scotland, 1975-2002', in Hake, B., Van Gent, B. and Katus, J. (eds.), *Adult Education and Globalisation: Past and Present,* Frankfurt: Peter Lang

Craik, G.L. (1830) *The Pursuit of Knowledge under Difficulties,* London: Charles Knight

Crowther, J., Martin, I. and Shaw, M. (eds.) (1999) *Popular Education and Social Movements in Scotland Today,* Leicester: NIACE

Crowther, J. (2004) '"In and Against", lifelong learning, flexibility and the corrosion of character', *International Journal of Lifelong Learning,* 23(2)

Davie, G. E. (1964) *The Democratic Intellect. Scotland and her Universities in the Nineteenth Century,* 2nd Edition, Edinburgh: Edinburgh University Press

Davie, G. E. (1986) *The Crisis of the Democratic Intellect. The Problem of Generalism and Specialisation in Twentieth Century Scotland,* Edinburgh: Polygon

Davies, N. (1997) *Europe. A History,* London: Pimlico

Davies, P. (ed.) (1995) *Adults in Higher Education: International Perspectives in Access and Participation,* London: Jessica Kingsley

Defoe, D. (1717), *Memoirs of the Church of Scotland,* (1844 edition) Perth: James Dewar

Defoe, D. (1724-6) *A Tour Through the Whole Island of Great Britain,* (1971 edition) London: Penguin

Devine, T.M. (ed.) (1991) *Irish Immigrants and Scottish Society in the Nineteenth and Twentieth Centuries,* Edinburgh: John Donald

Devine, T.M., (1999) *The Scottish Nation 1700-2000,* London: Penguin

Dick, T. (1824) *The Christian Philosopher: The Connection of Science and Philosophy with Religion,* Glasgow and London: Collins

Dick, T. (1833) *On the Improvement of Society by the Diffusion of Knowledge,* (1869 edition) Glasgow: William Collins

Dickinson, W. Croft (ed.) (1949) *John Knox's History of the Reformation in Scotland,* 2 Volumes, London: Thomas Nelson

Donaldson, W. (1986) *Popular Literature in Victorian Scotland,* Aberdeen: Aberdeen University Press

Donnachie, I. (1979) 'Drink and society 1750-1850: some aspects of the Scottish experience', *Scottish Labour History Society Journal,* 13: 5–22

Donnachie, I. (2000) *Robert Owen. Owen of New Lanark and Harmony,* East Linton: Tuckwell Press

Donnachie, I. (forthcoming) *Robert Owen and New Lanark: The Lessons of History*

Ducklin, A. and Wallace, S. (2000) 'Ivory tower or wasted asset? Why did residential adult education fail to take root in Scotland?' in Cooke, A.J. and MacSween, A. (eds.), *The Rise and Fall of Adult Education Institutions and Social Movements,* Frankfurt: Peter Lang

Duncan, R. and McIvor, A. (eds.) (1992), *Militant Workers. Labour and Class Conflict on the Clyde 1900-1950,* Edinburgh: John Donald

Duncan, R. (1992) 'Independent working class education and the formation of the Labour College Movement in Glasgow and the west of Scotland, 1915-1922', in Duncan R. and McIvor, A. (eds.), *Militant Workers. Labour and Class Conflict on the Clyde 1900-1950,* Edinburgh: John Donald

Duncan, R. (1999) 'A critical history of the Workers' Educational Association in Scotland, 1905-1993', in Crowther, J., Martin, I. and Shaw, M. (eds.), *Popular Education and Social Movements in Scotland Today,* Leicester: NIACE

Duncan, R., (2003) 'Ideology and provision: the WEA and the politics of workers' education in early twentieth century Scotland', in Roberts, S. K. (ed.), *A Ministry of Enthusiasm. Centenary Essays on the Workers' Educational Association,* London: Pluto Press

Edwards, R. (1997) *Changing Places? Flexibility, Lifelong Learning and a Learning Society,* London: Routledge

Farquhar, B. (A Labourer's Daughter) (1848) *The Pearl of Days or the Advantages of the Sabbath to the Working Classes,* London: Partridge and Oakey

Ferguson, W. (1978 edition) *Scotland 1689 to the Present,* Edinburgh: Oliver and Boyd

Field, J. (2000) *Lifelong Learning and the New Educational Order,* Stoke on Trent: Trentham Books

Field, J. and Schuller, T. (1995) 'Is there less adult learning in Scotland and Northern Ireland? A preliminary analysis', *Scottish Journal of Adult and Continuing Education,* 2(2): 71–80

Field, J. and Schuller, T. (2000) 'Networks, norms and trust: explaining patterns of lifelong learning in Scotland and Northern Ireland', in Coffield, F. (ed.), *Differing Visions of a Learning Society: Research Findings,* Volume 2, Bristol: Policy Press

Fieldhouse, R. (1996) *A History of Modern British Adult Education,* Leicester: NIACE

Fiennes, C. (1982 edition) *The Illustrated Journeys of Celia Fiennes, c. 1682-c. 1712,* London: Macdonald

Fife County Council (1964) *Report by Working Party on Adult Education,* Fife: Fife County Council

Fisher, D. (1999), '"A band of little comrades": socialist Sunday schools in Scotland"', in Crowther, J., Martin, I. and Shaw, M. (eds.), *Popular Education and Social Movements in Scotland Today.* Leicester: NIACE

Fleming, Sir J. (1922) *Looking Backwards for Seventy Years 1921-1851,* Aberdeen: Aberdeen University Press

Flinn, M.W. (ed.) (1977) *Scottish Population History from the Seventeenth Century to the 1930s,* Cambridge: Cambridge University Press

Foster, J. (1992) 'Red Clydeside, Red Scotland', in Donnachie, I. and Whatley, C. A. (eds.), *The Manufacture of Scottish History,* Edinburgh: Polygon

Foster, J. (1998) 'Class', in Cooke, A.J. et al. (eds.), *Modern Scottish History 1707 to the Present, Volume 2: The Modernisation of Scotland, 1850 to the Present,* East Linton: Tuckwell Press

Fraser, D. (ed.) (1988) *The Christian Watt Papers,* Collieston: Caledonian Books

Fraser, W.H. (1988) *Conflict and Class: Scottish Workers 1700-1838,* Edinburgh: John Donald

Fraser, W.H., (1990), 'Developments in leisure' in Fraser, W.H. and Morris, R.J. (eds.), *People and Society in Scotland Volume II 1830-1914,* Edinburgh: John Donald

Fraser, W.H. (1998) 'Social Class', in Cooke, A.J. et al. (eds.), *Modern Scottish History 1707 to the Present, Volume 1, The Transformation of Scotland: 1707 to 1850,* East Linton: Tuckwell Press

Fraser, W.H. (2000), *Scottish Popular Politics,* Edinburgh: Polygon

Freer, W. (1929) *My Life and Memoirs,* Glasgow: Civic Press

Friedenthal-Haase, M. (2000) 'Mediating an institutional and professional identity between reich and region: The Thuringian Association of folk high schools in the Weimar Republic 1919-1933', in Cooke, A.J. and MacSween, A. (eds.), *The Rise and Fall of Adult Education Institutions and Social Movements,* Frankfurt: Peter Lang

Fyffe, J.G. (ed.) (1942) *Scottish Diaries and Memoirs 1746-1843*, Stirling: Eaneas Mackay

Fyffe, J. (ed.) (1980) *Autobiography of John McAdam (1806-1883) with Selected Letters,* Edinburgh: Scottish History Society

Gallacher, W. (1936) *Revolt on the Clyde*, London: Lawrence and Wishart

Gallacher, W. (1966) *Last Memoirs,* London: Lawrence and Wishart

Galloway, V. (1999) 'Building a pedagogy of hope: the experience of the adult learning project', in Crowther, J., Martin, I. and Shaw, M. (eds.), *Popular Education and Social Movements in Scotland Today,* Leicester: NIACE

Galt, J. (1821) *Annals of the Parish*, (1919 edition) London and Edinburgh: T. N. Foulis

Gauldie, E. (ed.) (1969) *The Dundee Textile Industry 1790-1885: From the Papers of Peter Carmichael of Arthurstone,* Edinburgh: Scottish History Society

Geddes, P. (1890) *Scottish University Needs and Aims. Closing Address at University College, Dundee,* Perth: Cowath and Co.

Geddes, P. (1904) *City Development. A Study of Parks, Gardens and Cultural Institutes. A Report to the Carnegie Dunfermline Trust,* Birmingham: St George's Press

Geddes, P. (1911) *The Civic Survey of Edinburgh*, Edinburgh: University of Edinburgh

Geddes, P. (1913) *The Masque of Mediaeval and Modern Learning,* Edinburgh: The Outlook Tower

Geddes, P. (1915) *Cities in Evolution. An Introduction to the Town Planning Movement and the Study of Civics,* London: William Norgate

Gerver, E. (1992) 'Scotland', in Jarvis, P. (ed.), *Perspectives on Adult Education and Training in Europe*, Leicester: NIACE

Gifford, D. and McMillan, D. (eds.) (1997) *A History of Scottish Women's Writing,* Edinburgh: EUP

Gilmour, D. (1876) *Paisley Weavers of other Days, The Pen Folk,* Paisley and London: Alex Gardner (Paisley) and Houlton and Sons (London)

Glasgow Museum Service (1998) *The People's Palace Book of Glasgow*, Edinburgh: Mainstream

Goldman, L. (1995) *Dons and Workers, Oxford and Adult Education since 1850,* Oxford: Clarendon Press

Gramsci, A. (1973), *Letters from Prison,* New York: Harper and Row

Grosart, A. (ed.), (1865) *The Works of Michael Bruce*, Edinburgh: William Oliphant

Guthrie, T. (ed.) (1858), *The Street Preacher. The Autobiography of Robert Flockhart,* Edinburgh: Adam and Charles Black

Guthrie, T. (1877) *Autobiography and Memoir*, London: Daldy, Isbister and Co

Hamilton, J., (1868) *Poems and Ballads,* Glasgow: James Maclehose

Hammond, W. (1904) *Recollections of a Glasgow Handloom Weaver*, Glasgow: Citizen Press

Harrison, J.F.C. (1961) *Learning and Living, 1790-1960. A Study in the History of the Adult Education Movement,* London: Routledge and Kegan Paul

Harrison, J.F.C. (1969) *Robert Owen and the Owenites in Britain and America. The Quest for the New Moral World,* London: Routledge and Kegan Paul

Harrison, J.F.C. (1971) *Underground Education in the Nineteenth Century. The Eighth Mansbridge Memorial Lecture,* Leeds: Leeds University Press

Harvie, C. (1994) *Scotland and Nationalism: Scottish Society and Politics 1707-1994,* (2nd edition), London

Harvie, C. (1998) 'Culture and Identity', in Cooke, A.J. et al. (eds.), *Modern Scottish History 1707 to the Present, Vol. 2, The Modernisation of Scotland 1850 to the Present,* East Linton: Tuckwell Press

Harvey, W.S. and Downs-Rose, G. (1980) *William Symington. Inventor and Engine Builder,* London: Northgate Publishing

Hayes, E. and Darkenwald G.G. (1988) 'Participation in basic education: deterrents for low literate adults', *Studies in the Education of Adults,* 20(1)

Herman, A. (2003) *The Scottish Enlightenment: The Scots' Invention of the Modern World,* London: Fourth Estate

Hodgson, G.B., (1908) *From Smithy to Senate: The Life Story of James Annand, Journalist and Politician,* London: Cassell and Co.

Hogg, J. (1972 edition) *Memories of the Author's Life and Familiar Anecdotes of Sir Walter Scott,* Edinburgh: Scottish Academic Press

Hollis, P. (1997) *Jennie Lee: A Life,* Oxford: Oxford University Press

Holmes, H. (ed.) (2000) *Scottish Life and Society: Education,* East Linton: Tuckwell Press

Hope, J. (1851) *The British League Evening Classes or Water versus Whisky and Tobacco. An Answer to the Right Honourable Fox Maule, the Duke of Argyll and Rev Thomas Guthrie,* Edinburgh: Blackwood

Horobin, J. (1980) 'Adult education in Scotland from 1968 to 1978', *Scottish Journal of Adult Education,* 4(4): 5–15

Horobin, J. (1983a) 'Adult Education in Scotland from 1976 to 1981', *Scottish Journal of Adult Education,* 6(1): 5–10

Horobin, J. (1983b) 'The education of adults in Scotland', in Tight, M., (ed.), *Education for Adults, Volume II: Educational Opportunities for Adults,* (reprinted 1990) London: Routledge

Houston, R.A. (1985) *Scottish Literacy and Scottish Identity: Illiteracy and Society in Scotland and Northern England 1600-1800,* Cambridge: Cambridge University Press

Houston, R.A. (1994) *Social Change in the Age of Enlightenment: Edinburgh, 1660-1760,* Oxford: Clarendon Press

Hudson, J.W. (1851) *The History of Adult Education* (1969 reprint), London: Woburn Press

Inglis, J, Cooke, A.J. and Inglis, A. (1989) *Pulling Together in Adult Education. A History of the Scottish Institute of Adult and Continuing Education 1949-1989,* Edinburgh: SIACE

Ireland, J. (1878) *The Life of a Dundee Draper,* Dundee: W. Kidd

Jacobsen, B. (1992) 'Denmark', in Jarvis, P. (ed.) *Perspectives on Adult Education and Training in Europe,* Leicester: NIACE

Jackson, K. (1995) 'Popular education and the state: a new look at the community debate', in Mayo, M. and Thompson, J. (eds.) *Adult Learning, Critical Intelligence and Social Change,* Leicester: NIACE

Jackson, T.A. (1953) *Solo Trumpet. Some Memories of Socialist Agitation and Propaganda,* London: Lawrence and Wishart

James, P. (ed.) (1966) *The Travel Diaries of Thomas Robert Malthus,* Cambridge: Cambridge University Press for the Royal Economic Society

Johnson, R. (1979) '"Really useful knowledge": radical education and working class culture, 1790-1848', in Clarke, J., Critcher, C. and Johnson, R. (eds.) *Working-Class Culture: Studies in History and Theory,* London: Hutchinson

Johnson, S. (1775) *A Journey to the Western Islands of Scotland,* (1984 edition) London: Penguin

Johnston, E. (1867) *Autobiography: Poems and Songs of Ellen Johnston, the 'Factory Girl',* Glasgow, published by subscription

Jolly, W. (1883), *The Life of John Duncan, Scotch Weaver and Botanist,* London, Kegan, Paul, Trench

Kelly, T. (1957) *George Birkbeck, Pioneer of Adult Education,* Liverpool: Liverpool University Press

Kelly, T. (1973) *A History of Public Libraries in Great Britain 1845-1965,* London: The Library Association

Kelly, T. (1992) *A History of Adult Education in Great Britain,* (3rd edn) Liverpool: Liverpool University Press

Kenefick, B. (1998) 'Demography', in Cooke, A.J. et al (eds.), *Modern Scottish History 1707 to the Present Volume 2: The Modernisation of Scotland, 1850 to the Present,* East Linton: Tuckwell Press

Kett, J. (1994) *The Pursuit of Knowledge under Difficulties. From Self Improvement to Adult Education in America 1750-1990,* Stanford: Stanford University Press

King, E. (1987) 'Popular culture in Glasgow', in Cage, R.A. (ed.), *The Working Class in Glasgow 1750-1914,* London: Croom Helm

Kirkwood, C. (1990) *Vulgar Eloquence: From Labour to Liberation. Essays on Education, Community and Politics,* Edinburgh: Polygon

Kirkwood, D. (1935) *My Life of Revolt,* London: Harrap

Kirkwood, G. and Kirkwood, C. (1989) *Living Adult Education: Freire in Scotland,* Milton Keynes: Open University Press

Knox, W.W. (ed.) (1984) *Scottish Labour Leaders 1918-39: A Bibliographical Dictionary,* Edinburgh: Mainstream Publishing

Knox, W.W. (1990) 'The political and workplace culture of the Scottish working class, 1832-1914', in Fraser, W.H. and Morris, R.J. (eds.), *People and Society in Scotland, Vol. II, 1830-1914,* Edinburgh: John Donald

Knox, W.W. (1999) *Industrial Nation: Work, Culture and Society in Scotland, 1800-Present,* Edinburgh: EUP

Lally, P. *Lazarus Only Done it Once,* London: Harper Collins

Laqueur, T. (1976) *Religion and Respectability: Sunday Schools and Working Class Culture 1780-1850,* New Haven: Yale University Press

Laslett, P. (1969) 'Scottish weavers, cobblers and miners who bought books in the 1750s', *Local Population Studies,* 3

Lee, J. (1963) *This Great Journey,* London: MacGibbon and Kee

Leech, M. (1999) 'Further education in Scotland post-incorporation', in Bryce, T.G.K. and Humes, W.M. (eds.), *Scottish Education,* Edinburgh: EUP

Lenman, B.P. (1981) *Integration, Enlightenment and Industrialisation: Scotland 1746-1832,* London: Arnold

Leonard, T. (1990) *Radical Renfrew: Poetry from the French Revolution to the First World War,* Edinburgh: Polygon

Lewis, G. (1834) *Scotland: A Half Educated Nation,* Glasgow: William Collins

Lewis, G. (1902) *The Life Story of Aunt Janet (Authoress of 'Aunt Janet's Legacy'),* Selkirk: James Lewis

Lindsay, M. (1968) *Robert Burns 1759-1796,* 2nd edn, London: MacGibbon and Kee

Little, J. (1792) *The Scotch Milkmaid: Poetical Works,* Ayr, published by subscription

Livingstone, D. (1857) *Missionary Travels and Researches in South Africa,* London: John Murray

Lockridge, K.A., (1974) *Literacy in colonial New England,* New York

Logue, K.J. (1979) *Popular Disturbances in Scotland 1780-1815,* Edinburgh: John Donald

Lucas, J. (1920) *Co-operation in Scotland,* Manchester: Co-operative Union Limited

McConnell, C. (ed.) (1997), *Community Education: The Making of an Empowering Profession,* Aberdeen: Scottish Community Education Council

Macdonald, J. (1927) *Memoirs of an Eighteenth Century Footman,* London: Routledge and Sons

Macdonald, M. (1999) 'The significance of the Scottish generalist tradition', in Crowther, J., Martin, I., and Shaw, M. (eds.), *Popular Education and Social Movements in Scotland Today,* Leicester: NIACE

Macdonald, M. (2000a) 'The patron, the professor and the painter: cultural activity in Dundee at the close of the nineteenth century', in Miskell, L., Whatley, C.A., and Harris, B. (eds.), *Victorian Dundee: Image and Realities,* East Linton: Tuckwell Press

Macdonald, M. (2000b) *Scottish Art,* London: Thames and Hudson

MacDougall, I. (1985) *Labour in Scotland. A Pictorial History from the Eighteenth Century to the Present,* Edinburgh: Mainstream

McGonagall, W. (1969 edition) *Poetic Gems, More Poetic Gems and Last Poetic Gems: With Biographical Sketch and Reminiscences by the Author,* Dundee: David Winter

Macgregor, G. (ed.) (1883) *The Collected Writings of Dougal Graham: 'Skellat' Bellman of Glasgow,* 2 volumes, Glasgow: Thomas Morison

McIlroy, J. (1996) 'Independent Working Class Education', in Fieldhouse, R. et al., *A History of Modern British Adult Education,* Leicester: NIACE

McIlroy, J. and Westwood, S. (eds.) (1993) *Border Country. Raymond Williams in Adult Education,* Leicester: NIACE

Maclaren, A.A. (1967) 'Presbyterianism and the working classes in nineteenth century Scotland', *Scottish Historical Review,* 46: 115–39

Maclean, I. (1975) *Keir Hardie,* London: Allen Lane

Maclean, I. (1983) *The Legend of Red Clydeside,* Edinburgh

McPherson, A. (1983) 'An angle on the geist: persistence and change in the Scottish educational tradition", in Humes W.M. and Paterson, H.M. (eds.), *Scottish Culture and Scottish Education 1800-1980,* Edinburgh: John Donald

McShane, H. (1978) *No Mean Fighter,* London: Pluto Press

Malthus, T.R. (1826, 6th edition), 'An essay on the principles of population', Part II, in Wrigley, E.A., and Souden, D. (eds.) (1986), *The Works of Thomas Robert Malthus,* London: William Pickering

Marquand, D. (1977) *Ramsay Macdonald,* London: Jonathan Cape

Martin, I. (1996a) 'Creating space for the "Democratic Intellect": the Edinburgh biennial adult education conference', *Scottish Journal of Adult and Continuing Education,* 3(2): 99–113

Martin, I. (1996b) 'Community education: the dialectics of development', in Fieldhouse, R. et al., *A History of Modern British Adult Education,* Leicester: NIACE

Martin, I. (1999) 'Introductory essay. popular education and social movements in Scotland today', in Crowther, J., Martin, I. and Shaw, M. (eds.), *Popular Education and Social Movements in Scotland Today,* Leicester: NIACE

Marwick, W.H., (1930) 'Early adult education in the west of Scotland', *Journal of Adult Education,* 4(2): 191–202

Marwick, W.H. (1931) 'Adult education in Glasgow eighty years on', *Proceedings of the Royal Philosophical Society of Glasgow*, Vol. LIX: 87–94

Marwick, W.H. (1932) 'Early adult education in Edinburgh', *Journal of Adult Education*, 5(4): 389–404

Marwick, W.H. (1933a) 'Adult Education in Victorian Scotland', *Journal of Adult Education*, 6: 130–8

Marwick, W.H. (1933b) 'Mechanics' institutes in Scotland', *Journal of Adult Education*, 6: 292–309

Marwick, W.H. (1967) *A Short History of Labour in Scotland*, Edinburgh: W. & R. Chambers

Maxwell, W. (1910) *The History of Co-operation in Scotland*, Glasgow: Co-operative Union

Meller, H. (1993) *Patrick Geddes: Social Evolutionist and City Planner*, London: Routledge

Mill, J.S. (1994 edition) *Principles of Political Economy*, Oxford: Oxford University Press

Millar, J.P.M. (1979) *The Labour College Movement*, London: NCLC Publishing Society

Miller, G. (1833) *Latter Struggles in the Journey of Life*, Edinburgh: James Colston

Miller, H. (1847) *First Impressions of England*, London: John Johnstone

Miller, H. (1874) *My Schools and Schoolmasters*, London and Edinburgh: William Nimmo

Mills, C.W. (1959) *The Power Elite*, New York: Galaxy

Milne, W.J. (1901) *Reminiscences of an Old Boy. Autobiographical Sketches of Scottish Rural Life 1832-1856,* Forfar: John Macdonald

Milton, N. (1973) *John Maclean*, London: Pluto Press

Milton, N. (ed.) (1978) *John Maclean in the Rapids of Revolution. Essays, articles and letters, 1902-23,* London: Alison and Busby

Ministry of Reconstruction (1980 edition) *The 1919 Report: Final and Interim Reports of the Adult Education Committee,* Nottingham: University of Nottingham

Moffat, A. (1965) *My Life with the Miners,* London: Lawrence and Wishart

Moore, L. (2000) 'Women in education', in Holmes, H. (ed.), *Scottish Life and Society: Institutions of Scotland. Education,* East Linton: Tuckwell Press

Muir, E. (1940) *The Story and the Fable*, London: Harrap

Muir, E. (1954) *An Autobiography*, London: Hogarth

Muir, J. (1913) *The Story of My Boyhood and Youth*, Boston and New York: Houghton Mifflin

Munn, P. and Macdonald, C. (1988) *Adult Participation in Education and Training*, Edinburgh: SCRE

Munn, P. Tett, L. and Arney, N. (1993) *Negotiating the Labyrinth: Progression Opportunities for Adult Learners*, Edinburgh: SCRE

Murray, N. (1978) *The Scottish Handloom Weavers 1790-1850: A Social History*, Edinburgh: John Donald

Myles, J. (1850) *Rambles in Forfarshire, Sketches in Town and Country*, Dundee: James Myles

New, C. (1961) *The Life of Henry Brougham to 1830*, Oxford: Clarendon Press

New Statistical Account of Scotland (1845) Vol. VI, Lanarkshire, Vol. XII, Aberdeenshire, Vol. XIII, Banff, Elgin, Nairn, Edinburgh and London: William Blackwood and Sons

Nicolson, J. (1932) *Arthur Anderson, A Founder of the P. and O. Company*, Lerwick: T. and J. Manson

Open University (1976) *Report of the Committee on Continuing Education*, Milton Keynes: Open University Press

Osborne, M. & Gallacher, J., (1995), "Scotland", in Davies, P., (ed.), *Adults in Higher Education*, London, Jessica Kingsley

Osborne, M. and Edwards, R. (2003) 'Inquiry into lifelong learning', *Journal of Adult and Continuing Education*, 8(2): 165–78

Owen, R. (1966 edition) *A New View of Society and Other Writings*, London: J.M. Dent

Owen, R.D. (1824) 'An outline of the system of education at New Lanark', in *Robert Owen at New Lanark 1824-1838*, (1972 reprint), New York: Arno Press

Pae, D. (1858) *Lucy the Factory Girl; or The Secrets of the Tontine Close*, (2001 edn), Hastings: Sensation Press

Paine, T. (1995 edition) *The Rights of Man, Common Sense and Other Political Writings*, Oxford: Oxford University Press

Paterson, L. (2003) *Scottish Education in the Twentieth Century*, Edinburgh: EUP

Paterson, L., Bechhofer, F. and McCrone, D. (2004) *Living in Scotland: Social and Economic Change since 1980*, Edinburgh: EUP

Paterson, J. (1871) *Autobiographical Reminiscences: Including Recollections of the Radical Years in Kilmarnock*, Glasgow: Maurice Ogle

Paton, J.G. (1889) *Missionary to the New Hebrides*, (reprinted 1994), Cambridge: Banner of Truth Trust

Payne, P.L. (1998) 'Industrialisation and industrial decline', in Cooke, A.J., Donnachie, I., MacSween A. and Whatley C.A. (eds.), *Modern Scottish History 1707 to the Present, Vol. 2: The Modernisation of Scotland, 1850 to the Present*, East Linton: Tuckwell Press

Penny, G. (1836) *Traditions of Perth*, (1986 edition) Coupar Angus: Culross Press

Pollard, S. (1963) 'Factory discipline in the industrial revolution', *Economic History Review*, Vol. XVI: 254–71

Ramsay, J. (1888) *Scotland and Scotsmen in the Eighteenth Century*, Vol. II, Edinburgh and London

Reid, A. (1978) 'Newbattle – Scotland's Residential College', *Scottish Journal of Adult Education*, 4(1): 23–6

Reid, J. (1976) *Reflections of a Clyde-Built Man*, London: Souvenir Press

Roberton, H.S. and Robertson, K. (eds.) (1963) *Orpheus with his Lute: A Glasgow Orpheus Choir Anthology*, London: Pergamon

Roberts, S.K. (ed.) (2003) *A Ministry of Enthusiasm: Centenary Essays on the Workers' Educational Association*, London: Pluto Press

Rodger, R. (1998) 'Concentration and fragmentation: capital, labour and the structure of mid-Victorian Scottish industry', in Cooke, A.J. et al (eds.), *Modern Scottish History 1707 to the Present, Vol. IV, Readings*, East Linton: Tuckwell Press

Rose, J. (2002) *The Intellectual Life of the British Working Classes*, New Haven and London: Yale University Press, Nota Bene

Ross, D. (2002) *David Livingstone. Mission and Empire*, London: Hambledon

Rubenson, K. (1992), 'Sweden', in Jarvis, P. (ed.) *Perspectives on Adult Education and Training in Europe*, Leicester: NIACE

Sargant, N. (1996) 'The Open University', in Fieldhouse, R. et al., *A History of Modern British Adult Education*, Leicester: NIACE

Sargant, N. (1997) *The Learning Divide*, Leicester: NIACE

Saunders, L.J. (1950) *Scottish Democracy 1815-1840*, Edinburgh: Oliver and Boyd

Scottish Community Education Council (1995) *Scotland as a Learning Society*, Edinburgh: Scottish Community Education Council

Scottish Education Department (1975) *Adult Education: The Challenge of Change. Report of* a Committee of Inquiry under the Chairmanship of Prof. K.J.W. Alexander, Edinburgh: HMSO

Scottish Education Department (1980) Adult Literacy in Scotland, Edinburgh: HMSO

Scottish Executive (2003) The Lifelong Learning Strategy for Scotland, Edinburgh: HMSO

Scottish Historical Review (1920) 'The Fenwick Improvement of Knowledge Society', SHR, 17: 118–35

Scottish Institute of Adult Education (1968) Report by the Working Party on the Finance of Adult Education in Scotland, Edinburgh: SIAE

Scottish Office (1998) Opportunity Scotland: A Paper on Lifelong Learning, Edinburgh: HMSO

Scottish Office Education Department (1992) The Education of Adults in Scotland, Edinburgh: HMSO

Scottish Parliament (2002a) Interim Report on the Lifelong Learning Inquiry, Enterprise and Lifelong Learning Committee of the Scottish Parliament, www.scottish.parliament.uk/official-report/cttee/ enter-02

Scottish Parliament (2002b) Final Report on the Lifelong Learning Inquiry, Enterprise and Lifelong Learning Committee, http://www.scottish.parliament.uk/official-report/cttee/enter-02/elr02-09-01.htm

Schafe, M. (1982), University Education in Dundee 1881-1981, Dundee: University of Dundee

Shaw, M. and Crowther, J. (1995) 'Beyond Subversion', in Mayo, M. and Thompson, J. (eds.) Adult Learning, Critical Intelligence and Social Change, Leicester: NIACE

Shearer, G. (1969) 'The universities and adult education in Scotland', Studies in Adult Education, 1(2): 140–56

Sher, R.B. (1995) 'Commerce, religion and the enlightenment in eighteenth century Glasgow', in Devine, T.M. and Jackson, G. (eds.), Glasgow: Vol. I: Beginnings to 1830, Manchester: Manchester University Press

Shinwell, E. (1955), Conflict without Malice, London: Odhams Press

Shinwell, E. (1981) Lead with the Left, My First Ninety Six Years, London: Cassell

Silver, H. (1965) The Concept of Popular Education: A Study of Ideas and Social Movements in the Early Nineteenth Century, London: Macgibbon and Kee

Simon, B. (1960) Studies in the History of Education 1780-1870, London: Lawrence and Wishart

Simon, B. (ed.) (1990) The Search for Enlightenment: The Working Class and Adult Education in the Twentieth Century, Leicester: NIACE

Simpson, K. (1988) The Protean Scot, Aberdeen: Aberdeen University Press

Sinclair, Sir J. (1826) Analysis of the Statistical Account of Scotland, Part II, London: John Murray

Sinclair, Sir J. (ed.) The (Old) Statistical Account of Scotland 1791-1799, (reissued 1973-1982), Vol. II, The Lothians, Vol. IV, Dumfriesshire, Vol. VI, Ayrshire, Vol. VII, Lanarkshire and Renfrewshire, Vol. VIII, Argyll (Mainland), Vol. IX, Dunbartonshire, Stirlingshire and Clackmannanshire, Vol. X, Fife, Vol. XI, South and East Perthshire and Kinross, Vol. XII, North and West Perthshire, Vol. XIII, Angus, Vol. XIV, Kincardineshire and South and West Aberdeenshire, & Vol. XVII, Invernesshire, Ross and Cromarty, Wakefield: EP Publishing

Smart, R. (1968) 'Literate ladies: a fifty year experiment', St Andrews Alumnus Chronicle, 59

Smiles, S. (1859) *Self Help*, (1997 edition) London: Institute of Economic Affairs

Smiles, S. (1863) *Industrial Biography: Iron Workers and Tool Makers*, (reprinted 1967), Newton Abbot: David and Charles

Smiles, S. (1875) *Thrift*, London: John Murray

Smiles, S. (1878) *Robert Dick – Baker of Thurso, Geologist and Botanist*, London: John Murray

Smiles, S. (1882) *Thomas Edward – The Life of a Scotch Naturalist*, London: John Murray

Smiles, S. (1905) *Autobiography*, London: John Murray

Smillie, R. (1924) *My Life for Labour*, London: Mills and Boon

Smith, A. (1776) *An Inquiry into the Nature and Causes of the Wealth of Nations*, 2 Volumes, (1976 edition), Oxford

Smith, A. (1990) *Forty Years in Kincardineshire 1911-1951: A Bothy Loon's Life Story*, Collieston: Caledonian Books

Smith, J.V. (1977) *The Watt Institution, Dundee 1824-49*, Dundee: Abertay Historical Society, No. 17

Smith, J.V. (1983a) 'Manners, morals and mentalities. Reflections on the popular enlightenment of early nineteenth century Scotland', in Humes, W.M. and Paterson, H.M. (eds.), *Scottish Culture and Scottish Education 1800-1980*, Edinburgh: John Donald

Smith, J.V. (1983b) 'Reason, revelation and reform: Thomas Dick of Methven and the improvement of society by the Ddiffusion of knowledge', *History of Education*, 12(4)

Smith, V. (ed.) (1979) *Opportunities for Women*, Edinburgh: Scottish Institute for Adult Education

Smout, T.C. (1967) 'Lead mining in Scotland, 1650-1850', in Payne, P.L. (ed.), *Studies in Scottish Business History*, London: Frank Cass

Smout, T.C. (1969) *A History of the Scottish People 1560-1830*, London: Collins

Smout, T.C. (1982) 'Born again at Cambuslang. New evidence on popular religion and literacy in eighteenth century Scotland', *Past and Present*, 97: 114–27

Smout, T.C. (1986) *A Century of the Scottish People 1830-1950*, London: Collins

Somerville, A. (1848) *The Autobiography of a Working Man*, (1967 edition) London: McGibben and Kee

Spackman, A. and Paul, S. (2000) 'Education for women in late Victorian Dundee', in Cooke, A.J. and MacSween, A. (eds.), *The Rise and Fall of Adult Education Institutions and Social Movements*, Frankfurt: Peter Lang

Standish, P. (1999) 'Adult and continuing education in Scotland', in Bryce T.G.K and Humes W.M., (eds.), *Scottish Education*, Edinburgh: Edinburgh University Press

Steele, T. (1995) 'Cultural struggle or identity politics: can there still be a 'popular' education?', in Mayo, M. and Thompson, J. (eds.), *Adult Learning, Critical Intelligence and Social Change*, Leicester: NIACE

Steele, T. (1997) *The Emergence of Cultural Studies 1945–65: Adult Education, Cultural Politics and the English Question*, London: Lawrence and Wishart

Steele, T. (1999) 'With "real feeling and just sense": rehistoricising popular education', in Crowther, J., Martin, I. and Shaw, M. (eds.), *Popular Education and Social Movements in Scotland Today*, Leicester: NIACE

Stewart, R. (1985) *Henry Brougham. His Public Career 1778-1868*, London: Bodley Head

Stewart, T. (1893) *Among the Miners*, Larkhall

Struthers, J. (1850) *Poetical Works with Autobiography*, London

Stuart, J. (1883) *Inaugural Address at the Opening Ceremony of University College, Dundee,* Dundee: John Leng

Stuart, J. (1901) *Address in Gilfillan Memorial Hall, Dundee, 25 October 1901,* Dundee: John Leng

Stuart, J., (1911), *Reminiscences,* London: Chiswick Press

Tannahill, R. (1874) *Complete Songs,* Glasgow: John Cameron

Taylor, J. (1980) 'The making of the report' in Wiltshire H. et al. (eds.), *The 1919 Report, The Final and Interim Report of the Ministry of Reconstruction,* Nottingham: University of Nottingham

Thom, W. (1880) *Rhymes and Recollections of a Handloom Weaver,* Paisley: Alexander Gardner

Thompson, A.R. (1963) 'The use of libraries by the working class in Scotland in the early nineteenth century', *Scottish Historical Review,* 42: 21–9

Thompson, E.P. (1968a) *Education and Experience. The Fifth Mansbridge Memorial Lecture,* Leeds: Leeds University Press

Thompson, E.P. (1968b) *The Making of the English Working Class,* London: Pelican

Thompson, E.P. (1993) *Customs in Common,* London: Penguin

Thompson, J. (1995) 'Feminism and Women's Education', in Mayo, M. and Thompson, J., (eds.), *Adult Learning, Critical Intelligence and Social Change,* Leicester: NIACE

Thomson, A. (1895) *Random Notes and Recollections,* Glasgow

Thomson, R. (2001) 'From arcadia to wonderland: reflections on a decade of continuing education in Scotland', *Journal of Adult and Continuing Education,* 7(1)

Tranter, N. (1998) 'Demography', in Cooke, A.J., Donnachie, I., MacSween, A, & Whatley, C.A., (eds.), *Modern Scottish History 1707 to the Present,* Vol. 1, East Linton: Tuckwell Press

Tyrell, A. (1969) 'Political economy, whiggism and the education of working class adults in Scotland 1817-40', *Scottish Historical Review,* 48: 151–65

Usher, R., Bryant, I. and Johnston, R. (1997) *Adult Education and the Postmodern Challenge. Learning beyond the limits,* London: Routledge

Vincent, D. (ed.) (1978) *James Dawson Burn. The Autobiography of a Beggar Boy,* London: Europa Publications

Vincent, D. (1981) *Bread, Knowledge and Freedom. A Study of Nineteenth Century Working Class Autobiography,* London: Europa Publications

Walker, W.M. (1979) *Juteopolis. Dundee and Its Textile Workers 1885-1923,* Edinburgh: EUP

Walsh, A.D. (1968) 'Notes on the first visit of the British association to Dundee and the early history of University College, Dundee', in Jones, S.J., (ed.), *Dundee and District,* Dundee: British Association for the Advancement of Science

Webb, R.K. (1954) 'Literacy among the working classes in nineteenth century Scotland', *Scottish Historical Review,* 33: 100–14

Webb, R.K. (1955), *The British Working Class Reader 1790-1848,* London: George Allen and Unwin

Weber, M. (1992 edition) *The Protestant Ethic and the Spirit of Capitalism,* London: Routledge

Whatley, C.A. (1988) 'The experience of work', in Devine, T.M. and Mitchison, R.M. (eds.), *People and Society in Scotland, Volume 1, 1760-1830,* Edinburgh: John Donald

Whatley, C.A. (1995) 'Labour in the industrialising city', in Devine, T.M., & Jackson, G.,

Glasgow Volume 1: Beginnings to 1830, Manchester: Manchester University Press

Whatley, C.A. (ed.) (1996) *The Diary of John Sturrock, Millwright, Dundee, 1864-65,* East Linton: Tuckwell Press

Whatley, C.A. (2000a) *Scottish Society 1707-1830: Beyond Jacobitism, towards industrialisation,* Manchester: Manchester University Press

Whatley, C. A. (2000b) 'Altering images of the industrial city: the case of James Myles the "Factory Boy" and mid-Victorian Dundee', in Miskell, L., Whatley, C. A. & Harris, B. (eds.) *Victorian Dundee: Image and Realities,* East Linton: Tuckwell Press

Williams, R. (1967) *Culture and Society 1780-1950,* London: Chatto and Windus

Wilson, A. (1970) *The Chartist Movement in Scotland,* Manchester: Manchester University Press

Wilson, V. (ed.) (1981), *Recent Developments in New Opportunities for Women in Scotland,* Edinburgh: SIAE

Withers, C.W.J. (1998) *Urban Highlanders: Highland-Lowland Migration and Urban Gaelic Culture,* East Linton: Tuckwell Press

Withers, C.W.J. (2000), "Education and the Gaelic Language", in Holmes, H., (ed.), *Scottish Life and Society. Education,* East Linton: Tuckwell Press

Withrington, D.J. (1987) "Scotland: a half educated nation?" *Scottish Economic and Social History,* Vol. 7

Withrington, D.J. (1988) 'Schooling, literacy and society', in Devine, T. M. and Mitchison, R. (eds.), *People and Society in Scotland 1760-1830,* Edinburgh: John Donald

Withrington, D.J. (1998) 'Education', in Cooke, A.J., Donnachie, I., MacSween, A., & Whatley, C.A. (eds.), *Modern Scottish History 1707 to the Present,* Vol. 1, East Linton: Tuckwell Press

Young, J.D. (1992) *John Maclean, Clydeside Socialist,* Glasgow: Clydeside Press

Younger, J. (1849) *The Light of the Week or the Temporal Advantages of the Sabbath Considered in Relation to the Working Classes,* London: Partridge and Oakey

Newspapers, magazines and yearbooks

Chambers Edinburgh Journal

Dundee Year Books, 1883-1902

Forward, 11 June 1910, 'Rambling Recollections of an Agitator', (Dr G.B. Clark)

Perthshire Courier

The Chartist Circular, Glasgow, 1839-41

The Cheap Magazine, 1813 – 1814

The Glasgow Journal, 1755 - 1756

The Glasgow Mechanics' Magazine, 1825

The Herald to the Trades Advocate and Co-operative Journal, Glasgow, 1830-1831

The Saturday Evening Commonwealth, Glasgow, (Prize Autobiographies of Working Men; 'Narrative of a Miner', 25 October 1856, 'Jacques, Glimpses of a Chequered Life', 1 & 8 November 1856, and 'The Life of a Journeyman Baker', 13 December 1856)

Parliamentary papers

Reports from the Assistant Hand-Loom Weavers' Commissioners, South of Scotland and East of Scotland, *Parliamentary Papers,* 1838-39, (1970 reprint, Irish University Press, Industrial Revolution, Textiles, Vol. 9)

Report of Robert Hugh Franks on the Employment of Children and Young Persons in the Collieries and Iron Works of the East of Scotland, *Parliamentary Papers,* 1842, Vol. XVI

Tremenheere Report on the Mining Districts, *Parliamentary Papers,* 1849, Vol. XXII

Report from the Commissioners for Education (Scotland), *Parliamentary Papers,* 1867, Vol. XXV

Index

(Index notes: *a* = autobiographer)